COLUMBIA UNIVERSITY STUDIES

IN ENGLISH AND COMPARATIVE LITERATURE

Number 125

PHINEAS FLETCHER

PHINEAS FLETCHER

MAN OF LETTERS, SCIENCE
AND DIVINITY

BY

ABRAM BARNETT LANGDALE

1968
OCTAGON BOOKS, INC.
New York

Reprinted 1968

by special arrangement with Columbia University Press

OCTAGON BOOKS, INC.
175 FIFTH AVENUE
NEW YORK, N. Y. 10010

PR
2275
'L3
c.2

Library of Congress Catalog Card Number: 68-15890

Printed in U.S.A. by
NOBLE OFFSET PRINTERS, INC.
NEW YORK 3, N. Y.

PREFACE

PHINEAS FLETCHER's life and works have caught the interest of many, but few have whole-heartedly labored in the investigation of this clergyman, scientist, and poet. Their company is as choice as it is small: Alexander Grosart, Frederick Boas, and Ethel Seaton. Professor Boas' work dealt with the text of the poems, and his two volumes, published in 1908-9, have proved definitive. Miss Seaton's *Venus and Anchises* grew from her discovery of a Fletcher manuscript in the Sion College Library. *Venus and Anchises* supplied a number of fresh biographical and critical facts, and yet the author's study was restricted to the several poems of her manuscript. Her accomplishment suggested that a similar research into the bulk of Fletcher's works would be proportionately rewarding. Grosart's writings upon Phineas Fletcher, his brother, and his father, are set forth in a number of volumes. These storehouses of fact and error are tributes to Grosart's tirelessness as a collector. On the other hand he overlooked many of the pertinent pieces of evidence and was unaware of the relative importance of those which he possessed.

The present work supplies the dates of events and poems, and the names of acquaintances and relatives, that have been hitherto unknown. It clarifies the most troublesome mysteries of Fletcher's biography: the apparent double marriage to Elizabeth Vincent; his early familiarity with Norfolk; the editions of *Brittain's Ida* and *Sicelides*, formerly supposed to have been pirated; the interest of Sir Henry Willoughby in Phineas Fletcher; the interest of Sir Francis Bacon in the younger Giles; and the identity of the ever-present Fusca. It traces Phineas Fletcher's dependence upon the Latin classics, redefines the term *Spenserian* as applied to a seventeenth-century poet, and examines Fletcher's innovations, as yet unconsidered, in prosody and the pastoral. Important, also, is the establishing of two crises: the elder Giles Fletcher's near ruin along with Essex's absolute ruin, and Phineas' break with Cambridge University. Both catastrophes have gone without telling; indeed, their existence has scarcely been suspected. Finally there is the chief fact about Phineas Fletcher's life and writing, also unsurmised until now, his interest in dissection, and his intimate connection with the new inductive science, a circumstance not the less arresting when it is found that Fletcher may have known both William Harvey and Francis Bacon.

Since I happened upon unexplored territory, my one accomplishment has been entering therein, remaining for a space, and considering. It has been a pleasant sojourn. Instead of feeling the imprisonment of critical writings, I have enjoyed the *Piscatorie Eclogs* and *The Purple Island*. More than once I have quit the British Museum for the quadrangles of Cambridge and the hamlets of Kent, Derby, and Norfolk. I hope that I have communicated to the following pages some of the mellowness of the collegiate halls, the peace of Cranbrook, Risley, and Hilgay, and the delights of *The Purple Island* and *The Apollyonists*.

Professor Frank Allen Patterson's lectures on the seventeenth century first interested me in the subject, and since that time he has been my unfailing guide, helper, and friend. Whenever the difficulties of the way became wearisome, I have looked to the heroic, even Miltonic fortitude which has enabled him to carry on with his edition of John Milton. I am indebted to Professors Ernest H. Wright, Jefferson B. Fletcher, Frederick S. Boas, and Henry W. Wells for their courtesy and generosity, and I have profited from their rich scholarship.

A. B. L.

Brooklyn, N. Y.
November 2, 1936

CONTENTS

PHINEAS FLETCHER

GENEALOGICAL TABLE OF THE FLETCHER FAMILY

Vicar Richard Fletcher

- **Bishop Richard**
  b. 1545
  d. 1596
  m. (1)
  Elizabeth Holland
  m. (2)
  Mary Baker

- **Dr. Giles**
  b. *c.* 1548
  d. 1611
  m.
  Joan Sheaffe
  b. 1562

- **Phebe**
  d. 1610

- **A daughter**
  m.
  Pownall

- **Priscilla**
  m. 1573
  William
  Atkinson

- **John**
  b. 1566
  d. 1566/7

Children of Bishop Richard:

- **Phineas**
  b. 1582
  d. 1650
  m.
  Elizabeth Vincent

- **Anne**
  b. 1584

- **Giles**
  b. 1585
  or
  1586
  d. 1623

- **Elizabeth**
  b. 1587

- **Joan**
  b. 1588

- **Judith**
  b. 1591

- **Nehemias**
  d. 1596

Children of Phineas:

- **Anne**
  b. 1616

- **Elizabeth**
  b. 1621

- **Edmund**
  b. 1623
  d. 1638

- **Phineas**
  b. 1626

- **William**
  b. 1628
  d. 1695

- **Frances**
  b. 1631

- **Edward**
  b. 1634

- **Sarah**
  b. 1636

I

A SON OF KENT
1582–85

"April 8, 1582. Phineas Ffletcher filius bb Egidij."

THE half dozen words, quite legible against a paper yellowed by the passing of three centuries, record the beginning of a poet's life. The Latinity, the casual orthography, and the efficiency of the entry are characteristic of the temper of 1582; and so, too, was the mature Phineas Fletcher long after his coevals had outlived the year. The poet was born in the age of the Virgin Queen and died in that of Oliver the Protector, and yet he remained an Elizabethan to the end. The same religion, politics, esthetic and personal philosophy which hovered over his cradle were in the air about his deathbed. The roots of the man's intellectual life struck deep into these early times and scenes, and he ever persisted in drawing spiritual sustenance therefrom. Thus the events of the Civil War had less influence upon the middle-aged poet than those of the Marian persecutions had upon the Fletcher as yet unborn. Though he resided in his birthplace no longer than five years, the locality colored his writings to a greater extent than Hilgay, where he lived for thirty years. His grandfather and uncle, both of whom were dead before he reached his majority, proved to be more powerful factors in his career than any persons whose years paralleled his own. Because of these paradoxes, an account of Phineas Fletcher's life cannot properly begin with the record of his nativity; it must travel backward as well as forward from that point.

The author of *The Purple Island* was born in Cranbrook, fifteen miles from the Channel cliffs and fifty odd from London, but altogether remote from either of those doorways to the larger world. Although his kinsmen were filled with an almost Viking urge for change of scene, the capital of the Kentish weald was long the center of their movements. The town lies like a jewel with its circlet of sister hamlets, Frittenden and Marden to the north, Hawkshurst to the south, to the east Sissinghurst and Tenterden, and Glassenbury to the west. The church, inn, shops, and houses are set on a level stretch of ground, which soon breaks into steep little hills. The uneven terrain shuts off Cranbrook from the outside and also serves as an excellent hop land. The slopes are overgrown by vines, and the curious, lopsided cones of the oast houses or hop kilns rise above the luscious vegetation that feeds them.

In 1582 the upper stratum of the townspeople comprised not only the landowners with near-by seats, like the Robartses at Glassenbury, but also the prosperous merchant families such as the Sheaffes. One is surprised to find these two groups, whose ideas and ideals must have clashed, meeting on a plane of equality and frequently intermarrying. Presumably the gentlemen farmers nursed a sense of superiority, conscious of an ancestry that could be traced to the followers of the Duke of Normandy. It was, however, the age of Queen Bess, when trade took on a new importance, and the Robartses and Knatchbulls swallowed their ancestral pride and wed their sons to Sheaffe daughters.

The parsonage, built with a solidity that bordered on the luxurious, was a token of the prosperity of the gentry. In 1648 it consisted of "a hall, kitchen, buttery, milkhouse, with several rooms over them, an orchard, little garden, two great barns, one stable and fodder house, with several rooms over them." [1] The poet probably saw the light of day in one of those "several rooms." At the present time a footpath leaves the vicarage grounds to the north, winds between graves that were less numerous in 1582, and leads to a small door built into the wall of the church.

St. Dunstan stands upon a twenty-foot mound which rises abruptly from the main thoroughfare of Cranbrook, giving the structure a fine prominence. It is supposedly the oldest church in that quarter of the county and boasts a clock famous throughout southern Kent for its gilt decoration. On the east wall and to the right of the altar is a tablet bearing an account of the life of Richard Fletcher, vicar, and founder of his family.

In the year of the poet's birth, his grandfather was the dominating figure in the parsonage, ruling with an ascendancy that was not

[1] Hasted's *History of Kent*, III, 55.

so much the result of his office or venerable years, as a tribute to his foursquare character. His acts are partly hidden in the mists of the early sixteenth century, but through these he looms like a patriarch of the Old Testament. He was the father of a renowned ambassador and one of Elizabeth's favorite bishops, and the grandfather of three important poets. He is never mentioned in Phineas Fletcher's verse, and yet his spirit haunts sentence after sentence and adds a perspective to all of the grandson's work. The vicar was the fountainhead of the characteristic family traits.

Richard Fletcher's first known act is typical in its influence upon his descendants unto the third generation. He traveled down from the North to Cambridge and thereby established a family tradition. Not only were eight or more of his tribe Cantabrigians, but the elder Giles and his two sons devoted large parts of their lives to teaching at the university. The Yorkshire youth left behind him a family of Fletchers joined by marriage with three other great kindreds, the Nevilles, Molyneuxes, and Willoughbys. The intricate, but at present indistinct relationship was to provide patrons for three of his offspring, including Phineas Fletcher.

The old records provide only the barest account of the vicar's life, but the events known to follow his commencing M.A. form a curious sequence. He married; in 1545 had a son christened Richard; went off on an embassy to the Sophi of Persia; and returned to enter the Church. It was like a Fletcher to venture to a remote corner of civilization, and more so to do this while his young wife remained to rear his offspring. He passed on the wanderlust to his progeny, and it led his son Giles, under similar circumstances, to Moscow. The same restlessness, suppressed by the limitations of a more conventional age, can be recognized in the many passages of Phineas' poetry which deal with Russia, Poland, Turkey, and other remote lands.

As a churchman Richard Fletcher was born with the Reformation, lived to be, in a small way, one of its champions, and died the incarnation of Protestantism. His career provides a commentary upon the life of the grandson. It makes clear much that has remained dark and palliates much that has been condemned. Hatred of the papacy became the family heritage; it seems to have cost the vicar's eldest son his life, and to have led the second son, Giles, perilously close to the execution block. The bitterness found immortality in *The Apollyonists* and *Locustae* of Phineas Fletcher, who scarcely wrote a poem or prose work that was not modified by it in one way or another. In 1547 the young man, fated to lay up this patrimony, having just returned from Persia, entered the Church. The ceremony was one of dramatic fitness; he stood with John Fox and was ordained by Nicholas Ridley, the martyr bishop.[2] His first living was Watford, Herts., where a second child, Giles, the father of Phineas, was born in 1548 or the following year. Shortly afterward he was preferred to the neighboring town of Bishop Stortford,[3] but on February 23, 1556/7, he was forcibly deprived and became a wanderer.

The glimpses we obtain of Richard Fletcher during the next few years are scattered, but sufficient to show that he lived in darkness. He was one of the sufferers by the Marian persecutions, and his own sorrows were deepened by communings with other victims whose agonies were greater. John Fox mentions him several times in his *Book of Martyrs;* in 1555, before his deprivation, the Bishop Stortford incumbent was present at the martyrdom of Christopher Wade at Dartford, and two years later he was at Frittenden. He had spent part of the interim in prison [4]—he was fortunate to escape the bloody fate of Wade. Richard Fletcher had been a warm Protestant before Mary's reign, but after that holocaust he must have become an extraordinary hater of Romanism. It tempered his spirit, making of it a sword which he handed on to his sons and their sons, and the blade kept all its sharpness for one hundred years.

The attraction which drew the unbeneficed clergyman to Frittenden in 1557 is unknown. Frittenden was only four miles distant from the Cranbrook destined to become a family seat of the Fletchers. Perhaps Richard Fletcher was already living in the neighborhood as an unofficial minister to the Protestants. In 1558, shortly after her accession, Elizabeth presented him to the living of Cranbrook. The new queen had opened the Promised Land, and Phineas Fletcher never tired of offering poetic sacrifices in her

[2] Strype's *Ecclesiastical Memorials*, II, 402.

[3] Lansdowne MS 982, f. 190. Richard Fletcher held the additional benefice of Ugley, Essex, from February 7, 1552/3, to April 18, 1554.

[4] Igglesden's *Saunter through Kent*, VI, 41.

name. So far as can be determined, the remaining twenty-six years of Richard Fletcher's life were placid.[5]

Such was the man who, in 1582, sat at the head of the table in the vicarage hall, a veteran of some sixty winters. Around the board gathered a numerous family, many of whom were only occasional guests because the urge which had led the vicar to Persia was already stirring within them. The eldest son, Richard, thirty-seven years old and a doctor of divinity, had been presented to the living of Rye in 1569 by Lord Buckhurst, the poet. In 1583 he was preferred to the deanery of Peterborough, the change evidently upsetting his domestic arrangements at Rye so that he stationed his family in Cranbrook for the several years immediately following Phineas Fletcher's birth. His wife, the former Elizabeth Holland of Cranbrook,[6] was the mother of four little children: Nathaniel, destined to be chaplain to Sir Henry Wotton at Venice; Theophilus; Elizabeth; and John. The last, who became the great dramatist, was only three years old, so that for several years Phineas Fletcher and his first cousin may have shared the same nursery. Three more babies were born to Elizabeth Holland Fletcher during her residence at Cranbrook, and all were baptized by their grandfather: Thomas, on September 29, 1582; Sarah, January 19, 1583/4; and Anne, November 22, 1584. If his three years of majority made the infant dramatist somewhat overbearing, Phineas Fletcher did not lack for companionship more nearly of his own age, both masculine and feminine.

The vicar's daughter Priscilla had left his home—its buttery, milk house, orchard, and garden—in October, 1573, to marry William Atkinson. Probably the husband carried his bride afar, because there are no further records of their presence in Cranbrook. It is evident that there were two other daughters: Phebe, who seems to have died a spinster; and a second who married, the lady called "my sister Pownall" in Richard Fletcher's will.[7] Her son Henry

---

[5] On July 19, 1556, the Cranbrook incumbent was nominated to the additional benefice of Smarden, a village five miles away.

[6] The marriage took place on May 25, 1573. There is an equal likelihood that the lady and her children lodged in the Holland house. If such were the case, they were probably frequent visitors at the vicarage. It is likewise possible that Phineas Fletcher was born in the home of his maternal grandparents, the Sheaffes.

[7] Lansdowne MS 982, f. 191.

was buried on August 21, 1583, at Cranbrook; and another son, Nathaniel, was baptized on October 28, 1584. In the old church registers, where marriage, birth, and death are ironically contiguous, the business of living becomes foreshortened. Nathaniel later was admitted to Oxford, died in promising young manhood, and left behind him a book which was edited by Phineas Fletcher's brother, Giles. The Pownalls apparently lived at Hollingbourn,[8] some fourteen miles to the north, and thus could readily visit the vicarage. The patriarch had two other sons: one, John, baptized on October 14, 1566, who lived but three months; and another, Giles, the parent of Phineas, who left Eton to enter King's College, Cambridge, on August 27, 1565, proceeded B.A. in 1569/70, M.A. in 1573, and D.C.L. on June 23, 1581.

Both brothers, Giles and Richard, came home to their father close to 1582, but the manners of their returning were in sharp contrast. The elder established his family temporarily in Cranbrook because his talents had won him recognition, and in his recent preferment to the Peterborough deanery, he had received a notable presage of future success. Giles, a man of thirty-one years or so, was running away from failure. He had devoted half of his life to a university career, had met with disappointment, and worse, with public humiliation.

It is evident that Giles Fletcher's ambitions, rather than being blighted by the Cambridge winter, had actually grown, and even now he projected greater things than the university had ever offered. His destination was the court, but for him the road to London lay through Cranbrook and Rye. Richard Fletcher's influence, perhaps too time-serving but certainly pervasive, has never been reckoned with in estimating the lives of his brother and nephew. This churchman's idea of administering the spiritual affairs of the Worcester see involved an unbroken residence in London and a faithful attendance upon the queen. Such a man would never have counseled his brother to turn his back upon the way of the world. He opened to Giles Fletcher not the priesthood, but certain temporal offices afforded by the Church, which served as

---

[8] Although there is no further record of the Pownall family at Cranbrook, Hasted notes that they rented lands at Hollingbourn in 1645.

stop-gaps while he cast around for a means of getting his unhappy relative to London.

Once a man had abandoned his fellowship, he was free to enter upon matrimony, and Giles Fletcher lost little time. Quitting Cambridge in the late summer or autumn of 1580, he married Joan Sheaffe of Cranbrook on January 16. He had irrevocably surrendered his college rights, although it was not until the following September that his name was removed from the King's College account books. His alliance with the Sheaffes was a practicality. The young woman—she was born on October 10, 1562—was the daughter of a well-to-do clothier. This Edmund Sheaffe presided over the largest family in Cranbrook—between the years 1559 and 1592 there are forty-four recordings of the name in the Church register. Although it was a merchant tribe, its children were entering the Church and marrying among the landed gentry. As early as 1560 another Joan became the wife of Sir Richard Knatchbull of Mersham, Kent, and shortly afterward Sir Richard's brother took to himself one of Joan's sisters. Of greater consequence was the union of Richard Sheaffe and Margery Robarts in February, 1581/2, because from time immemorial the Robartses of Glassenbury had been the little monarchs of Cranbrook and its environs. Richard was probably the brother of Phineas Fletcher's mother, and thus the poet's aunt was a Robarts, a kinship of which he made much throughout his life.

If the vicarage entertained a numerous company of adults and children, the first-born of Giles and Joan found even larger society in the household of his maternal grandfather. The boy paid frequent and long visits to Edmund Sheaffe's home during his childhood. The clothier had married a widow, Joan Kitchell Jordan, who brought with her five children. Three of them were daughters that subsequently married, one of these, an Elizabeth Rucke, emigrating to New England. By Joan, the tradesman had much increase. As far as can be learned from the Cranbrook register, she bore him three girls and seven boys.[9] Of the young men, Thomas,

[9] These included Richard and Thomas, both of whom were born before 1559; Edmund, born in 1559; John, 1565; Alexander, 1566; Harman, 1570; Samuel, 1573/4; Katherine, 1564; Mary, 1567/8; and Anne, 1571/2.

Edmund, and Harman proceeded to King's College, influenced, no doubt, by their brother-in-law, Giles. Harman left a fellowship to become rector of the Chapel of Totham, and later of Goldhanger, Essex. One feels some of the *Deserted Village* melancholy upon finding that the Sheaffes had vanished from Cranbrook as early as 1640. In 1580, however, they were not only numerous but well-connected, and his marriage may easily have given Giles Fletcher part of the influence in the region which was to send him to Parliament and to the London of his new ambitions.

Immediately before leaving Cambridge and the fenlands, the poet's father had tried his hand at managing the affairs of the Church. Since the records of his university career have mentioned only the man's enemies, we should be tempted to ascribe to him a cold, pushing nature were it not for this proof that he had at least one solicitous friend. Richard Bridgewater, whom he had served as deputy orator, became vicar general and chancellor of Ely in 1579, and on July 3 of the following year he made Fletcher his commissary. Thereafter until 1585, when he went to London, his opportunities seem to arrive by way of Rye. Richard Fletcher's vicarage belonged to the diocese of Chichester, and on July 5, 1581, Giles was one of the party that made the visitation to the cathedral church. By the following year he had become the chancellor of the West Sussex cathedral, but his family did not remove from Cranbrook, because not only Phineas but a second child, Anne, baptized on November 22, 1584, were born in Kent during this period. The father must have made frequent circuits from his diocesan town to Rye and to Cranbrook, a forty-mile journey. His hope for a future existence in his offspring, which rested in the infant Phineas, drew him to Cranbrook, but his prospects for the present life lured him to Rye, to Richard Fletcher, and the near-by Winchelsea.

This household, to which the poet was born on April 8, 1582, has been reconstructed from the evidence furnished by the Cranbrook register. It remains to be seen that the characteristics of the mature Phineas sprang from one member or another of the group.

II

LIFE BECOMES METROPOLITAN
1585-1600

FOLLOWING the registration of his birth, tne next specific record concerning Phineas Fletcher occurs under the date of August 25, 1600, when he proceeded from Eton to King's College. Since the passing of more than three centuries has rendered it hopeless that the hiatus of eighteen years will ever be filled, we must investigate the father's life in order to bridge the gap. The elder Giles Fletcher left abundant material, much of which has gone unused, for such a biography. Since he, too, was no mean poet and prose writer, his activities, notable in themselves, are of more than ordinary interest to the student of English literature. The father's changes in residence, the additions to his family, the sudden rises and declines of his success, with their subsequent joys and anxieties, must have comprised much of the youth's life during his first eighteen years. Rarely has there been a son like Phineas Fletcher for adopting the paternal philosophy, politics, and theology, for becoming a champion in his father's disputes, and for modeling his own in the very image of his parent's course of life. All this is visible in the *Piscatorie Eclogs,* where Phineas wrote a biography of Thelgon, the elder Giles Fletcher, expounding his academic, diplomatic, and civic careers in veiled terms which demand elucidation.

On November 23, 1585, Parliament opened and there on its benches was Giles Fletcher sitting for Winchelsea. The die had been cast. He was in London, the gateway to opportunity, the focal point of court favor. He had left far behind him the ingrown life of the university, which would have been peaceful enough had he not been so ambitious. Less remote, but likewise given over, was a secure, comfortable existence amid the cloisters and bell towers of the southern cathedral. Before him lay a career of hazardous journeys, of intrigues, of political warfare, of endlessly varied employment, of rapid flights on the wings of prosperity and more speedy plunges into poverty—in short, the life of a gambler in Elizabethan policy. There is no reason to suppose that the newly elected Member of Parliament ever regretted his choice. It was another story with the young Cranbrook mother. She journeyed up to London in the fall of 1585, or in the following summer, with her baby boy and girl, ignorant of the sorrows and anxieties that her husband's recent success was to entail upon her.

From 1585 to his death, London became Giles Fletcher's permanent home, at least as regular a residence as he was ever to have. For many years of his life he was destined to be a diplomatic Ishmael, but his journeys began and ended in the metropolis. His early identification with its affairs explains the part he played in the politics of after years, when Essex employed him as a leader of the citizens. His wife, however, frequently returned to Cranbrook, and half of her children were born there. Hers was a distorted domestic régime, and repeatedly she bore offspring to a husband who had been long absent on some perilous pilgrimage. Evidently she quit the city for Edmund Sheaffe's roof each time Giles Fletcher departed upon an embassy.

It is doubtful whether the lady came up to London at all in the autumn. She must have made her residence in the city during some part of the year because her third child, born at this time, was not baptized in Cranbrook. This second son was none other than the younger Giles, who lived to write *Christs Victorie and Triumph*. The date of his birth has never been established, many authorities placing it as late as 1588. The error has an important implication, for his great poem was written as early as 1608 or 1609, and we are asked to believe that it was the work of a boy of twenty. Since it now can be stated that he first saw the light of day between November 23, 1585, and November, 1586, it is less difficult to understand the maturity of his masterpiece.[1]

[1] Our only authority for the 1588 date is Fuller, who claims to have had it from John Ramsay, husband of Giles Fletcher's widow. He states that the Trinity College poet was born in London in that year. I knew that Fuller had made a gross error when I came upon the following entry in the Cranbrook register: "December 22, 1588: Joan Fletcher filia b. doctor. Egidij Fletcher." If Giles had been born in the weald town, a record of his baptism would probably be found in the register. Until November 23, 1585, the mother was resident there. In all likelihood she had returned by February 1, 1585/6, and stayed until the following June, because her husband was in Scotland during those months. Furthermore, on account of his absence, the birth could not have taken place between November, 1586, and the following March, but by that time another child, Elizabeth, had been conceived. This daughter was baptized on November 19, 1587, and a second, Joan, on December 22, 1588. On the

For a newcomer, Dr. Fletcher was a reasonably active member of the House of Commons and was appointed to divers committees.[2] He immediately aligned himself with the immoderate anti-Romanists by pledging fealty to Francis Walsingham, leader of that party, torturer of papists, and by Spenser called the Maecenas of the age. This important action of Giles Fletcher affected the entire life of Phineas. We are less surprised by the promptness of the father's decision when we recollect that it had been long prepared, having its inception in another era when a Bishop Stortford incumbent was deprived and sent to prison. To Walsingham, Fletcher owed his next several appointments, which carried him into more promising employment as an ambassador.

The story of his diplomatic career, fully documented in the state papers, has been told only in the *Piscatorie Eclogs* [3] of Phineas Fletcher. The son would have us believe that his father went first to Germany, secondly to Russia, and finally to Scotland. This sequence fails to correspond with fact, for the elder Fletcher traveled to Scotland, then to Germany, to far-off Moscow, and lastly to Holland. The son's reasons for distorting his father's biography are obvious: he must have regarded the Dutch embassy as less important than the others and so omitted it, and he must have moved the Caledonian expedition to the end because he wished to devote the latter half of the eclogue to an acquaintance, Amyntas, whom Thelgon met beyond the Tweed.

After preparing himself for the journey to Edinburgh, where he was to act as secretary to the ambassador, Thomas Randolph, Fletcher was left behind by Randolph's party. He had received word from Cranbrook that his father was desperately ill. He hastened home and was at the vicar's bedside on February 12, the day of his death. If his wife and children had not been in Cranbrook all through the winter, they very probably came down from the city at this time. Henceforth the lady's refuge during her husband's

---

latter date the father was in Russia, and he did not return until September, 1589. Giles Fletcher could not have been born in 1590 or later because he entered Trinity College, Cambridge, in September, 1601. Thus his birth date is restricted to the eleven months following November 23, 1585. Moreover there is little likelihood that it occurred between February and June, so that we are left with two periods of approximately three months.

[2] D'Ewes' *Compleat Journal*, pp. 361, 372.

[3] *Piscatorie Eclogs,* I, st. 11-22; II, st. 13-14.

absences was probably the house of Edmund Sheaffe, because with the patriarch's death a new family took possession of the vicarage. After interring his father's remains near the altar of the church, the grief-stricken Fletcher made posthaste for Edinburgh—a journey which carried him from the chalk cliffs of the Channel to the Tweed, through the flood, snow, and mud of all England.

The secretary joined his new chief in the Scottish capital not long before March 13. Randolph was an astute and grizzled veteran of diplomacy, trained by the plots and crimes of Holyrood, in which he had been personally involved. It was a brief conjunction of the new and the old, since Randolph, who had gone as ambassador to Russia and Germany, was nearing the end, but his young secretary was soon to be sent to both Hamburg and Moscow. The object of the 1586 mission was to secure James the Sixth's signature to a treaty drawn up by Elizabeth. For several months the business went on in Edinburgh, and then in June the negotiators removed to Berwick-upon-Tweed, where the pact was formally signed. There is a record of Fletcher's presence in the border town on June 20, according him first mention among the English attendants.[4]

In July, 1586, with his foreign service temporarily at an end, Fletcher needed more than promises of future employment, however sincere. For the first, but by no means the last time he became aware of the unpleasant aspect of the adventurous life which he had chosen. Even from Edinburgh, he had written a letter to Walsingham begging frantically for a new place.

How many months he waited in desperation is not known, but before the following spring he was made an extraordinary master of the court of requests. Probably he owed this office to the queen's secretary. He now had charge of a debt court, and his work threw him into the flood tide of commerce that surged from Leadenhall, through Cheapside, to Newgate, not sparing St. Paul's, which lay in its course. Henceforth he served two powers whose interests were more or less the same—the extreme Protestant party and the merchants. Fletcher's alliance was with a new character in London of whom Buchan draws a picture in his *Oliver Cromwell*: "The city merchant on the grand scale, with a holding in companies that traded in the ends of the earth," who "had now so many points of

---

[4] *Calendar of State Papers: Scottish*, Vol. VIII.

contact with public affairs that he had perforce to become something of a politician." He and his fellows were the Gargantuan
progeny of Elizabeth's reign, the men who were to finance Oliver
at Naseby and who were even then hewing out the British Empire.
Fletcher's shift in allegiance reveals an admirable readiness to sense
the realities.

In the same spring he received a second diplomatic appointment,
the direct result of his expanded interests. He went to Hamburg
bearing the letters of Elizabeth and her ministers, but primarily as
the employee of the great Society of Merchant Adventurers, a company which he was to serve for many years.[5] Giles Fletcher's fourth
child, Elizabeth, was baptized at Cranbrook on November 19, 1587.
The register entry suggests that the mother and her three offspring
had spent the summer under the Sheaffe roof. It is likely that they
soon rejoined the father in London and remained there through
the winter and the following spring. Did the lady know how soon
she was to return to the Kentish weald to live through more than a
year of extreme anxiety?

In the summer of 1588 Giles Fletcher left for remote, dangerous
Moscow, and he went alone. Russia was different from Scotland or
Germany; it was a realm that offered itself as subject matter for
Purchas, his Pilgrimage, a land where the Englishman might
well expect to see monstrosities like "the Anthropophagi and men
whose heads do grow beneath their shoulders." Fletcher described
himself as the queen's own ambassador, but, as in Germany, his
object was a trade alliance.[6]

After many months' residence in Moscow, during which he experienced a variety of difficulties, the ambassador was granted all
of the trading rights which he sought. He reached England in September, 1589. His own anxiety and that of his family during his
absence is evident in his first act. He sent for his intimate friend,
Henry Wayland, prebendary of St. Paul's and the tutor of Thomas
Fuller's father, and together they "thanked God for his safe return." Again his wife brought her family up from Cranbrook, including a fifth child, Joan, who was now almost a year old and had
never seen her father. The lady's relief must have been unbounded,

[5] For an account of this mission, see Wheeler's *Treatise of Commerce,* pp. 64-68.
[6] Hakluyt's *Principal Navigations,* I, 473.

especially since the Russians had denied her husband the privilege of sending letters out of the country. The reunion was a blessed day in her life for another reason. It inaugurated seven halcyon years during which Fletcher remained in London, had good employment, prospered modestly, and rose steadily in municipal affairs.

Phineas Fletcher's interest in distant principalities, a prominent aspect of his poetry, had its origin in his grandfather's mission to the Sophi of Persia; but it sprang more directly from his father's diplomatic career, and particularly from his Russian journey, which caused a domestic upheaval that must have been one of the son's first memories. Two long sections of *The Apollyonists* and *Locustae* [7] develop the history of Russia's political background, while other passages deal with the contemporary affairs of different European countries.[8] America interested him, and he refers to Virginia on several occasions. One of the most curious of his foreign excursions is a lament for the fair, sad relic of departed worth, Greece, "where once the lovely Muses us'd to sing," [9] an early sounding of a note which was to grow more insistent in English letters.

The seven years of peace gave Giles Fletcher an opportunity to return to the literary pursuits which he had abandoned in Cambridge. Almost immediately after his return he wrote two books, *Of the Russe Common Wealth* and *Israel Redux,* which presented the facts and speculations of his Muscovite experiences. Having completed these accounts, he gathered together the manuscripts of his Cantabrigian years and, in 1593, published a volume entitled *Licia and the Rising to the Crown of Richard the Third.* Long after, Phineas Fletcher did likewise, waiting for twenty years before putting his poetry into print. We have the son's statement to prove that his father's historical verses were written at the university, and it is probable that the love sonnets had the same origin. The father dedicated his little volume to Sir Richard Molyneux of Sefton, and expressed gratitude for important favors from his Lancashire patron. Sir Richard's kindnesses, whatever they were, came as an acknowledgment of kinship. The two men sprang from the tribe that Richard Fletcher left behind him as he journeyed from York

---

[7] *Apollyonists,* III, st. 5-12; *Locustae,* p. 108.

[8] *Apollyonists,* IV, st. 24-28; *Locustae,* pp. 107-8.

[9] *Apollyonists,* III, st. 13.

to Cambridge—the united families of Fletcher, Molyneux, Neville, and Willoughby—which was to produce patrons for both the younger Giles and Phineas.

In Giles Fletcher's scheme of life, there was an insistence upon the necessity of providing himself with a patron, and we shall find the same characteristic dictating the conduct of both his sons. Since he admittedly lacked the genius, birth, and the private fortune to become a Bacon, a Burghley, or an Essex, he regarded himself as belonging to the retainer class. Upon leaving Cambridge he hurried to Rye to serve his brother, and no sooner had he arrived in London than he declared himself Walsingham's man. The prosperity, poverty, triumph, and anxiety that alternately marked his days, rose or fell with the achievements and failures of the powerful persons to whom he was attached.

When Fletcher returned from Moscow, Secretary Walsingham was sinking, and he died during the following summer. Without a master, the ambassador felt something akin to panic, and made an abortive attempt to secure Burghley's interest. Phineas Fletcher's poetry seethes with hatred for Elizabeth's great minister—

> . . . thy great foe shall sink
> Beneath his mountain tombe, whose fame shall stink;
> And time his blacker name shall blurre with blackest ink.
> *The Purple Island,* I, st. 20.

but the passion has never been traced to its source.

Insignificant as the elder Giles Fletcher may have seemed in the statesman's eyes, the former must have regarded Burghley as persistently malevolent. During Fletcher's academic life he had been humiliated by the minister who was acting as chancellor of the university. Years later, upon his return from Russia, the ambassador made several attempts to recover the great man's favor and failed. Almost immediately upon reaching London, he wrote out a letter or brief setting forth his accomplishments and sent it to Burghley,[10] but so far as we know, it brought him no return. A year or so later the indefatigable suppliant forwarded to the minister an outline for a history of Elizabeth's reign, which he proposed to undertake. Once again Cecil must have been deaf to his plea, because the book

---

[10] This interesting letter is printed in Sir Henry Ellis' *Original Letters of Eminent Literary Men,* pp. 79-85.

was never written. Shortly thereafter the Eastland merchants, fearing that Fletcher's *Of the Russe Common Wealth,* with its harsh picture of the Russian court, would harm their trade, petitioned Burghley for its suppression.[11] He promptly acceded, thereby entering once more into the author's life, and still as an enemy. Nor was this the last time he did so.

If the minister was unwilling to offer his suitor even the crumbs of patronage, there were others more favorably disposed. The years following Giles Fletcher's return from Russia have been left blank by his biographers, and so we have remained unaware of his two most important patrons. Richard Fletcher was the benefactor who replaced Walsingham and cared for his dependent's interests with all the solicitude of a blood kinsman. Neither the queen's secretary nor Giles Fletcher's later master, the Earl of Essex, had the same vital concern for his retainer's affairs. Thus the 1589-96 era brought more employment and contentment to Giles Fletcher than any other period of his life.

We last heard of the elder brother when he was at a transitional stage of his career, having established his family at Cranbrook while he prepared to remove them from Rye to Peterborough. The records that have come down to us present Richard Fletcher's rise in a series of matter-of-fact titles, but one needs little imagination to determine the causes and to sense the drama of his success. For several years he filled his new office quietly, until opportunity came to him in his cathedral town, and he was not the man to turn his back upon that goddess. When Mary, Queen of Scots, was imprisoned at near-by Fotheringay Castle, the dean managed to represent the holy Church in every scene of the sad last act. Probably he had few competitors for so ugly a rôle, and perhaps he is to be condemned for seeking it. The Fletchers went to gross excesses in their Protestantism, but the sights that their patriarch had seen during the days of that other Mary are some justification for the brutality of his descendants. On October 12, 1586, Fletcher preached the sermon at the royal prisoner's arraignment. Four months later Elizabeth commissioned him to stand at the scaffold, where he threatened and cajoled the unfortunate woman, urging her to abjure the Roman faith. She refused, with an idealism and shining

[11] Ellis' *Original Letters,* pp. 76-79.

serenity that make the priest's self-seeking seem the blacker. After wasting his words of persuasion and denunciation, he cried, "So perish all the Queen's enemies!" To himself he must have said, "So live and prosper the Queen's friend," for he was a made man. Having assisted at the interment of Mary in his own cathedral church, he became Elizabeth's chaplain and in several years was elevated to the see of Bristol.

This prelate, the last refinement in worldliness, rarely went near Gloucestershire. Shortly after his consecration we find him at Wandsworth, a few miles from London, in attendance upon Arnold Cosbie, about to be hanged for the murder of Lord Bourgh.[12] Although he was officially assigned to divers seats, the bishop, who wanted to be close to the court, lived in the metropolis from this time on. His presence there had no little influence upon the family of his brother, Giles Fletcher. Richard built himself a house in Chelsea where he was visited by Elizabeth herself, and for the occasion he cut a door through a bay window and erected a staircase. Shortly after his wife's death, in 1592, he was preferred to the see of Worcester. John Aylmer, Bishop of London, died in 1594, and Fletcher was the chief mourner at his funeral. The intensity of his grief can be imagined when it is learned that he succeeded immediately to the vacant episcopacy.

Whatever were the defects of the prelate's character, he was a loyal party and family man. Upon his father's death he became head of the family, and his Chelsea establishment replaced the Cranbrook vicarage as its center. His brother and his nephews, Giles and Phineas, must have been familiar with the premises, the more so because they may have lived there after 1594, when the new Bishop of London fell heir to his houses at Wycombe, Hadham, Fulham, and in the city.

Probably it was the great, though not all-powerful, influence of his brother which brought to Giles Fletcher a number of preferments.[13] For instance, beginning in January, 1587, he served for eighteen years as remembrancer to the city of London, acting as

---

[12] Collier's *Bibliographical and Critical Account,* I, 160. For additional evidence of his early establishment in London, see Strype's *Life of Whitgift,* II, 214; and Faulkner's *Chelsea,* II, 127.

[13] The bishop wrote a fervent letter urging his brother's claims for the office of extraordinary master of chancery. See Strype's *Annals of the Reformation,* IV, 373 ff.

collector of debts for the municipal corporation. The poet's father was never the man to be entirely satisfied, and we soon find him complaining about his position. He claims to have had "much pain and employment," and he disliked drawing on himself the displeasure of great personages to whom he was compelled to deliver what he called "denying messages." Accordingly he threw all of his strength into securing the office of extraordinary master of chancery, an appointment controlled by Burghley. He lost; Sir Thomas Ridley, an old rival of whom we shall hear more, won; and the flames of his hatred for the minister were fanned afresh.

Throughout the seven years of comparative security there was being prepared the climax of the man's life—his service under Essex, which was to lead him far from surety, to prison and within sight of the scaffold. The Bishop of London was an ardent member of the Earl's party, and probably his brother counted himself a supporter of the cause long before he became active in it. Giles Fletcher was to work for Essex under the lieutenancy of his secretary, Anthony Bacon. On March 30, 1595, Lady Bacon, mother of Sir Francis and Anthony, wrote to the latter, "I am sorry I cannot speak with Dr. Fletcher for your horse." [14] Trivial, but intimate, the remark suggests that the warm friendship which existed between the men several years later had already been founded. The closeness of the ties binding the two households is apparent in the fact that some fifteen years later Sir Francis became the younger Giles' patron. Although excitement, fear, and hardship were in the making, the remembrancer's family lived on placidly enough during this year. What new brothers or sisters Phineas then acquired cannot be fully determined. On August 1, 1591, Judith was baptized at St. Thomas Apostles, and evidently two other children were born before or after. The mother brought forth five infants in London, but Judith's is the only baptismal record now extant.

Matters might have run on in this pleasant and uneventful manner for an indefinite time, were it not for the fact that there is some justice. Giles Fletcher doubtless deserved all the profits that came to him in this life and more, but those of the 1589-96 era were the fruit of another's hypocrisy. Although he had them from a divine, they were not blessed, and his benefactor spent his hours with the

[14] Birch MS 4120, f. 183.

world rather than with heaven. Elizabeth was too willing to condone, even to smile upon the bishop's unscrupulousness in forwarding her own policies, but the queen's attitude changed when he applied the same methods to his private interests. Soon after elevation to his last office, he proceeded to marry the wealthy Lady Baker, widow of Sir John. (The London Fletchers must have maintained contact with their old home, since the Baker seat was at Sissinghurst, a short mile out of Cranbrook.) This lady's fame had spread far beyond the bounds of the Kentish weald, a reputation less unblemished than her beauty.[15] The match became a court scandal. Elizabeth banished the prelate from her presence and suspended him from his episcopal functions on February 23, 1594/5. Though he was restored to his office after six months, the queen refused to see him for a year. He was grief-stricken. Was it for his sins and for the shame he had brought upon the Church, or was it because he had lost favor at Whitehall?

Shortly afterwards the bishop took a leading part in the conference which drew up the Lambeth Articles, and their extreme Calvinism was largely his work.[16] Here, for a change, he seems to have been motivated, not by greed or self-interest, but by the deepest principle of his creed. Elizabeth's anger, which had slightly cooled, now fell upon him with redoubled fury. On June 15, 1596, Anthony Bacon wrote to Dr. Hawkins, "The Bishop of London died the other day very sodenly, having satte in commission till sixe o'clock at night and deceased at seaven." [17] It has been supposed that the royal disfavor, which grew out of his marriage and his tempering of the Lambeth Articles with Calvinism, was the real cause of his death.[18] The smooth-tongued eulogist might say that Richard Fletcher gave up his life for love, religion, and queen.

The same week was doubly grievous for Giles Fletcher. He buried his son, Nehemias, at St. Luke, on June 12 (possibly an indication that he was living in the bishop's old house), and three days later he learned of his brother's death. Considering his natural

---

[15] Fuller's *Worthies*, II, 138-39.

[16] This is the opinion of Sir Philip Warwick (*Memoirs*, p. 86).

[17] Lansdowne MS 982, f. 190.

[18] This is Mullinger's conclusion. See his *University of Cambridge*, II, 338-39. The great sorrow suffered by the bishop as a result of Elizabeth's anger (*vide* Strype's *Life of Whitgift*, II, 215 ff.) substantiates Mullinger's opinion.

affection for Richard, his dependence upon the prelate's influence, and the suddenness of his passing, it must have been a sad blow. The new era in his life, our knowledge of which is to be obtained from petitions, balance sheets, and actions at law, was ushered in under a black augury, and in truth he had fallen upon evil days.

Giles Fletcher was named the executor of his brother's will, but he must have anticipated much pain and little profit. He knew the economy of the episcopal household too well. The churchman, who had scarcely observed a New Testament rule of poverty after his elevation to London, had spent £1,438 for first fruits, £3,100 to the queen's attendants for "gratifications," great sums for the repair of his various houses, and greater for hospitality. The first inventory of the estate proved the executor's forebodings to have been well-founded, the accounts barely balancing: [19]

INVENTORY OF THE ESTATE OF RICHARD FLETCHER, BISHOP OF LONDON

DEBTS OWING:

	£	s.	d.
To the Queen	600		
To the Dean and Chapter of St. Paul's	100		
To Mr. Aylmer	200		
To Mr. Kemp	135		
To the Upholsterer	121		
To the Goldsmith	55		
To Servants wages	32	12	6
To the Draper	70	10	
To the Taylor, Mercer, Divers others	150	10	
Legacies	10		
	1,474	12	6

ASSETS:

	£	s.	d.
In plate beside one Bowl given to St. Bennet's College by Will	414	17	—
In ready money	223		
In other household stuff	453	2	—
The Stable	120		
Wood felled at Highgate	60		
Arrearages of Rent and other small Debts, whereof a great part was turned over by the Dean and Chapter of Paul's the last Vacation and is like to prove desperate	102		
A Bond of T. Griggs, with the Date uncertain	—		
	1,412	19	4

[19] The inventory is to be found in the Birch MS 4120, ff. 222-23. Parts of the manuscript are illegible, and I have been compelled to leave several blanks. The more substantial sums, however, are plain.

Worse followed. As Fletcher probed further into the dead man's affairs, the assets shrank while the debts kept growing.

The remembrancer had contracted to settle the estate, and accordingly he was beset by the bishop's creditors.[20] The professional debt collector, who for many years had been a dunner, was dunned. Prison, fines, and poverty confronted him. Once again he fell into a panic and wrote to Burghley, who, as usual, made no move in his behalf. On August 21, he turned to his friend, Anthony Bacon, then living at Essex House and a man of considerable influence. By this date the £1,474 credited to the estate had diminished to less than £900, and Fletcher did not know where he was to secure the £500 or £600 demanded of him. He sent Bacon a paper entitled, "Reason to move her majesty in some comisseration towards the orphans of the late bishop of London." The philosopher's half brother took immediate action, and handed the complaint on to Edward Reynolds, another of the Earl's secretaries, who was to convey it to Essex, and thus it would reach her majesty. A month later Essex had agreed to intercede with the queen, but Fletcher was still tormented by creditors, Bacon writing again to Reynolds. Shortly after this Elizabeth dictated a letter stating why she was moved to compassion for Giles Fletcher's plight, and he breathed freely for the first time in four months.

It was only a respite, because Sir John Fortescu, Chancellor of the Exchequer, sent his men to collect the £600 the bishop had owed to the queen. On December 6, process was out against Fletcher, the under officers had given him exactly five days to pay, and once more he could see the shades of the prison walls closing in upon him. He went to Bacon, who moved in his behalf as speedily as before, and the Earl did likewise. Two days later Bacon wrote to Essex, thanking him for what he had accomplished. On April 27, 1597, Elizabeth released Fletcher from payment of the £600, and on July 9 was forced to repeat the order. At the same time she remitted additional indebtedness to the extent of £509 14s. 2d., and two bonds in which he was bound. The last act of grace settled the estate and brought an end to his anxieties.

The fearful business had gone on for more than a year. The ambassador, who had successfully negotiated perils by land and water,

[20] Birch's *Memoirs*, II, 77, 98, 100-1.

who had survived the trickery of Holyrood and the barbarism of Moscow, very nearly lost his liberty and possessions in his own London and at the hand of his nearest kinsman. He was saved by the Earl of Essex, and from 1596 on, Fletcher was the favorite's servant as well as suitor.

In the meantime Phineas Fletcher had entered Eton College. Having thus been removed from the immediate sphere of his father's activities, his mind was now taken up with rising at six in the morning, saying *Deus misereatur*, the collect, *De profundis*, and confronting the admonitions of "the prepositors for yll kept hedys, unwasshid facys, fowle clothis, and sich other." [21] These embarrassments left no lingering distaste, and his later reminiscences about Eton were pleasant. He thought of her primarily as the place where he learned to versify, calling her the sweetest Nurse of the Muses.[22] He proceeded from Eton to King's, following the traditional rules of the royal founder and also the footsteps of his father. He was enrolled as a pensioner on August 25, 1600.

[21] Morgan's *Readings in English Social History*, pp. 240-41.
[22] Phineas Fletcher's recollections of Eton found expression in the dedication of his father's *De antiquis literis Britanniae*.

III

CHANGING WORLDS
1600

TO PHINEAS FLETCHER the first year of the new century was momentous for two reasons. During February and March his father was living in constant dread of punishment, perhaps of the execution block; and in August the poet entered Cambridge, where he was to remain for a lengthy period, the most memorable of his life.

We have no account of the elder Giles Fletcher's connection with Essex, although it is the critical fact of his history. It left deep marks upon the character of the son as well. About 1596 the remembrancer entered into his new allegiance to Robert Devereux. It entailed no hypocrisy, for the Earl was the champion of everything anti-Spanish, nationalistic, and ultra-Protestant in England. On the other hand, Essex found Fletcher useful as a medium of control over the corporation and citizens of London. This last patron was the most powerful the poet's father had known, was indeed the brightest star in the contemporary political firmament, but so brilliant that his sudden, utter decline was already imminent.

The elder Fletcher had long been dissatisfied with his place as remembrancer, and now had reason to be even more so. He had had enough of collecting debts and far too much of being dunned. Wielding an influence greater than any he yet had known, he secured the finest preferment of his career. On May 23, 1597, the queen's grant made him treasurer of St. Paul's, an office void by the promotion of Dr. Bancroft.[1] After experiencing many varieties of employment, Fletcher returned to the Church in a capacity somewhat similar to that which had launched him into his life at Chichester, fifteen years before.

---

[1] Our knowledge of Giles Fletcher's dependence upon patronage and of the date when Essex took him under his wing (i. e., a few months before he entered this office) leaves little doubt as to whose influence brought him the treasurership.

In the meantime, Giles Fletcher was toiling steadily in the fatal interests of Robert Devereux, and we have a few glimpses of him at work. Essex returned from his triumph at Cadiz on July 28, 1596, and with him he brought an army. Always desirous of having a military power at beck and call, he proposed to keep his men under arms for a future attack upon Calais. His political enemies favored an immediate demobilization, and through Reynolds he instructed Fletcher to line up the city men.[2] Fletcher, a kind of party leader, went to Burghley before August 10 and set before him the desires of the Londoners. He represented his constituents as being eager for the capture of the French port and ready to make contributions to that end, but the great statesman was noncommittal. Having been unsuccessful with his enemy, Fletcher told Bacon that he would persuade the Lord Mayor to appear before the Privy Council in the same cause. One Nicholas Faunt served as intermediary between Bacon and Fletcher in the matter. In 1599 Essex, about to leave upon his blundering Irish expedition, was concerned over the training of the city troops. He called in the poet's father for personal interviews, and through him succeeded in winning the city's support. Thus until the very hour of his patron's fall, Fletcher became more and more his man. The retainer scheme of life, after fifteen insecure and ofttimes dangerous years, at last seemed to be functioning. In 1599 he must have had visions of an affluent and distinguished old age, safe under the glittering wings of a favorite— perhaps of a prince consort.

The whole structure of his ambitions crashed on that summer eve of 1599 when Essex flung himself, mud bespattered, at Elizabeth's feet and found he had lost her grace forever. Loyal to the end, Fletcher spent his energies in carrying out the insanities of the Earl. The story of his activities during those final six months will never be told; and, if it could have been, he might have died elsewhere than in his bed. He must have played an important rôle in the weird last act of rebellion, because its success depended upon the London citizens. The coup d'état was an immediate, dismal failure, and retribution was immediate. Sir Walter Raleigh implicated Fletcher, and there is a note by Coke stating that Sheriff Smythe,

---

[2] Birch's *Memoirs*, II, 77, 98, 100-1.

Giles Fletcher, and others would have to be examined. After being questioned by Lords Egerton, Buckhurst, Nottingham, and Hunsden on February 13, the sheriff testified that Fletcher had told him Essex was in danger of being murdered by Jesuits. Thus on the unlucky thirteenth, the finger of suspicion was pointed at Fletcher, and for three weeks his thoughts must have centered upon the gray battlements of Tower Hill and the two-handed ax.

On the twenty-fourth he was taken into custody by Alderman Lowe and cast into prison.[3] He set about writing a confession, which he sent off on March 3, attributing all of his information about Essex's peril to William Temple. The latter finally admitted to Popham and Coke that he had originated the story. Fletcher, on the other hand, pleaded that he had no real connection with the Earl's armed uprising: "Neither did the Earl judge me a fit man to impart to me any such ungodly practises, knowing well that I would reveal them." The blind and undeviating service Fletcher rendered to Essex in all the Earl's London affairs makes one suspicious of the foregoing allegation. At any rate, it saved Fletcher from charges of treason, but did not bring him release. Once his major anxieties were relieved, others took their places. He owed £200 on forfeiture of double bonds before Lady Day; he was confined and thus could not raise the funds. His wife, Joan, went to Sir Robert Cecil to plead her plight, and on March 14 the husband wrote a pitiful letter [4] to Cecil, who was moved to release his suitor and did so. Freedom put a permanent end to Giles Fletcher's troubles and also to his accomplishments.

It appears that Richard Sheaffe, Joan's brother and the husband of Margery Robarts, was called upon to help in the pecuniary crisis. In the same year he made Giles Fletcher a gift of the benefits from the Ringwood, Hants., vicarage, a lease worth £75 5s. 5d., which he had obtained from King's College in 1596. He renewed it five years later and again in 1611 after his brother-in-law's death, this time in the name of the widow.

If Fletcher had lived for nothing else, he at least had won a favor from the Cecil family in securing his release from prison. Perhaps

[3] Cooper's *Athenae Cantabrigiensis*, III, 36.
[4] Additional MS 6177, f. 79.

it was fortunate for him that the father had given way to the son, because Burghley's perfect consistency in refusing him favors might never have been broken.

By August twenty-fifth Phineas Fletcher had entered King's College. From then on, it was as if some mysterious power, emanating from the Giles Fletcher of the 1560's and 1570's, vibrated across three decades to govern the acts of his son. For twenty years Phineas' history was curiously analogous to what his father's had been. On the other hand, it is not so easily followed, because deeds, which leave indelible marks on the pages of history, are fewer and less positive in the son's life. The Fletcher family is a striking example of a hereditary cycle that is not altogether unusual. The originator was a plain, pious being whose life was largely spiritual. His two sons, Giles and Richard, were men of action, men who found expression in physical accomplishment. Three of their sons, Phineas, Giles, and John, became artists and worked in the material of thought. The unhappy culminations in the progression, Phineas, Giles, and John, although greater than their antecedents, all experienced the sense of defeat that so often accompanies unrequited literary achievement.

If Alma Mater Cantabrigia ever recovered one of her own children, she did so on that summer's day. Neither Cambridge nor King's College was strange to the youth of eighteen years. His grandfather, father, three of his Sheaffe uncles, numerous Knatchbull cousins from Mersham, the bishop, and his dramatist cousin had all preceded him. Perhaps John was still resident at St. Bene't's; and Phineas' uncle, Harman Sheaffe, was a fellow of King's until 1617. The Cranbrook vicarage, Richard Fletcher's Chelsea house, and Eton College were so many outposts of the fenland university, where the new pensioner had been drenched in her influence. Although most of his college lore pertained to an earlier day, changes came very slowly along the banks of the Cam. In 1600 the customs, the academic procedures, and the rivalries were much the same as those which Giles Fletcher had abandoned in shame and disappointment.

Among the collegiate and university authorities, there must have been many friends of the poet's father and uncle who would make the newcomer welcome. Phineas Fletcher's attachment for Samuel

Collins and Playfere, expressed many years later, might very naturally arise from such a beginning. The former, called by Fuller "the most fluent Latinist of our age," was the pensioner's senior by nine years. In 1600 Collins was a busy contributor to the collections of academic poetry, while Dr. Thomas Playfere was the foremost preacher at Cambridge. Four years earlier he had succeeded Peter Baro as Lady Margaret Professor, but there awaited him a dismal fate.

In addition, Fletcher already owned, or later made, new friends more nearly of his own age whose names are introduced to us in his poems, where they are oftentimes disguised. William Woodford, of London, and the poet were of exactly the same age. Woodford had proceeded from Eton to King's in the preceding year. Not only were the two good companions, but they had a common interest in poetry. Woodford contributed to the academic collection of 1603, *Threno-Thriambeuticon,* and also to *Epicedium Cantabrigiensis* of 1612.[5] The poet did not come up from Eton alone, but in the company of Edmund Cook of Pusey, Berks. The relationship between these two was close, and has perplexed the biographers because Fletcher alludes to Cook as his "sonne by the University." His attitude of friend-father towards a classmate is understandable after we learn that Cook was three years younger, a very considerable difference when both were youths.

There is reason to believe that the newcomer recognized still another person at Cambridge, whose presence was not only significant but even baleful—Roger Goad, the provost of King's College. It becomes necessary once more to turn back the pages of history. We find, away back in 1576, that Goad was provost, even then having completed a six-year tenure of his office. Under his command was a restless, youthful fellow, Giles Fletcher.

The *Piscatorie Eclogs* of Phineas Fletcher provide the only account of the father's university career, the whole concealed under a pastoral disguise which is both the despair and the justification of the Fletcherian student. Shadowy figures, such as Griphus, play

---

[5] Woodford left King's College to become chaplain to Viscount Doncaster. He later served as minister to St. Faith's, London, and was finally beneficed in Worcestershire. Fletcher addressed his friend with "Ad. Gul. Woodfordum Cantiae agentem," which was a verse letter written from Cambridge at a time when the other was residing in Kent.

shady tricks upon Thelgon, Giles Fletcher. Boats, nets, fishermen, shepherds, are all intermingled with the roaring of the seas which beat upon the shores of an imaginary continent, echoing and re-echoing through the rocky caves until their accents become indistinguishable. The very pains taken by Phineas Fletcher in chronicling his father's failure at Cambridge suggest that he saw a connection between it and his own academic mishaps.

Both Giles Fletcher and his two sons placed a strange value upon their poetic talent: it was to be the avenue of academic advancement.[6] The contemporary university powers must have felt that poetic ability, however desirable, was scarcely a recommendation for promotion. Rhymes did not further the ambitions of father or sons, although each was separately recognized as Cantabrigian laureate. The eclogues make it plain that Fletcher proposed to satisfy his ambition by poetizing, but they do not specify the heights he sought to scale. A fellow might hope to advance within his own college or in the university at large, but a King's man had another opening. His provost owned the right of nominating to places in the related foundation of Eton. It appears that Fletcher's aspirations were pointed in all directions, that he engaged in a threefold struggle, and met triple frustration. It is therefore natural that the *Piscatorie Eclogs* biography should dwell long upon Thelgon's grievances against his so-called Alma Mater. The critical passage, however, is that which places the responsibility for the defeat upon a single individual, one enemy who forced Giles Fletcher out of Cambridge and dogged him through a large part of his life. The author of the eclogues dubs him Gripus or Griphus, and, with a passionate and manifestly real hatred, calls him the basest and most dunghill swain that ever lived.[7] Phineas Fletcher abominated three men above all others—Guy Fawkes, Burghley, and Griphus. The following stanzas from the piscatorial biography introduce one of these villains, Griphus:

---

[6] Although George Herbert is a famous instance of a poet's winning academic promotion, university preferment was usually the reward of virtues other than metrical.

[7] Several years after the completion of *Piscatorie Eclogs*, Phineas Fletcher gave the obnoxious name of Gryphus to a rude servant in his play, *Sicelides*. Did he still find it necessary to vent a spite that had no end, or was this a piece of sardonic humor?

When *Thelgon* here had spent his prentise-yeares,
Soon had he learnt to sing as sweet a note,
As ever strook the churlish *Chamus* eares:
To him the river gives a costly boat,
That on his waters he might safely float,
The songs reward, which oft unto his shore
He sweetly tun'd: Then arm'd with sail, and oare,
Dearely the gift he lov'd but lov'd the giver more.

Scarce of the boat he yet was full possest,
When, with a minde more changing then his wave,
Again bequeath'd it to a wandring guest,
Whom then he onely saw; to him he gave
The sails, and oares: in vain poore *Thelgon* strave,
The boat is under sail, no boot to plain:
Then banisht him, the more to eke his pain,
As if himself were wrong'd and did not wrong the swain.
> *Piscatorie Eclogs,* II, st. 11-12.

Obviously the wandering guest, Griphus, is a key personage to the father's life, and an identification is imperative. The heat and prolixity of the parent's ambition, instead of making the task easier, confuse it. Evidently at one time or another he craved three different offices, none of which he secured. Thus he had three successful rivals, any one of whom may have been Griphus.

In the eclogues the affair did not end with the banishment of the unfortunate fisher, but had a sequel many years later:

Yet little thank, and lesse reward he got:
He never learn'd to sooth the itching eare:
One day (as chanc't) he spies that painted boat,
Which once was his: though his of right it were,
He bought it now again, and bought it deare.
But *Chame* to *Gripus* gave it once again,
Gripus the basest and most dung-hil swain,
That ever drew a net, or fisht in fruitfull main.
> *Piscatorie Eclogs,* II, st. 14.

An identification of the villain must provide an explanation for the second loss of the "painted boat," an event which the author places definitely after Thelgon's return from Moscow in 1589, as well as the "wandring guest" and "boat possest" and "again bequeath'd."

In her *Venus and Anchises,* Miss Ethel Seaton makes several interesting attempts to identify Griphus, suggesting the names of Anthony Wingfield, Thomas Ridley, and Roger Goad.[8] She seems to favor Wingfield's claim to the questionable distinction because he succeeded Richard Bridgewater as public orator in 1580. Giles Fletcher had become deputy orator in 1577 and had reason to hope for this university post, once it should fall vacant. Standing beside the deputy orator, with less right to the oratorship but with an equally greedy appetite, was none other than Gabriel Harvey. Fletcher had a real claim upon the office, and his son might well say that Chamus gave Thelgon a costly gift which it later took away. On the other hand, Harvey wrote that he had three rivals for the office, all of whom were younger than he. (In quoting this evidence, Miss Seaton has greatly weakened her argument.) Fletcher being two or three years older than Harvey, the latter apparently did not regard the deputy as a serious competitor. Since Wingfield's term expired in 1589, the former ambassador to Russia may have renewed his efforts to secure the university post, but for this no one can offer a scrap of proof. Accordingly there is nothing to link Wingfield with the second loss of the "painted boat."

I have come upon new evidence in connection with Goad and Ridley, which rather definitely removes Wingfield from the running, but it leaves two close competitors.

The most likely avenue that opened before the restless Giles Fletcher lay within the walls of his own foundation and led to the provostship. Roger Goad was a man of tempestuous and unethical nature.[9] Throughout his life he was a storm center, but in 1576 his youth and his questionable practices made him a more tempting target for Fletcher, officially his subordinate but in every other respect his superior. There can be no doubt that the thane would gladly have assassinated the monarch in the approved academic fashion. The walks and quadrangles of King's College, supposedly

---

[8] Miss Seaton seems to favor Anthony Wingfield's claim for much the same reasons that I give. I am indebted to her for the suggestion of Ridley's name, which put me on the track of certain corroborative evidence. She seeks an etymological link between "gripus" or "griphus" and "Ridley" or "Wingfield," but Fletcher rarely modeled his pastoral names upon the real names of their owners. Furthermore, his reason for using "griphus," "vulture" in medieval Latin, is obvious.

[9] Heywood and Wright, and Leigh (see the latter's *King's College*) agree in condemning the provost.

given to the Muses and divine philosophy, were throughout the sixteenth and seventeenth centuries a battle ground of warring ambitions. Active minds, confined by an archaic program of studies, found release in strife with one another. The history of the college during those two hundred years is punctuated by eruptions, when the dissatisfied came into open conflict, and the most famous was the Goad riot of April and May, 1576.

The revolt involved five fellows, Robert Liless, Robert Johnson, Robert Dunning, Stephen Lakes, and the ringleader, Giles Fletcher. They drew up a lengthy bill of charges against their provost which they sent to the Bishop of Lincoln and to Lord Burghley, the Chancellor.[10] Many of the complaints seem trivial, while others—particularly those dealing with the preferment of the undeserving—are quite the opposite; indeed they have much of the earnestness of Milton's attack upon the blind mouths who scrambled at the shearers' feast. The plaintiffs sought the summary removal of Goad, and there can be little doubt that at least one of them, their chief, had designs upon the office which he hoped to make vacant.

The provost was worried, deeply so, and labored over his defense, answering each of the charges categorically. After a brief consideration, Burghley sustained him and humbled the wretched fellows, compelling them to write letters of apology. Giles Fletcher composed not one but many, each succeeding expiation more self-reproachful and humiliating than the last.[11] He had played his hand and lost because he had not reckoned with the one factor which left Goad the winner. The provost was unpopular, unworthy, and unprincipled, but he had influence at court, while his opponent had little more than ambition and a flair for poetizing. Fletcher lingered on at Cambridge for several years, still striving for promotions which never came. Since Goad was an enemy and not unpowerful, there is reason for suspecting him of working against Giles Fletcher during these closing years. What is more, there is reason for suspecting that the provost was unfriendly to Phineas Fletcher twenty-four years later.

[10] The charges are printed in Heywood and Wright's *Ancient Laws for King's and Eton*, pp. 227-39.
[11] Heywood and Wright likewise print the letters of apology, *loc. cit.*

It is incredible that the *Piscatorie Eclogs* should not allude to an incident which affected the lives of both father and son. Equally unbelievable is it that Roger Goad, a foe of Giles and Phineas Fletcher, should have escaped mention in the poetic biography, and therefore I feel sure that Griphus, the dunghill swain, must have been the provost. On the other hand, the events of the rebellion, as we know them, agree imperfectly with the piscatory account, where it appears that Thelgon actually obtained what he sought, only to lose it to one called a "wandring guest." Some allowance can be made for the incompleteness of our information about the Goad riot.

On September 17, 1594, Goad wrote to Burghley concerning Robert Liless, one of the conspirators in the earlier affair. He had since proved himself a troublesome sort and had been expelled from King's, by sentence of John Bell, for slandering one Thomas Moundeferd. Within or without, Liless insisted upon having his finger in the politics of the stormy foundation:

he . . . hath now in this late distraction of our company, entered into another plot of greater importance, touching one that should succeed in my roome, who for his strength and authoritie by his frendes should so prevail, as howsoever could not be withstood; whereof by the rejoysing in conference of hym and his adherents, about the success thereof, that is come to my knowledge which they thinke is yet secreate.

Harleian MS 7031, f. 31.

There is a bare possibility that the exile's candidate for the provostship was the same man whom he supported in 1576. With the passing of time, Giles Fletcher had become more than a poet; indeed he was a politician of influence, and his may have been the strength and authority which so genuinely worried Goad. Burghley spent only ten days in snuffing the ambitions of both Liless and his unnamed office seeker. We have had other and more certain evidence that William Cecil was even colder to Fletcher, the servant of Essex, in this later year than he had been in 1576.

Giles Fletcher's third quest for preferment offers a new Griphus, and one whose superficial qualifications fit the *Piscatorie Eclogs'* description much better than Wingfield's or even Goad's. One of the items in the bill of attainder drawn up against the provost in 1576 accused him of being "an approbatour and partaker in selling places at Eaton." Perhaps the conspirators had hoped for some of those offices, but had not been able to outbid and outbribe competitors. Apparently their leader was eyeing the royal school, and his interest there must have centered upon the provostship. This office, too, was filled in 1580. Thomas Ridley, native of Ely and fellow of King's, pursued a career at Cambridge remarkably parallel to Fletcher's, although he achieved his various degrees, including the doctorate in civil law, several years behind his rival. Despite Thelgon's slight seniority, it is easy to see why Ridley, whose record remained unblemished by riot, secured the Eton College post.

Like the Goad identification, the Ridley fails to agree with the "wandring guest" and the boat "possest" and "taken away" details of the eclogue. On the other hand it best fulfills the second loss of the "painted boat." Shortly before 1599 Giles Fletcher bent every effort to obtain the post of master of chancery, but by an extraordinary coincidence, he lost it to the same Thomas Ridley. The Ridley explanation of the obscure but vital passage is mechanically superior to the Goad. If the matter is viewed in its real proportions, however, we shall recognize that the riot of 1576 was a far more important fact in Giles Fletcher's life than either his Eton or university failure. Since the son specifies only one incident of his father's Cantabrigian career, we are forced to conclude that Griphus was Goad, and that lack of information prevents us from completely reconciling the pastoral with the historical account.

In 1600, though aged by the years, Goad was the same contentious, unreliable storm center, and King's College was still a battlefield of endless civil strife. Shortly after the poet arrived, a dispute was waged over the interpretation of the founder's rules. In 1604 William, Bishop of Lincoln, the visitor of King's, sent up a lengthy brief setting forth his understanding of the contested regulations, but the fellows and the provost were enjoying their wrangle too much to be pacified. On June 10 King James issued a summary command that the college abide by the visitor's interpretations. The curtness of the letter suggests that Goad's quarrelsome character was well known to the king, and that the royal patience had begun to tire.

Since Goad had been so inimical to Giles Fletcher, it seems odd that there has been no speculation about how Phineas got on with the provost. The poet's refusal to acknowledge Goad in his own writings is an indication that the provost harbored the grudge. Phineas Fletcher showered complimentary verse on all sides, and particularly upon influential persons who could do him good turns. If he had had the slightest hope of winning his superior's favor, if he had not known that the provost was an irreconcilable foe, he would have hammered out at least several lines of flattery, but he never wrote a measure to please the old man. Now why did Giles Fletcher subject his son to an ancient bitterness, still unforgotten and slumbering like embers beneath the ashes? The unfortunate move did not occur in 1600 but some years before, when Phineas enrolled at Eton. Thenceforth there was no retracting from the scholarship regulations that would lead him to King's, and on that day it was the least likely of possibilities that Goad would still be in the saddle when the boy reached his academic destination. In 1590 his tenure of the provostship had been unusually long. He managed to survive until 1600 and even until 1610, as if he and the fates were plotting Phineas Fletcher's eventual failure at Cambridge.

IV

FRIENDSHIP, LOVE, AND POETRY
1601-10

FLETCHER's undergraduate days were properly spent in learning in perfecting his talent for English and Latin verse, and in obscurity. The college year began on October 10 with the Michaelmas term; was interrupted for a Christmas vacation of almost four weeks; continued until the second Friday before Easter, when a three-week intermission occurred; and then ended on the Friday after the first Tuesday in July. One pictures Fletcher hurrying away from the fenland town to spend elsewhere his month in December and January, his three weeks at Easter, and his three summer months. We find an accurate and valuable record of his absences from table in the commons books of King's College, which provide an almost day-by-day check upon Fletcher's movements during the entire fifteen years of his university career.

None of the poet's biographers have been aware of these documents, and they have innocently fallen into the grossest errors concerning the creative era of Fletcher's life. The most consequential of these blunders has been the assumption that he was resident at King's without interruption, other than the regular vacations, during the entire fifteen years of his fellowship. Actually, he was absent for periods that varied from several days to several years, periods that rarely corresponded with the regular college holidays. No biographical evidence, outside the poet's own writings, is more useful than these commons books. The volume for 1601-2 has been lost, but from the others we ascertain that he was regularly present during the vacations of his undergraduate years. Throughout his first year, his residence in Cambridge was unbroken except for a five-week holiday in the early summer, from May 20 to June 24, 1601.

Three months after his return, on Michaelmas Day, Giles matriculated at Trinity College. It is possible that Phineas Fletcher escorted his younger brother to the university on June 24, and that he had gone to London for that purpose. At any rate Giles' presence marked a reunion of great importance in the lives of both. So thorough was their companionship at Cambridge that Phineas described it as two joined in one, or one disjoined in two. The affinity developed into an unusual literary collaboration, less definable than that of John Fletcher and Francis Beaumont, but probably more thorough. For the time being, Giles' appearance meant the resumption of a boyhood association that had been broken when Phineas went to Eton.

The younger brother had entered Westminster School, and from there had gone on to Trinity College. One of the father's closest London friends, Henry Wayland, the first man whom he sent for upon his return from Moscow, had been a senior fellow of Trinity, and he may have opened the boy's way through Westminster School into Henry the Eighth's foundation. On the other hand, the newcomer found an immediate patron in the master of his college, Thomas Neville, "the magnificent Neville," who was famous because of his extravagant outlays for Trinity buildings and banquets. Some of his interest may have been due to the youth's premature poetic talent, and more to a connection between Richard Fletcher and Neville's father, who succeeded the bishop as dean of Peterborough. Probably most of his partiality, however, was the result of a distant kinship between pensioner and master, Thomas Neville being a descendant of Anne Preston, the granddaughter of Richard Molyneux. Thus he belonged to that Molyneux, Neville, Willoughby, Fletcher kindred that had already yielded Sir Richard Molyneux as a patron to the elder Giles. Perhaps the master, rather than Wayland, started the youth on his road to Trinity College. Certainly the younger brother enjoyed happier prospects under Neville than did the elder under Goad.

During the same year James Lakes came up to King's from Eton. He and Phineas Fletcher had much in common and probably they were comrades from the start. He seems to have been the nephew of Stephen Lakes, who was one of Giles Fletcher's fellow conspirators in the Goad riot. His father, Osmund Lakes, also a King's College alumnus, was the vicar of Ringwood, Hants., and in 1600 the elder Fletcher owned the rights to the Ringwood income. James subsequently married in the Hampshire village and practiced physic.

Although Phineas Fletcher has left us without a certain key to the dates of his poems, it is possible to formulate an accurate chronology. A few of his minor versifications, most of them frankly experimental, can be fixed in the neighborhood of these under-graduate years. Slight as they are, they reveal an important evolution that was going on within the author's mind.

His *Sylva Poetica* of 1633 prints three little Latin works, seem-ingly written to fulfill opponencies or responsions: "Veritas omnis cognitionis est in judicio," "Mors est malum," and "Anni tempo-rum mutationes, variorum causa morborum." They are exactly similar to Milton's "Naturam non pati senium," prepared for the same purpose. Their composition therefore probably occurred in 1604, Fletcher's year as a senior sophister, or in any one of the fol-lowing three, the period of his candidacy for the master's degree. The last is scientific and medical in subject matter, and will be of help in our investigation into the author's anatomical studies. It was an era of trial and error, and two other versifyings show an un-certainty as to whether Latin or English was to be his eventual me-dium: "Upon the picture of Achmat the Turkish tyrant" and "In effigiem Achmati Turcarum tyranni," the same poem with parallel versions in the two languages. This first Achmet, after ascending to the throne at the age of thirteen, showed flashes of brilliance. By 1608, however, he revealed weakness, when he abandoned an in-vasion on the Asiatic side of the Bosphorus; and again on Novem-ber 11 of the same year, when he permitted himself to sign the peace of Sitvatorek with Austria. Where Fletcher saw a picture of Achmet the First is not known, but when he refers to the Turk as a dangerous, unbridled tyrant, we can be practically certain he was writing prior to 1606.

Fletcher's initial appearance in print was the first real milestone of his poetic development. He contributed three Latin versifica-tions to *Threno-Thriambeuticon*, an academic collection bemoan-ing the passing of Elizabeth and hailing the accession of King James. It was brought forth in 1603 by John Legat, university printer. Like his brother, Phineas Fletcher wrote an English poem for a similar collection, *Sorrowes Joy*, issued in the same year. Each of the four was an unblushing bid for favor within and without the university. It is interesting to note that King's College had extraordinary success in turning out poets, both in Latin and English. A full half of the items in *Threno-Thriambeuticon* were the contributions of the fellows and scholars on the royal foundation, nor in this respect was *Threno-Thriambeuticon* unusual.

Although there is no record of Fletcher's activities during his second year at Cambridge, we have scattered glimpses of him in the following two. During the summer of 1603 he left King's on three different occasions for brief periods. One of these in June, sixteen days in duration, gave him sufficient time to make the London trip; but the others of four days each, indicate that nearer places offered him hospitality. His first quarterly payment of ten shillings as a fellow is noted in the mundum books under the date of August 25. In October the university was scourged by a fearful outbreak of the plague, which was no stranger to Cambridge. By November all sermons and public exercises were halted. Caius College and perhaps other foundations granted leaves of absence until January 12, but Fletcher stayed on. The bachelor's degree was conferred upon him on the Thursday preceding Palm Sunday in 1604.

The 1604-11 era, set off at one end by the bachelor's degree and at the other by ordination, was the springtide of the poet's life, although there proved to be no summer, but only autumn and winter. The seven years were bright with dignified friendships, love affairs, and literary triumphs. The bulk of his poetry—*The Purple Island*, *The Apollyonists* and *Locustae*, *Brittain's Ida*, and part of the *Piscatorie Eclogs*—was produced during these years. Furthermore he was projecting some magnum opus, a source of pride, even though it never took shape. Like his father, Phineas Fletcher entertained high ambitions, and to achieve them it seemed necessary only to prove his poetic power. His friends and superiors increasingly praised his genius, calling him the foremost singer of the Cam, and, according to his theory, the future was filled with promise. If only Fletcher, with all his talent, had been able to rid himself of the idea that the chief guerdon of the poetic art was worldly place, a fame on mortal soil, how different would have been his life and his accomplishments!

The commons book for 1604-5, like that for 1601-2, has been lost, but the following volume provides us with a compensating fullness of information about the poet's activities. These records are not only of value in tracing Fletcher's goings and comings, but they also assist in fixing the dates of some of his major poems and major love affairs. The plague reappeared in the autumn of 1606, and on November 6 Caius College again granted leaves of absence until the end of the Christmas vacation. Fletcher departed on November 3 and did not reappear in the college hall until Christmas Day. It is almost certain that the events described in the third piscatory eclogue belong to this winter holiday.[1] There we learn that the poet went to the shore of silver Medway, which, no doubt, was his piscatorial way of saying Cranbrook and its environs.

Fletcher may have avoided London and passed on to the south because the city menaced him with the contagion from which he fled. On the other hand, the trip is more probably one of the many indications that his ties with the weald, instead of having long been severed, as has been generally believed, were still strong and active. Although the sons had gone off to the city and the father had died, the Fletchers never pulled up their roots from Kentish soil. A few years before, the poet's uncle had taken a second wife in Sissinghurst, and his father owned property in the county until his death.[2] Phineas Fletcher had spent a large part of his first eight years in his mother's Cranbrook home, and he had many relatives in the neighborhood. Some of them were persons of position, and the more mature Fletcher believed in using his connections with gentry to the utmost. From 1604 on, he took annual summer holidays of several months which made possible frequent and long sojourns at the place of his birth.

Dr. Giles Fletcher's sister, a Pownall, probably lived at Hollingbourn, some fourteen miles from Cranbrook, and the poet seems to have stayed with her during large parts of his visits.[3] She had a

---

[1] The writer of the eclogue dropped a hint which enables us to fix its date. Myrtilus says that he had "leave to play" by Medway's shore when the madding winds shook the madder ocean. Apparently his holiday was granted during the storms of the winter season. It could not have occurred after 1608, because Fletcher swore allegiance to a new ladylove during or before that year. Prior to 1608 the only known winter absence of sufficient length to permit a visit to Kent was that of 1605.

[2] Additional MS 24, 487, ff. 118, 121, 124.

[3] There are two references to the Pownall family in the Cranbrook register; the first is dated August 21, 1583, and the second, October 28, 1584. Since there are no

son, Nathaniel, several years younger than Phineas Fletcher, who entered Christ Church College, Oxford, in 1600. He and his Fletcher cousins were intimates, sharing common academic and literary interests. In addition there were numerous Sheaffes, who might offer hospitality nearer Cranbrook.[4]

The Robartses were related by marriage to the Sheaffes, and Sir Walter, son and heir of Sir Thomas, the high sheriff of Kent, was the poet's cousin. Fletcher was repeatedly lured across a hundred miles of English country by affection for the Pownalls and Sheaffes, by romantic sentiments which several young Kentish ladies aroused, but above all by the wealth and position of this chief Cranbrook family. Whether or not he lodged at their Glassenbury house is not known, but he would have been content to linger about its gates. He could also call Margaret, daughter of George Robarts of Moatlands at Brenchley, his cousin. She was the Gemma of the *Poeticall Miscellanies,* who married Sir Walter some years later. Before and after their wedding, Fletcher addressed the young

---

further entries of the name, Phineas Fletcher's aunt and her family seem to have removed to a new location, which may have been Hollingbourn. (See pp. 7-8 above, and Chap. I, f. n. 8.) Fletcher's allusion to the shore of silver Medway in *Piscatorie Eclog* II may place him at Hollingbourn, which was eight miles distant from the river, rather than at Cranbrook, which was twenty-five miles distant. All this has a bearing upon the identity of the mysterious Fusca.

[4] Perhaps in the course of these visits the poet became intimate with Thomas, the son of Richard Sheaffe and Demmie Smythe, who may be the chief character in the "Nisa Ecloga." One of the author's most curious works, it tells a story that is plainly based on fact. A certain William, who lives in London and owns property where the Thames is narrow, complains of his wife, Nisa. She has deserted his bed, has sued him at law, and he suspects her of infidelity. Both her mother and father have been active against him. It may be a mere coincidence that many years after the composition of "Nisa Ecloga" Thomas Sheaffe of London, and late of Cranbrook, wrote a letter—never before connected with the Fletchers—to Archbishop Laud and the Commissioners for Causes Ecclesiastical, complaining that his wife, Mary, had been persuaded by her mother, Elizabeth Gibbon of Westcliffe, to quit his bed and board. For twelve months they had refused him access to their home and detained his goods (*Calendar of State Papers,* 1640-41). The domestic tragedy recounted in the letter is remarkably similar to the burden of "Nisa Ecloga." It seems unlikely that the circumspect King's College fellow should have been on intimate terms with two families so grievously divided. The official letter must have been written after 1633, when Laud entered the primacy, and the eclogue before 1633, when it was printed. Since practically all of Fletcher's poetry was completed close to 1610, this work can hardly be assigned to the years immediately preceding 1633. It is possible that the poem alludes to an early bickering which led eventually to a break between husband and wife.

couple in three poems and a prose work. His relations with them were affectionate, but apparently he mixed his friendly yearnings with certain hopes of private profit. The family had influence, wealth, and connections with persons of high station. The ambitious youth would have been happy to share any or all of these desirable possessions.

One aristocratic dame of Hollingbourn was distantly allied to the poet and less remotely to Sir Walter Robarts—Lady Colepeper. Evidently she was the object of three of the author's most unusual poems. In these his solemn genius takes on a courtly gaiety like that of Suckling or Carew. The first installment of the sequence, "On womens lightnesse," was an indictment of the sex which he sent to Lady Colepeper. She answered in mock anger, and Fletcher retaliated with "A reply upon the fair M. S.," and again with "An Apologie for the premises to the Ladie Culpepper." These compositions have not been recognized as sequels, because of the deceptive title of the middle link.[5] The "fair-sweet" flattered in the series belonged to an ancient family associated with Goudhurst and Hollingbourn, and related to the Sidneys of Penshurst. She seems to have been Elizabeth, the daughter of John Cheyney of Guestling in Sussex, and the wife of Sir Thomas of Hollingbourn. Not only was Fletcher intimate with the Pownalls, who probably lived in the same village, but Sir Walter Robarts' aunt had married into the Colepeper family.[6]

Lady Colepeper was destined to play a vital rôle in the poet's life, but in the winter of 1606 she was merely a friend, one of the group which drew him from the plague-infested fens to the hills of Cranbrook or Hollingbourn, where he was introduced to the mysterious Coelia. Though it was the season when poets are not supposed to be susceptible, Fletcher fell in love. He promptly altered the pastoral designation of Coridon, which he had taken unto himself in 1603,

---

[5] There can be little doubt that "A reply upon the fair M. S." was addressed to Lady Colepeper. It has never been connected with her, probably because the title is deceptively arranged. The title leads the reader to believe that the lady's initials are "M. S." The poem is printed between the other two and is obviously part of the series. Furthermore, the author's lines refer to her as "a Daintie maid, that drawes her double name from bitter sweetnesse," apparently an allusion to *Colepeper*. By "M. S." perhaps Fletcher meant MS, that is, the lady's manuscript letter.

[6] For the relationship, see Griffin's *Visitation of the Arms of Kent*, p. 30.

to that of Myrtilus. The lady's identity is still a riddle,[7] but it matters little since she was to have no effect upon his future. The winter winds produced less warmth in her heart than in her swain's, and the names of Coelia and Myrtilus never reappear in Fletcherian verse. By 1608 he was pledging allegiance to another lady.

The months following the poet's return to the university were marked by the entrance into his life of "W. C.," probably William Cappell,[8] and John Tomkins. Both became his friends, but Fletcher and Tomkins grew to be a David and Jonathan. Cappell matriculated during the Easter quarter, and several years later Fletcher addressed him in "To Master W. C." It is a reassuring glimpse of a finer, unselfish side of the poet's nature. Evidently he was Cappell's instructor, and in the poem he takes his charge to task because he has gone off, bent on love, to Little Haddam in Herts., and to Maddingly, three miles from Cambridge. The teacher admonishes his erring scholar, his "deare Willy," with tact, humor, and winning enthusiasm for academic tasks.

John Tomkins was the Thomalin who appears again and again in the Fletcherian poems.[9] In his "To Thomalin" the author wrote:

> I love my health, my life, my books, my friends,
> Thee; (dearest *Thomalin*) *Nothing* above thee.

Tomkins shared the poet's inmost thoughts, became the confidant of his love affairs and his consolation in disappointment. For a time he was more intimate with Phineas Fletcher than any man except Giles had ever been. The relationship was all the more vital because it was concentrated within Fletcher's creative years and colored nearly all of his major works. Fletcher could scarcely have heard of Tomkins before his appearance at Cambridge in the fall of 1606. Four years younger than the poet, he came to fill Orlando

---

[7] One is at first tempted to read an allegory into the third eclogue, identifying Coelia as the Church and the love affair as the author's taking of the cloth. The extreme worldliness of the latter part of the poem renders such an interpretation absurd.

[8] There were two "W. C.'s" at King's College between 1600 and 1616, the span of Fletcher's residence. The second was a William Coppin, admitted on Lady Day in 1608. Since Coppin was so much Fletcher's junior, it is unlikely that the poet would make him privy to his romance.

[9] John Tomkins has often been confused with Thomas Tomkis, author of two plays, *Lingua* and *Albumazar*.

Gibbons' place as organist of King's College chapel. The two were not kinsmen; they had had no common friends; indeed their backgrounds were completely unlike. Tomkins, not a university man, was the son of Thomas, chanter of the choir at Gloucester cathedral, who traced his origin to Lostwithiel, Cornwall. Despite all these differences, the two must have entered into a community of interest and feeling almost immediately, because within a year their relations were at their closest.

Tomkins was a talented youth and was hailed by Thomas Nash [10] as the greatest organist of his day. Furthermore Fletcher mentions "Eupathus' Complaining" [11] and "The Dirge of Pasilia," [12] which seem to have been poems composed by the organist, and, with a surprising vehemence, praises their author as a great poet. The foregoing is an unhappy sample of Fletcher's critical judgment, and yet it suggests that the friendship grew largely out of mutual literary interests. Tomkins had numerous brothers who, like him, were musicians. Of these, Thomas was then at Magdalen College, Oxford. He developed into one of the first composers of his day, and at present is better known than John. The King's College organist maintained contact with Magdalen,[13] and consequently Thomas became a friend of the poet at this time. He dedicated the twenty-first piece in his *Songs of 3, 4, 5, and 6 Parts,* published at London in 1622, to Fletcher. Its words, with their reference to Fusca, whom we are soon to meet, prove that it was written close to 1610:

> Fusca in thy starry eyes
> Love in black still mourning dies
> That among so many slain
> Thou hast loved none again.

---

[10] *Quaternion,* p. 63. This Thomas Nash (1588-1648) was a friend of Rous, of the Bodleian.

[11] "To Mr. Jo. Tomkins." "To E. C. in Cambridge."

[12] "To E. C. in Cambridge."

[13] An Edward Othen of Magdalen wrote out the following inventory of goods (printed in Bloxam's *Register,* IV, 238) which he had left in the hands of John Tomkins between 1606 and 1610:

"One gown of black cloth faced with velvet	xxvi	s.	viii	d.
A frock gowne of cloathe of a puatre culler	xv	s.	
	xli	s.	viii	d."

Having familiarized ourselves with Giles Fletcher and Tomkins, we have already penetrated the Cambridge society of poets who surrounded Fletcher and celebrated him as their president. This clique was founded in accordance with the traditional laws of the pastoral cult. The organist and the author's brother were the chief subordinates, and both Woodford and Cook were members—each long-established friends of Fletcher and also contributors to the academic collections. Even Samuel Collins,[14] though older than the rest, may have been enrolled as a sort of honorary associate; but there were others whose names and dates of admission are obscure. One of these may have been the "H. M." who contributed complimentary verses to the 1627 edition of *Locustae,* and who has never been satisfactorily identified.[15] Fletcher addressed another of the brethren, his "beloved Thenot," on several occasions.[16] Although it has not been suggested before, there is reason for believing Thenot was Francis Quarles, the emblem writer.

In his stanzas addressed to this mysterious friend, Fletcher takes the young man to task for celebrating him as a second Colin or Spenser. Though the author of *The Purple Island* was commonly reputed to be a reincarnation of his master, we have but a single written statement to that effect. Quarles composed three complimentary poems, which were printed with the anatomical geography, one of which bears the title: "To the ingenious composer of this pastorall, the Spenser of this age." There can be little question that the emblem writer and his second Colin were intimates in after years. Since the former matriculated at Cambridge some time before 1613, it is entirely possible that the later familiarity was an outgrowth of a university amity.[17] Whether or not Quarles was a

[14] Collins wrote complimentary verses on *Locustae,* and he was a frequent contributor to the academic collections.

[15] Various commentators, including William Thomson of Queen's College, Oxford, have identified "H. M." as Henry More. It is true that the Platonist, years later, knew the work of both Fletchers. When *Locustae* was published, he was only thirteen and could scarcely have written the verses signed with his initials.

[16] *Purple Island,* VI, st. 4; "To my beloved Thenot."

[17] It might be objected that one of Quarles' complimentary poems addresses the author of *The Purple Island* in these words:

"I Vow (sweet stranger) if my lazie quill."

The anatomical poem, however, was printed anonymously, and apparently the encomiasts had been instructed to keep up the pretense. We shall have other evidence to prove that in 1633 Fletcher was no "stranger" to the emblem writer.

member of the pastoral society, Fletcher cannot be blamed for a pride in his small group, which included at least three or four persons who were to become nationally famous as artists in words or music.

In the year 1606 the poet entered upon a larger life of romance and friendship, such as he had never known. Our next bit of information concerning him is afforded by the matter-of-fact college records, which take no cognizance of a passion for Coelia or a fraternal fondness for Thomalin: throughout the twelve months following Christmas, 1606, he was receiving quarterly payments of five shillings *pro lectura*. In the meantime, the ambitions, apparent in his tributes to James, had grown, and so had his confidence in literary accomplishment as a means of fulfilling them. Nothing brought quicker fame than success in the field of the academic drama. Three entries in the King's College account book for the Annunciation term of 1607, concern disbursals for a comedy written by Phineas Fletcher. The author received forty-five shillings for his part, and a watchman named Elam was paid tenpence. The work is not extant today, nor is mention of it to be found anywhere other than in the college ledger. As the writer's first offering to the theater, it was probably an amateurish *tour de force,* the more so since his mature play, *Sicelides,* is itself a mediocre accomplishment. Since Fletcher must have recognized its deficiencies and since he was never willing to acknowledge his later piscatory drama,[18] it is not strange that the first comedy has disappeared.

Although the compensation paid to Elam was no strain upon the bursar, one wonders, for a moment, why it was necessary to hire a policeman for a sedate, academic entertainment. Despite the stringent restrictions placed upon Jacobean university students, their antics would put to shame the most exuberant of modern collegians. They eagerly awaited the gathering of an audience and the opportunity for stirring up a quarrel with the members of a rival foundation or with the populace of Cambridge town. The most sensational outburst of the kind during the poet's residence occurred while a comedy was being presented at King's College. The enemy attended in numbers, fortified with auxiliary troops of townsmen

[18] The single edition of *Sicelides* published during the author's lifetime appeared anonymously.

and supplied with stones. The ammunition, which was at first concealed beneath the dignified robes, soon made its appearance and filled the air. The college accounts make no mention of the heads broken during the exchange of pleasantries, but are chiefly concerned with the shattered windows. A soul-stirring climax was reached when "a great post of timber was violently pulled out of the ground, and there with divers running at a strong gate, the same was broke open." [19]

The great riot of King's has been connected with Fletcher's comedy by Professor Moore-Smith,[20] and rightly so. The outburst occurred on February 20, 1606/7, and the bills for the drama were settled during the Annunciation term of the same year, possibly as early as March. It is unlikely that the accounts would be closed until one or two weeks after the performance which they concerned. Although there may have been several King's College dramatic presentations within a few days of one another, there is more likelihood that Phineas Fletcher sat amidst the whirring of stones, the crashing of windows, and the thundering of the battering-ram, lamenting the fate of the project upon which he had pinned his ambitions.

In March, 1607/8, the poet proceeded Master of Arts and at about the same time entered upon a new human relationship which to him was immeasurably more important than any academic degree. The feminine spirit that guided the singer through his literary career was a certain Fusca. Their affinity may have been both real and Platonic; it was certainly the latter. The lady, dark in complexion, trails clouds of brunette loveliness through poem after poem, but the identity of Fusca has withstood numerous attempts at solution. Dan Cupid brought Fusca in one hand, and in the other a new name, Thirsil. It was neither Coridon nor Myrtilus, but Thirsil, who wrote *The Purple Island,* large parts of the *Piscatorie Eclogs,* and most of the *Poeticall Miscellanies.*

The poet referred to Fusca in many of his poems.[21] From the matter-of-fact nature of such remarks, it is plain that she was a real

[19] Cooper's *Annals,* III, 24.

[20] Boas (II, v, n. 1) states that Professor Moore-Smith held this opinion. Boas does not give Moore-Smith's reasons.

[21] Specific allusions to Fusca occur in "To my ever honoured Cousin," "To E. C. in Cambridge," "To Master W. C.," "To my beloved Thenot," and "Fusca Ecloga."

person, but they do not prove that the two were actual lovers. Since it was the poet's curious custom to alter his own name with each new mistress,[22] the attachment could not have been formed before 1603, when Fletcher was Coridon, nor could it have been prolonged after 1615 when he became Algon. Furthermore, we can assign a more precise date to one of his references, that contained in "To my ever honoured Cousin," an address written prior to Robarts' marriage, which occurred shortly before 1610. Other signs point to 1608 as the year when Fletcher first swore his allegiance.[23] Of course he may have known the lady long before succumbing to her charms.

There are equally definite clues to Fusca's habitation. In "Fusca Ecloga" the author describes their first meeting in an oak grove upon a holiday, and hints at the actual location:

> Ipse agro forte errabam, qui fronte Triones
> Spectat, et illota nomen sortitur ab ursa.

The "name derived from the bear" is an almost positive allusion to Bearden in Kent, a short mile out of Hollingbourn, the probable residence of the author's Pownall kin. His reference to a holiday can only mean that he was enjoying a vacation from the university, and since he seems to have spent most of his real leisure time in his birthplace and the surrounding neighborhood, there is further reason for believing Fusca to have been a daughter of the weald. Fletcher writes to Robarts about her in a manner which indicates that the young landowner knew her. Sir Walter would have had no familiarity with a fenland or a London lass, but only with a Kentish lady, and one of breeding. Finally in a verse letter, written to Edward Cook from Brenchley, there are several significant lines:

[22] Fletcher calls attention to his peculiar custom of changing his own pastoral name in "To my beloved Thenot," lines 13-15. Whatever may be the appropriateness of his habit, it enables us to date a large number of his poems. The poet adheres religiously to this rule in all of his English poems, but in "Myrtillus Ecloga" Myrtillus pledges love to a Daphne; and in "Lusus Ecloga," to a Nerine. Neither of these poems seems to have any biographical importance.

[23] See Fletcher's definite statement that he called himself Myrtilus, before changing to Thirsil ("To my beloved Thenot," lines 13-15). Thus there must have been a sufficient lapse of time between the Coridon baptism in 1603 and the later Thirsil baptism to permit an intermediate love affair. Most of the poems in which the author appears as Thirsil belong to the neighborhood of 1608.

> And often while my pipe lies idle by me,
> Read *Fusca's* deep disdain, and *Thirsil's* plaining;
> Yet in that face is no room for disdaining;
> Where cheerfull kindnesse smiles in either eye,
> And beauty still kisses humilitie.

> Then do not marvel *Kentish* strong delights
> Stealing the time, do here so long detain me:

When vacationing near Cranbrook, the swain had an opportunity to see his mistress' face.

We have a reasonably full measure of indices by which to locate Fusca, both in time and space, but the poet seems to have taken pains to shield her name from the public. He overlooked the fact that Miss Ethel Seaton would find, three centuries later, a manuscript of his *Brittain's Ida* in the Sion College Library, and would skillfully recognize it as his work. The opening stanza of the new version, which was carefully deleted in the printed version, proves to be the essential clue:

> Thirsil hidde in a willowes shaddowing
>
> . . .
>
> Thus ganne to trye his downie Muses wing,
> For soe the fayre Eliza deign'd desire
> Hir wishes were his lawes, hir will his fire,
> And hiding neerer Came his stranger name
> He thought with song his raging fire to tame.

Miss Seaton did not realize that the Eliza was Fusca but such must have been the case because Fletcher has called himself Thirsil, a name inseparably bound with this lady.

We are now in a position to piece together the several fragments. The fair one seems to have been a resident of the Hollingbourn locality, a gentlewoman and an acquaintance of Robarts, a person of whose friendship the poet would never tire of boasting to his Cambridge associates, and an Eliza or Elizabeth. The beautiful kinswoman of the Sidneys and the Robartses, Elizabeth Cheyney Colepeper, lived at Hollingbourn, and she had already been the object of Platonic addresses from Fletcher's pen. True enough, she was a married woman with a little daughter, but so perfect and so constant a poetic mistress could scarcely have been found in a real love affair. There is an orderly sequence in the poet's deportment, if Lady Colepeper was Fusca. The series of poems that bear her name probably followed close upon the holiday meeting under the oak trees, because the author makes no mention of Thirsil or Fusca, nor does he protest his love. *Brittain's Ida* was an outgrowth from the second stage. Fletcher has become Thirsil and hides his stranger name, Myrtilus, no doubt, in Cambridge. The opening stanza seems to be an announcement of the shift in nomenclature, and as yet he has not hit upon the title of Fusca which he was to press upon the fair one. By this time, however, she has filled his heart with a raging fire. The allusion to his "downie Muses wing" would also suggest that the poem preceded *The Purple Island, The Apollyonists,* and his other more mature works. Finally, in 1608 Fusca had been securely installed as the divinity of the young man's poetizing, a position which Thirsil, the goddess herself, her husband, her relatives, and the King's College Platonic poets, recognized and celebrated. Customs have changed since the day when a circumspect Fletcher could regard a sensuous love narrative as an offering proper to a matron.

Having been introduced to Fusca, we are again thrust, whether we will or no, into the problem of the chronological order of Fletcher's poetry. The most pervasive and most consequential error about Phineas Fletcher is the notion that he wrote his verse close to the years of its publication—1627 and 1633. Actually nine-tenths of his work was turned out between 1607 and 1612, some twenty years before the date erroneously ascribed to it. It is the product of a youth, and Fletcher, speaking of all his poems long after he had deserted Fusca and the Muses, called them "the raw essays of my very unripe youth." The rawness or ripeness is a matter for subsequent consideration. Since the so-called essays were concentrated within a brief span of years and since Fletcher was a patient reworker, the poems probably overlapped one another. For example, he was still perfecting *The Purple Island* after he had begun its successor, *Locustae.*

The author himself is of little help in the present inquiry, having left but one statement, and that the airiest. At the opening of the versified anatomy, he tells us that he has hitherto uttered "soft sighs of love unto a looser strain," alluding to his third eclogue, one or more of the Latin eclogues, and above all to *Brittain's Ida.*

He has also lamented upon "poore Thelgons wrong," a subject treated in three of the piscatory eclogues, although the larger part of each of the trio was certainly written several years after the completion of *The Purple Island*. The most valuable feature of Fletcher's autobiographical account is his silence about the twin works in which he seems to have had the greatest pride—*Locustae* and *The Apollyonists*. Thus there can be little doubt that *The Purple Island* preceded them. Since the author stated that he was busy upon the Gunpowder Plot poem late in 1610, the other must have been started several years earlier. *Christs Victorie and Triumph*, published in the same year, provides corroboration because it contains a reference to Eclecta's "Hymen," the grand climax of the anatomical epic.[24]

The "isle of man," therefore, was conceived prior to 1610; and what is more, its climax was in final form in 1609 or before. On the other hand, at least one part of the first canto was inspired by the author's ordination in 1611.[25] What seems to be a confusion in dates, with conclusion and introduction turned topsy-turvy, is no other than an indication that Fletcher was following his usual method of composition—subjecting his work to a process of elaboration and adaptation that went on for years. Izaak Walton, later a friend of the poet, quoted seventeen lines from *The Purple Island* in his *Compleat Angler*, but almost one-half of the lines of the Angler's rendition contain important variations from the text that we know.[26] The author appears to have written at least two versions of the work, although only one is now extant.

The conclusions concerning the creation of *The Purple Island* are the result of inference and deduction. *Locustae* and *The Apollyonists* came into being through the same accretion, but here the evidence concerning the methods used has survived in full. In addition to the 1627 edition of *Locustae*, there are three known manuscript versions—each an autograph and each materially different from the others—and an English paraphrase, *The Apollyonists*. All can be dated with reasonable accuracy. The author began the

---

[24] "Christs Triumph after Death," st. 49-50.
[25] *The Purple Island*, I, st. 33.
[26] The quotation is to be found in the 1655, or second, edition of *The Compleat Angler*, p. 296. The lines were taken from *The Purple Island*, XII, st. 2-6.

first shortly before March, 1610/11, and developed it while he watched at his father's bedside. Having completed his work, he furnished it with a dedication to James Montagu, Bishop of Bath and Wells, and a friend of his deceased parent. The second, addressed to Prince Henry, was turned out during the ensuing year. It proved to be an abortive gesture, because Henry died in November; whereupon Fletcher produced a third variant,[27] which he inscribed to Charles and to the Prince's tutor, Thomas Murray. This and *The Apollyonists* [28] probably were written within a year of 1612. It has been supposed that the poet began to enjoy the beneficence of Sir Henry Willoughby in 1615. We shall find that he won the squire's patronage three years earlier, and that from then on he refrained from such open hunting expeditions for a new master.[29] Although the young man's four attempts to secure a patron, concentrated as they were within a few months, clarify the development of his anti-papist poem, they have a wider significance, casting a strong light upon the development of his life as well. They are our first indication that through these quiet years of friendship, love, and literary productivity, a crisis was in the making.

One last incident, serene in nature, must be recounted before we turn to a stormier era. Walter Robarts took Margaret Robarts, the poet's Gemma, as his bride in 1610 or shortly before.[30] Apparently Fletcher made the long journey to Cranbrook or Glassenbury so that he might be present at the nuptials,[31] and as his offering he wrought his lovely "An Hymen at the Marriage of my most deare

[27] All three of these manuscripts are now owned by the British Museum: Sloane 444, Egerton 2875, and Harley 3196.

[28] *The Apollyonists* contains a reference to the death of Henry of Navarre (IV, st. 26), which occurred in 1610. Its last three stanzas are in praise of King Charles, but these were added shortly before the publication of the poem.

[29] The printed *Locustae* and *Apollyonists* have new dedications to Sir Roger Townshend and his bride. These, unlike the earlier dedications, seem to be expressions of gratitude, rather than solicitations for patronage.

[30] There is no record of the date of this marriage at Cranbrook, but the couple's first child, Thomas, was baptized in 1611. Miss Seaton erroneously gave this year as 1615. A monument in the Cranbrook church plainly indicates that Thomas was born in 1611 and died in January, 1637/8.

[31] The verse letter, "To E. C. in Cambridge" (lines 43-44), contains an explicit reference to "An Hymen." While conveying news to his correspondent, the poet informs "E. C." of the epithalamium which he has just written.

Cousins, Mr. W. and M. R." His absence from commons from March 5, 1609/10, to April 19 suggests the precise time and duration of his visit.[32] From his verse letter to Cook, written during his stay in Kent, it is plain that he is lingering on after the marriage celebration, loath to return to the striving and disappointment of university life. His allusions to the grief, white-headed caring, and black disdain, waiting to greet him at Cambridge, indicate that he already sensed his impending destiny. He procrastinated, finding an anodyne in the wood nymphs and graces, the Kentish strong delights.

[32] Fletcher was away from commons for unusually long periods on three different occasions, during the years 1609 and 1610. The first absence extended from January 19, 1608/9, to February 26. Since most of the fellows and scholars were likewise away, the cause was probably plague rather than marriage. The second began on the following September 16 and ended on the thirteenth of the next month. This may be the time of the Robarts wedding, but Fletcher's letter to Cook during his absence appears to describe a Kent colored by the soft tones of spring. Again he reports a visit which was more leisurely than was possible, if he allowed himself less than four weeks. Finally, the September absence also may be ascribed to the plague which descended upon Cambridge during the autumn of 1610.

V

THE CRISIS
1610-15

BY THE closing months of 1610, *Brittain's Ida* was completed, *The Purple Island* largely so, *Locustae* and "Elisa" were well under way, portions of the *Piscatorie Eclogs* and the Latin eclogues had been finished, a comedy had been written and presented, and what later were to comprise the *Poeticall Miscellanies* were for the most part in existence. The poet had not yet attained his twenty-eighth birthday, and he had already composed four-fifths of his life's work, enough to immortalize him. Nevertheless, he returned to Cambridge to face, once and for all, the reality—or at least what he deemed the reality—of his academic failure. The increasing bulk of Fletcher's achievement, the very circumstance which should have served to fill his cup of content, was one of the principal reasons why he suddenly decided his university career was hopeless. Since he had pinned material expectations upon each manuscript which he caused to be circulated, he regarded the mounting heap as a monument of disappointment.[1] In addition, several new influences focused upon 1610 and 1611, each of which would tend to make Fletcher self-critical and introspective.

To the poet the era was laden with the significance of mortality, as one after another of his closest friends and relatives sickened and died. The strange concentration of these deaths must have sobered him and made him conscious of the temporary lot of humankind and of the necessity for hasty achievement. Endowed with a mind that tended naturally toward melancholy, Fletcher probably became pessimistic and readier to render an unfavorable judgment upon his own accomplishments. The first blow came from an unexpected source. Dr. Thomas Playfere, whom Fletcher admired as one of the most brilliant thinkers in the university, developed insanity and died February 2, 1608/9. The poet wrote a heartfelt

[1] *Piscatorie Eclogs,* II, st. 8.

epitaph. Shortly afterward Edmund Cook, Fletcher's oldest friend at Cambridge and, with the exception of Tomkins, his closest, likewise lost his reason, though he lived on for several years.[2]

The third tragedy in the extraordinary sequence was the death of Sir Anthony Irby in 1610, which occurred amid heart-rending circumstances. Sir Anthony was the scion of an ancient Lincolnshire family and frequently had sat as Member of Parliament for Boston. His death was the subject of Fletcher's important elegy, "Elisa," and the woe, manifest in every stanza, is adequate proof that the author was no passive onlooker doing a piece of journeyman's work. Some years prior to 1610, Sir Anthony married Elisa, the third daughter of Sir John Peyton of Isleham, Cambridgeshire. In his poem Fletcher shows greater affection for the widow than for the deceased. Isleham was only nineteen miles distant from the university and Lady Irby's brother, Robert Peyton, matriculated at King's in 1609. Probably it was through the young scholar that Fletcher made Elisa Irby's acquaintance.

The remaining sorrows, likewise confined within these several years, proceeded from the deaths of three near relatives. On October 9, 1610, the poet lost his aunt, Phebe Fletcher. By her testament she left a Bible and the sum of fifty pounds to Phineas and an equal amount to the younger Giles. There followed an ugly domestic dispute with Nathaniel, eldest son of the late Bishop of London, successfully contesting the will in a court procedure. Evidently all was not well between the children of Richard and Giles. The incident might be connected with the ominous silence which the Cambridge brothers maintained concerning the writings of their dramatist cousin, John. They were, on the other hand, intimate with another cousin, Nathaniel Pownall, student of Christ College at Oxford. He died in 1610 or in 1611, still a youth whose years were luminous with promise. As a token of his respect and affection, the younger Giles Fletcher edited his kinsman's manuscript, *The Young divines Apologie for his continuance in the University with certain Meditations*, dedicated it to John King, Bishop of London, and in 1612 had it published by his own printer, Cantrell Legge. Perhaps this *in memoriam* tribute, so well conceived, suggested to the older brother a similar project, the editing of his late

[2] Additional MS 5816, f. 43.

father's *"De literis antiquae Britanniae."* He undertook the task close to 1611, although some twenty years elapsed before he carried the little poem to the press.[3] His pious labor consisted of scarcely more than addressing a dedication to Eton and King's Colleges.[4]

The sixth bereavement, by far the heaviest, came in the early months of 1611, when Dr. Giles Fletcher died, after a grievous and extended illness. Phineas went down from King's College to watch at his father's bedside, just as the doomed man had gone to Cranbrook to be with the vicar during his last days. Giles Fletcher was buried at St. Catherine Coleman, Fenchurch Street, on March 11. Before the end, the dying man had said to Phineas:

> My Son had I followed the course of this World, and would either have given, or taken bribes, I might (happily) have made you rich, but now must leave you nothing but your education.
>
> *A Father's Testament,* p. 2.

The loss of an admired scholar, two comrades of his own age, an aunt, and his father, all within the space of two years, removed some of the gaiety from Kentish and Cantabrigian strong delights.

One mortality remains to be accounted for, but it was not that of a friend or a relative, although it may have had an important effect upon Fletcher. The years of Roger Goad, which had stretched on through hatred, sedition, rebellion, and riot and had multiplied beyond all expectation, at last attained their destined number in 1610, an end that had been more hoped for than feared. He was succeeded by Fog Newton, who, in turn, gave way to William Smith two years later. The passing of such an enemy should have bound Fletcher closer to King's College, but apparently it operated in a contrary manner. If the poet had awaited the close of Goad's régime through weary years, expecting prompt recognition from a successor, and if he found Newton and Smith unappreciative of his merits, his disappointment would leave him less patient with the new provosts than he had been with the old. We shall learn that something like this took place, and Goad's death proved to be one more unsettling factor.

[3] It finally made its appearance in conjunction with Phineas Fletcher's *Sylva Poetica* of 1633.

[4] The dedication helps us in arriving at the date when he prepared the manuscript for publication because, while flattering King's College, Fletcher complains of his own lack of advancement.

The final influence which contributed to the crisis in Fletcher's life (although it may have been more a result than a cause) was his entrance into the priesthood on Trinity Sunday, the eighth week after Easter, in 1611. According to the university records, his ordination meant an additional quarterly income of three shillings and fourpence, but from other sources we know that it also entailed a great deepening of his spiritual life. In the sixth piscatory eclogue, the author implores Tomkins to turn from man to Christ; and in *The Purple Island,* he states that his sacred vow has moved him to abandon all wanton toys for a love to Him to whom all loves are wed.[5] Therefore, though Elizabeth Colepeper lived on for many years, Fusca had died as completely as Nathaniel Pownall or Dr. Thomas Playfere. Trinity Sunday marked the turning point in Fletcher's life. He seems to have spent the twelve months since the Robarts wedding in introspection, in reaching the estimate of his own worthlessness; but with the summer of 1611, he entered upon hectic activity.

From his own statements in the second piscatory eclogue, it is evident that Fletcher regarded himself a failure chiefly because his poems had brought him neither provostship, public oratorship, nor the like; and his first act was to rush into further versification, still expecting to secure employment by that method. He proposed to cure the disease by fresh and greater applications of the virus. Thus during the months following his father's death, he turned out three complete versions of *Locustae* with four different dedicatory addresses, each an undisguised bid for new patronage. In addition to its great rapidity, his work revealed another notable departure from past conduct. All of the appeals for service were directed toward agencies outside of Cambridge. Hitherto his poems, with scarcely an exception, were poured back into the university which had inspired them. By the summer of 1611, however, Fletcher had decided that his hope for advancement lay beyond the college walls, that at all cost he must break with the past.

Although the desire to find release from what he considered an academic bondage was unprecedented in its urgency, the poet had toyed with the idea before. Miss Seaton observed that the two obscure poems on Trinity College in *Sylva Poetica* seem to be requests

---

[5] *The Purple Island,* I, st. 6-7.

for a transfer from King's to the other foundation. No doubt the author saw greater promise in Neville than in Roger Goad, but there is no indication that his project advanced any further than such poetic hints. It has been noted that a verse petition, printed in *Sylva Poetica,* was addressed to Sir Henry Wotton, but the whys, whens, and wherefores of the matter have never been explained. From the poem it appears that the author first addressed an ordinary letter to the Venetian ambassador, the one-time colleague of the elder Giles Fletcher in Essex's service, requesting that he be nominated to the embassy chaplaincy. The office had been occupied by the same Nathaniel Fletcher who subsequently took his Cambridge cousins to court over Phebe Fletcher's will, and late in 1606 the bishop's son was "drawn home by his own urgent occasions." Wotton praised him "as the first that hath preached God's truth on this side the Alps, since the main deformities thereof." [6] The poet's appeal must have been written during this brief interval, because early in 1607 William Bedell arrived in Venice to fill the vacancy. The suit of Bedell, later the Bishop of Kilmore and Ardagh, had been supported by Sir Edmund Bacon, grandson of Sir Francis and the husband of Wotton's niece. As for the young Cambridge student, he received a letter from Sir Henry advising that he might improve his time by further study.

In 1606 Fletcher's desire to leave Cambridge was probably stirred more by the wanderlust which he had inherited from his grandsire and his father than by discontent with his environment. The same is not true of his second application to Wotton for the identical office. His new letter, "Dom. Observandissimo H. W. *Venetiis agenti*" of *Sylva Poetica,* was set out in a pedantic style, perhaps to convince the ambassador that the author had both studied and improved his time. Since the lines express a complete dissatisfaction with Cambridge and since Fletcher would not be overhasty about repeating his application after Wotton's rebuff, the missive must have been written close to 1610. It was plainly impossible for Sir Henry to accede, even had he been willing, because the petition reached him when he was on the brink of voyaging to England; nor did he return to Italy until 1616, when Fletcher had gone off to new and permanent employment.

[6] Birch MS 4160, f. 360.

In the *Piscatorie Eclogs'* account of the 1611 crisis, the poet wrote:

> I heard a voice, like thunder, lowdly say,
> *Thirsil,* why idle liv'st? *Thirsil,* away, away.
> *Piscatorie Eclogs,* II, st. 18.

His decision that he was an idler came largely from within, but it was hastened by certain external influences, and the same was true of his sudden conviction that the university was a prison from which he had to escape. For years he had gone on admiring Alma Mater: King's College was a royal temple, the Cam a soft water that laved the learned walls, and Cambridge was the seat of all the Muses. Every reference to his own foundation and to the corporate body of colleges was adulatory, and he was avid for opportunities to render homage.[7] After 1611 his remarks about Cambridge were as numerous, if not more so, yet a more complete reversal of attitude is difficult to imagine.[8] He no longer meets the Muses in the quadrangles, but

> Instead of those ambition, flatterie,
> Hate, ryot, wrong, oppression, briberie,
> Pride high as heav'n, Covetise deepe as hell
> Are those nine Muses which by Camus dwell.
> Seaton's *Venus and Anchises,* p. 62.

It is small wonder that such bold lines exist only in the manuscript version, and were suppressed in the quarto of 1633. The charges were not unfounded. His father had accused King's College of the same vices in 1576, and some fifteen years after the poet's disillusionment Thomas Rowe characterized the royal foundation in these words:

> The greater part of the fellows, sensible of the utter ruin of the college now approaching. . . . A show of discipline as remissly executed upon the vicious, as most severely upon such as least deserve their rigor. . . . The choice of officers and all business of moment more partially and preposterously swaied now than ever before.

Justification though there may have been for the poet's condemnation, the university had not rotted within the space of a year. It

---

[7] See Boas, I, 92, 122-23, 139, 178-79; II, 12, 223, 316.

[8] Other vicious attacks upon the university occur in *Piscatorie Eclogs,* II, V, and VII; and in "To Thomalin."

was the man who had changed, the scales having fallen from his eyes with startling suddenness.

The year following his ordination was a feverish period during which Fletcher lamented his own shortcomings, struggled for release from Cambridge, and wrote furiously upon his *Locustae*. It is from now on that the commons books prove especially valuable. Throughout the first six months he maintained—very much against his will—his regular residence at King's, but after Christmas his absences became increasingly longer. He was away for a week in January, a half week in February, the month of April, and all of June and July, intervals probably devoted to soliciting new employment.

The exact nature of the service sought can be partly determined from the poems and their dedications. Frequently Fletcher paints the placid joys of a country clergyman's existence:

> There may I, master of a little flock,
> Feed my poore lambes, and often change their fare:
> My lovely mate shall tend my sparing stock,
> And nurse my little ones with pleasing care.
> *The Purple Island*, I, st. 29.

If such was all he desired, his life became a success, because he eventually won a secure Norfolk rectory. In 1611, however, we know that his aspirations soared far beyond such an estate. Eager for greater things, he praised the pastorate because it offered an asylum from the storms of the world and from the pain of vaulting ambition, but it was to be a last resort.

The dedication of *Locustae* to Montagu reveals an author who hoped for a career in the Church, and its hasty transfer from the Bishop of Bath and Wells to Prince Henry and then to Charles suggests that he sought a footing at court. He was drawn toward the same spheres that his father had entered, but he had neither a brother like the one-time Bishop of London to sponsor him, nor the elder Giles Fletcher's capacity for furthering his own interests.

It was an era when crucial events occurred with rapidity, and at this juncture the poet quit King's College. Without the commons books, we should never have known of this move. He left on September 13, 1612, apparently with no intention of returning. There is little reason to suppose that he had a promise, even a hope, of new employment. Some years later his friend Tomkins was likewise to break away to become organist of St. Paul's, a departure that called for smiling congratulations. Fletcher, on the other hand, was a failure; he set his face toward a bleak future, and he left a trail of denunciations behind him. Evidently he had proposed to remain on at the university until he secured another position, but new events made even a temporary residence impossible. The second piscatory eclogue describes his retreat and explains it: [9]

> His stubborn hands my net hath broken quite:
> My fish (the guerdon of my toil and pain)
> He causelesse seaz'd, and with ungratefull spite
> Bestow'd upon a lesse deserving swain.
> *Piscatorie Eclogs,* II, st. 7.

In all probability the poet's enemy was the new provost, William Smith, who had just taken office. Smith would have the authority to humble a fellow of Fletcher's maturity and dignity. Furthermore a malcontent, who spent his time—when he was not off in search of outside employment—in bitterly criticizing the corruption of the college, must have been a thorn in Smith's side. A recently installed provost would incline to regard the poet's insubordination as a personal challenge. There is a curious analogy between this affair and the elder Giles Fletcher's break with King's thirty-five years earlier. The son recognized this and, while relating his own experiences, frequently alludes to parallel circumstances in his father's history. In "To Thomalin," a poem probably inspired by the same event,[10] the author pretends that he was leaving behind him only one regret—his broken comradeship with Tomkins, his brother, and several other persons. He is unwilling to confess that he also turned his back upon ten placid years of accom-

[9] Since Fletcher's commentators were not aware of this first break from King's College in 1612, the second eclogue has regularly been connected with his second departure in 1615. There are several circumstances which indicate that the eclogue was written in 1612 and not in 1615. *Piscatorie Eclog* V was definitely written in the spring of 1615. If *Piscatorie Eclog* II be compared with this later poem, one will note differences between them: the author's new pastoral name, the many references to Derbyshire, to Algon (probably Willoughby), to Nicaea (Elizabeth Vincent), and to the spring season. *Piscatorie Eclog* II makes no allusion to any of the foregoing, and was produced during the winter (st. 2). In the poem (st. 2) we are informed that it was composed several months after the author's removal. These facts harmonize with the first break of September 13, 1612, and not with that of March 25, 1615.

[10] Compare *Piscatorie Eclog* II, st. 5, with "To Thomalin," st. 6.

plishment in learning, teaching, writing—a decade of confidence in the successful academic career which he saw stretching endlessly before him.

For some nineteen months after the critical thirteenth of September, we lose sight of Phineas Fletcher, and his movements can only be inferred. His immediate destination may have been his mother's house in London:

> But thou, proud Chame, which thus hast wrought me spite,
> Some greater river drown thy hatefull name.
> *Piscatorie Eclogs,* II, st. 23.

We have no record concerning the whereabouts of Joan Fletcher after the death of her husband, of how long she lived, or of what became of her other children. Presumably the lady, having donned her widow's weeds, had the alternative of retaining her metropolitan residence or removing to her childhood home at Cranbrook. She was forty-nine years old, had not revisited Kent (so far as we know) for all of twenty years, and her people had scattered in every direction. Furthermore, if she had gone home to the weald, there ought to be some notice concerning her or her children in the Cranbrook registers of the seventeenth century, but there is none. Probably the widow ended her days in the city, and sweet Thames was the greater river in which Fletcher hoped to drown the name of Cam.

While in London the poet seems to have continued his office hunting and also his elaboration of *Locustae*. A few weeks after his arrival, England was shocked by the death of Prince Henry, and the members of the Cambridge society of pastoral poets hastily prepared contributions to fill out *Epicedium Cantabrigiensis*. Their erstwhile president, with equal expedition, wrote a third dedication for his Gunpowder Plot poem and addressed it to the new heir apparent, the ill-fated Charles. At the same time he added an epistle to Thomas Murray, in the course of which he gave expression to the deepest despair:

> Hinc est quod aut nulla aut perexigua mihi spes affulgeat; cui et vox nunqua importuna, et ingenium minus quam haec aetas postulat inverecundum semper fuit.
> Boas, *Poetical Works of Giles and Phineas Fletcher,* I, 282.

Those were the saddest words Phineas Fletcher ever wrote. He had whipped himself into a frenzy of ambition, he left Cambridge in disgrace,[11] for more than a year he steadily pounded at the doors of opportunity, both Church and state were deaf to his pleas, and now he knew not where to turn. He had reached the bottom of the pit.

Salvation came almost immediately and from an unexpected source. It has been known that Fletcher spent some considerable portion of his life in Norfolk long before he went to Hilgay in 1621. The date and cause of this earlier residence have been unsolved mysteries. The commons books provide the year, and Fletcher's own address to Sir Henry Willoughby offers the reason: "for my long continuous entertainment in your house (such as I never saw any gentlemen give unto their minister) or that I first initiated my weake Ministerie in your Familie and Hamlet" (*The Way to Blessednes,* dedicatory address). There is but one "long continuous" period in the poet's life before April, 1616 (at which time he "initiated" his "weake Ministerie" at Risley), when we are unable to locate him precisely, and that is the nineteen months from September, 1612, to April, 1614. Thus late in 1612 or shortly thereafter, Fletcher was honored with Willoughby's hospitality and patronage. He was to enjoy the fruits of the latter to the end of his days.

Sir Henry Willoughby of Wood-Hall at Hilgay, Norfolk, was the heir of a line of shrewd and prosperous country squires whose seat was Risley Hall in Derbyshire. Only one Risley Willoughby, so far as we know, was an adventurer. That was Sir Hugh, a celebrated navigator and discoverer of the preceding century. He sailed the north seas, was frozen in off the Lapland coast, and finally discovered a part of Greenland since called Willoughby Land. His kinsmen remained close to home, cultivated the glebe, refused to send their sons to court or to the wars, and prospered. Fletcher's patron was typical of the breed—solid, rich, and uninspired. Born at Risley along with Frances, Elizabeth, and Ursula, he was the son and heir of Sir John Willoughby and Frances Hawe of Hilgay. Sir John did not live to inherit his father's Risley Hall, which passed directly

[11] *Piscatorie Eclog* II, st. 7.

from George to the grandson, Sir Henry.[12] In the meantime the latter married Elizabeth Knollys, a niece of the Earl of Banbury, and established his residence at Risley. His first child, Frances, was baptized there on October 12, 1607, and died a half year later. Before January 9, 1610/11, he had taken possession of Wood-Hall at Hilgay, one of his mother's Norfolk properties,[13] where he buried another infant, John, on that date. His daughters, Margaret and Ursula, were baptized at Hilgay, the first on April 23, 1611, and the other on May 11 of the following year. Thus the Hilgay register enables us to place the squire in Norfolk during the critical year of 1612.

When Sir Henry Willoughby became the protector and patron of the despairing poet, he owned the gift of one benefice, the Hilgay rectory, and as the heir of Risley Hall, expected to become the donor of its chaplaincy in a short time, the days of his grandfather being numbered. Such were the favors that Fletcher might hope from his benefactor. Although the rectory was a comfortable living, it was insignificant and located in fields that were strange to the poet, while the chaplaincy was a gift poor indeed. Furthermore neither office was available at the time, there apparently being an incumbent in each. It is surprising that Fletcher could find comfort in the remote expectation of such preferments.

The belated acknowledgment of *The Way to Blessednes*, besides being the surest proof of Fletcher's earlier Hilgay residence, provides a glimpse into his activities during his stay. A clergyman, a teacher, and a writer, he came qualified to serve his patron in divers ways, but it is evident that Willoughby did not avail himself of any of these talents. Since there was a rector residing in the tiny village, the newcomer would have no occasion to perform the clerical functions, nor, according to his own statement, did he do so. Sir Henry's two daughters were of an age that required no university-trained tutor, but rather some red-faced, east-country nursemaid

[12] Frances Hawe Willoughby died on November 21, 1602, and was followed by her husband, Sir John, on January 28, 1605/6. The church registers of Hilgay and Wilne and the monuments of Wilne have provided most of the information concerning the Willoughby family. For additional and sometimes parallel material, see Thoroton's *Nottinghamshire*, II, 208 ff. and Cox's *Notes*, IV, 401 ff.

[13] Willoughby owned additional Norfolk property at both Medney and Southery.

like Peggotty. Finally, the collections of Fletcher's verse are barren of a literary project undertaken in 1612 to justify his benefactor's generosity. On the other hand, they do afford several slight pieces with illuminating suggestions as to what their author was doing. The Sion College Manuscript contains an epithalamium addressed to a Norfolk couple:

> Harke gentle sheppeardes that on Norwiche plaines
> In daintie verses sing your loves desiring
> And yow both Cause and part of those sweet flames
> Fayre Norfolke maydes.
>
> Seaton, p. 21.

The epithalamium hints that the writer was enjoying a holiday similar to those spent in the Cranbrook neighborhood, and was finding the Norfolk maids quite as delightful as the Kentish wood nymphs. It was another period of procrastination like the Robarts weddingtide, when he luxuriated in the pleasures of rural society. At such a time a more forceful man, a Dr. Giles Fletcher for example, would have kept working for preferment. If his son, with his talent, had persevered, he must eventually have secured a more promising opportunity than the country pastorate which Willoughby offered in a doubtful future. That he was not unconscious of the weakness of such idling is apparent in the lines which have always given commentators so much trouble, but which are plain enough in the light of this early Hilgay residence:

> Go little pipe, for I must have a new:
> Farewell ye *Norfolk* maids, and *Ida* crue:
> *Thirsil* will play no more; for ever now adieu.
> "To Mr. Jo. Tomkins," lines 69-71.

They were written some years later, when the poet had become a serious-minded minister. As he reflected upon the follies of his youth, he regretted above all else his *Brittain's Ida*, the sensuous love poem addressed to Fusca. Yet he laid almost equal blame upon the months of sporting with Amaryllises and Neaeras in the Hilgay neighborhood.

It is not easy to explain why Willoughby maintained this drone under his roof for so many months. We have noticed that Fletcher himself commented upon his patron's unusual hospitality, calling it an entertainment "such as I never saw any gentlemen give unto their minister." The squire could not have been motivated by a desire to have his name immortalized in verse, because, with all the author's propensity for celebrating his friends in rhyme and meter, he never so much as mentioned Willoughby's name in his poetry. He must have received special orders to the contrary. Possibly the hamlet of Hilgay was brightened by the graces the young man imported from London and Cambridge, or perhaps Sir Henry felt that Fletcher was so good a catch for the Risley chaplaincy that he was worth his bed and board in advance. Above all, there may have been some old bond between patron and poet, for we have not yet learned why the former showed his first interest in the young man.

Although Willoughby bursts into the records of Fletcher's life with astonishing suddenness, it is impossible that the two were utter strangers before 1612. Sir Henry's cousin, Peregrine Willoughby of Eresby, had been on cordial terms with Anthony Bacon, Dr. Giles Fletcher's friend and employer. Again one of the elder Fletcher's comrades was Maximilian Brook, heir to the title of Lord Cobham, whose manor was contiguous to Boreplace, the home of Sir Percival Willoughby. This Kentish baronet was related to the Risley family through his wife, Bridget Willoughby of Wollaton. Phineas Fletcher could have used such mutual ties to effect an interview with his benefactor, but they do not account for the squire's excessive interest.

The solution seems to rest in a fact of seeming insignificance: Sir Henry's great-grandmother was Margaret, daughter of Thomas Molyneux of Sawton, Notts. This lady was a first cousin of Anne Preston, who married Sir Richard Neville [14] of Liversedge, Yorks., and founded the line of descent which produced Thomas Neville of Trinity College, patron of the younger Giles Fletcher. Furthermore, Sir Henry's grandfather, George Willoughby, was a first cousin of Sir Richard Molyneux,[15] the benefactor of the elder Giles Fletcher. Most important, yet least clear in all these kinships, is the marriage of a second Margaret Molyneux to a Robert Fletcher [16] of Stoke Bardolph, Notts., about 1550. Whether or not he was related to the vicar Richard Fletcher, and if so, how, cannot be said, but the other families seemed to recognize the vicar's descendants as close kinsmen. The absurdity of the Wood-Hall squire's concerning

[14] Molineux's *Memoir*, p. 7.   [15] *Ibid*, p. 33.   [16] *Ibid*, pp. 38-39, 128-29.

himself with the blood ties of a great-grandmother is apparent, rather than real. The son of Margaret Molyneux was no other than George Willoughby, the lord of Risley Hall in 1612. The old man would be mindful of his mother's relations, and the young Sir Henry would be equally solicitous concerning the whims of a grandfather upon whom he depended for his inheritance. In all likelihood Phineas Fletcher and his patron recognized each other as distant relatives, and there were forces which tended to lessen the remoteness of their ties.

Since the references to Sir Henry's family disappear from the Hilgay register, since Phineas Fletcher began to revisit Cambridge, and since George Willoughby departed this life all at the same time, there can be little doubt as to when and why the Wood-Hall hospitality came to an end. In the absence of any other information, a tombstone of St. Chad near Risley has yielded the year of the grandfather's decease, 1613.[17] Thereafter, the poet's patron became the lord of Risley Hall, either closed the doors of Wood-Hall or transferred the estate to another tenant, and moved his family to the new manor house. In all probability he was then in a position to open the Derbyshire chaplaincy to his dependent. It is therefore somewhat significant that Fletcher did not go northward with Willoughby. Perhaps he was still too proud to accept so poor a living, or perhaps his hopes for a career at Cambridge were reviving.

There is full evidence that the self-exiled King's College fellow had recovered from his first rancor by the spring of 1614. In April he reappeared at commons for three days, then withdrew, returned for a week in June, for a like period in August, and for a fortnight in November. The increasing duration of his visits may reflect a steadily decreasing resentment. One of these calls coincided with Edmund Sheaffe's arrival at the royal foundation on August 31.[18] Perhaps the poet escorted his Cranbrook cousin to the university from Kent or London, or perhaps the occasion was simply an excuse for returning. It is not impossible that during his months at Hilgay he learned to regret his hasty departure, wished to sur-

---

[17] The month and day of George Willoughby's death are unknown.

[18] His father, Edmund, probably a brother of Phineas Fletcher's mother, graduated from King's in 1580, married an Elizabeth Taylor of Cranbrook in 1586, and their first child, Edmund, was born at Marden a year later.

render to homesickness for King's College, and yet was ashamed to give in without some pretext. More in harmony with his nature, however, is another explanation: that even thus early he scented an opportunity for writing a play to be presented before King James. For to Cambridge the *annus mirabilis* was about to come—that season of incessant comedies, disputations, feastings, and glamour, when the sober alleys and quadrangles of Cambridge were fired with color and activity, when the university became the focal point of the whole of England. The visitation of King James and his train was announced for the forthcoming March. Such was certainly the inducement which influenced Phineas Fletcher to return to permanent residence at King's College on December 16, and his earlier visits may have been motivated by the same irresistible attraction.

After two years and three months of absence, the wanderer resumed his old way of life on December 16, 1614. The day marked another turning point in his career. Some half dozen colleges were preparing plays to be presented upon each night of the king's stay. The university, ready to move heaven and earth in an effort to please the king, regarded these dramas as her supreme offering. They were impressive enough, being staged before an audience of two thousand persons that included the most distinguished figures in the academic, ecclesiastic, and political spheres. The contribution of King's was scheduled for the final night, the grand climax. How much it must have meant to Phineas Fletcher to be chosen its author! In the eyes of King's College, indeed of the whole university, he was the man of the hour. The miserable one who had gone off, shamed and obscure, returned in glory. What is more, the man who trusted in literature as an avenue to worldly advancement found himself nominated to write a play which was to be presented before the masters of every opportunity England afforded. He set about composing his piscatory comedy, *Sicelides.*

On March 7, 1614/15, James and his company, which included Prince Charles and John Donne, arrived amidst foul weather. The king was lodged at Trinity College, where the "magnificent Neville," Giles Fletcher's patron, made good his sobriquet, kept open house for the entire body of guests, and drew James' praise. Meanwhile the host lay upon a bed of pain, unable to leave his chambers during the course of the festivities. The various plays were run off according to schedule, all being presented in the hall of Trinity. The culmination, *Sicelides,* however, was to be performed at King's.[19]

At last the crucial March 11 arrived. Perindus and Thalander were prepared to excite the royal tears, Cancrone and Scrocca to tickle the royal sides, the chorus of priests and fishers to dazzle the royal eyes, and Phineas Fletcher to win the favor which was to launch him upon a career as courtier or ecclesiastic. Cancrone carried off his buffoonery, but Fletcher had no laughter for his own jests. King James, Prince Charles, and their train had departed Cambridge on the morning of the eleventh. Probably no man in the departing company ever heard of the piscatory drama which had been calculated to impress them all. Certainly none of them suspected the real drama that went on that evening: the disappointment of the author, who had foolishly cast all his hope into the success of this one play.

The scope of the man's disappointment is best measured by its effects. They were immediate and irrevocable. On March 25, just two weeks after the performance of *Sicelides,* the author left King's College for Risley, never to return as a fellow. It has been commonly supposed that his departure did not occur for many months, but again the evidence of the commons books is indisputable. Unlike the first, his second exodus was without rancor.[20] Spiritless and resigned, he accepted himself a failure. He went to occupy the chaplaincy, and, so far as we know, his aspirations never again rose beyond a modest country pastorate. Although he composed some scattered verses and several prose works during the thirty-nine years that remained to him, his creative life actually died with the fisher play. The two thousand persons who gathered in the hall of King's on that late winter night and laughed at the bold jests were attending, unknown to themselves, the funeral of a poet.

The statement that Fletcher never reappeared at Cambridge as a fellow is not quite correct. A year or so later he was back for several short visits, but by then he was a married man. A fellowship

[19] For a narrative of the king's visit, see Todd's *Account of the Deans of Canterbury,* p. 76.
[20] See *Piscatorie Eclog* V.

lapsed automatically with matrimony, although the person involved continued to enjoy his privileges throughout one year of
grace. Therefore the poet's name was not removed from the King's
College rolls until Lady Day of 1616. Even down to the end of his
days, Fletcher's divorce from Cambridge was never complete.
When he undertook the publication of his poetic works, he turned
to the university press, and probably he made more frequent visits
than the four of which we are aware.

There were always the strongest ties of kinship and friendship
to recall Fletcher either in spirit or in person. During this very
year, his brother, Giles, was enjoying an increasingly successful
academic career. Not only was he gaining recognition as a scholar,
but he was active in the official business of his foundation. In 1615
he was appointed Lector Graecae Grammaticae, and at about the
same time he traveled with Thomas Fortho, the bursar of Trinity
College, to Greenwich, where they met King James and Prince
Charles, delivering to them letters of congratulation. Furthermore
he began to preach sermons, famous for their grace of idea and
diction, at St. Mary's.

Giles remained at Cambridge until 1617, and Phineas Fletcher's
dearest friend, Tomkins, until 1619. One or more of the poet's
Sheaffe cousins were in residence at King's for the next twenty
years. Both Edmund and John Sheaffe died in college. The former,
having become a fellow, was buried in the chapel in 1625, and the
latter came to an untimely end while still a scholar. A Grindall
Sheaffe, who matriculated in 1633, achieved prominence as an
academic poet, subsequently entering the Church.[21] In the very
year Fletcher abandoned his fellowship, his friend Samuel Collins
was elected provost of King's and remained in office until 1644.[22]
The final bond between the poet and his Alma Mater was joined
long after 1615, when he sent his own son to the university.

[21] Grindall Sheaffe left King's College to serve as chaplain to the garrison of Jersey
Castle. He was presented by his college to the rectories of Colbeshall and Horsted,
Norfolk, in 1650. After living near Witney, Oxfordshire, he became Archdeacon of
Wells on August 12, 1660. He married Ann Woodward, the daughter of George
Woodward of Lee, Bucks. Anthony Wood mentions him in no pleasant terms.
[22] Collins became Regius Professor of Divinity on October 22, 1617.

VI

THE RISLEY SHEPHERD'S COT
1615-21

PHINEAS FLETCHER had chosen to exile himself, but his Siberia was a region of old England where friends waited to welcome him and where the farm lands were then faintly green with the new spring. At the end of his eighty-mile journey was Risley, a small Derbyshire village. Four or five hundred yards from Risley lay Wilne with its parish church, St. Chad. This homely, warlike structure owns a register containing important facts concerning the life of Phineas Fletcher, and a vault entombing the bones of many a Willoughby. In olden days a beacon flared from its tower to guide wayfarers to the ford over River Derwent, which meanders across the plain to meet the Trent a mile or so from the hamlet. If the poet found the buildings modest and sparse, the fields were widespread and luxuriant. Modern Risley, set midway between the industrial centers of Derby and Nottingham, offers but a faint suggestion of its older self. Factory chimneys can be seen from the pastures, themselves traversed by the main line of the London, Midland, and Scottish. Live cinders from the locomotives have scarred grass that must have been fresh and thick under the poet's feet.

After he had settled himself at Risley Hall, the newcomer passed beneath the stone doorway and the arch, upon which was inscribed

$$W$$
$$1593 -$$
$$M \quad K$$

that he might enter the chapel where he was to perform his holy offices. It had been erected by Katherine Willoughby in memory of her husband, Michael, and she died a few months after the completion of her pious labor. Fletcher was also supposed to act as schoolmaster, but the squire's household was composed of persons either too young or too old for the ministrations of the new teacher. There is a record of Sir Henry Willoughby's setting aside the sum of £13 6s. and 8d. for the maintenance of his chaplain, no doubt an addition to the perpetual endowment.[1] The poet's annual stipend must have been small.

The actual labor which Fletcher was called upon to perform was probably trivial, compared to what he had accomplished during his most active university days. Furthermore, to one who had spent his life amidst the thriving wool marts of Cranbrook, the bustle of Cheapside, and the eager youth of Cambridge, Risley and Wilne would seem lifeless. Yet to a certain extent the change had a salutary and chastening effect upon the author's turbulent spirit. His poem, "Against a rich man despising povertie," may have been the fruit of this era. Although it is brief and of slight merit, it reflects the serenity that was replacing the mad ambitions of earlier years:

> My little fills my little-wishing minde;
> . . .
> Poor are thy riches, rich my povertie.
> Lines 7-12.

His "To Mr. Jo. Tomkins," known to have been composed at Risley, strikes a similar note.

During Fletcher's earlier visit with the Willoughbys, he had no definite tasks like those set for him at Risley. Here, too, his duties were probably more or less nominal, and his life in Derbyshire was not unlike that in Norfolkshire. Most of his time seems to have been spent in nothing more arduous than entertaining his patron and Lady Willoughby, paying visits to the near-by gentry, and flirting with the damsels. Although the social round of Risley was more limited than that of Cranbrook and Hilgay, it provided some pleasures. If the "Damon, friendly Damon" of the fifth piscatory eclogue is Sir Henry, and probably he is,[2] then Fletcher met his patron on a common ground of friendship, even comradeship. The poem, "Upon the Contemplations of the B. of Excester, given to the Ladie E. W. at New-Yeares-tide," yields an

---

[1] Cox's *Notes*, pp. 409-11.

[2] The fifth piscatory eclogue was written shortly after Fletcher's arrival at Risley. The poem (st. 2) suggests that Damon was already a friend of long standing. Risley and its inhabitants—with the exception of Sir Henry Willoughby, his lady, and his infant daughters—were, so far as we know, strangers to the poet.

equally cheerful glimpse into the relations of the author with the manor-house family. His present to his mistress was the famous book of Bishop Hall, *Contemplations upon the Principall Passages of the Holy Storie,* eight volumes published at intervals between 1612 and 1626.[3]

A marginal note which the author entered upon his *Apollyonists* manuscript indicates that he ventured at least ten miles away from Risley when making polite calls. It alludes to a book found in the library of Sir Thomas Hutchinson of Owthorpe,[4] the father-in-law of Charles Cotton and of Mrs. Lucy Hutchinson. The squire was a friend of Sir Henry Wotton, who may have sent Fletcher to see him, although rural neighbors would scarcely have stood upon such ceremony. Sir Thomas was as interesting a character as the young chaplain might find in any shire:

After this, returning into the country, he there lived with very much love, honour, and repute; but having been tossed up and down in his youth and interrupted in his studies, he grew into such an excessive humour for books, that he wholly addicted himself to them; and deeply engaging in school divinity, spent even his hours of meat and sleep among his books.

Lucy Hutchinson, *Memoirs of Colonel Hutchinson,* pp. 38-39.

This scholar's wife died in 1619 and thereafter he became even more of a recluse. His books, "the choicest library in that part of England . . . drew to him all the learned and religious men thereabouts."

Phineas Fletcher was not a man to imitate his friend, Sir Thomas, and bury himself in books. Within a few weeks after his arrival, his heart, as he said, festered with a deeply hidden wound, and for once he seems to have meant what he wrote. He had taken the highroad to matrimony. The events of his courtship, largely internal and cardiac, are narrated in the fifth *Piscatorie Eclog,* where the swain dubs himself Algon, and his lady, Nicaea. She was the person subsequently addressed in a little anagram, "To my onely chosen Valentine and wife—Maystress Elisabeth

---

[3] It is possible that Fletcher presented Hall's book to Lady Willoughby prior to his arrival at Risley. Since she died in 1621, the poem must have been written before he left Derbyshire for Hilgay.

[4] *Apollyonists,* IV, st. 33.

Vincent." [5] On August 23, the following entry, labeled "marriage," was made in the Wilne register: "Feneas Flecher and Elizabeth Vincet, of Risley." Within less than six months after his arrival, he had carried off the redoubtable fair one who—according to his own statement—had captivated one thousand swains; and he might well say, *"Veni, vidi, vici."*

Although the poet's biographers have failed to account for her origin, there can be little doubt that the young clergyman first met his bride in Derbyshire. His eclogue describes her as a nymph of the Derwent, and the register entry also suggests that she was a resident of Risley. Because there is no other mention of the name in the same register, it is probable that her parents were not natives of the village. There were Vincents living in many places within twenty miles: at Hemington, Kegworth, Markfield, Beckenthorpe, Bottesford, Aylestone, and Sheepy Magna.[6] Since Damon seems to be familiar with Elizabeth, he may have imported her from one of these near-by hamlets to act in some capacity at Risley Hall, perhaps as governess to his daughters. Despite Fletcher's hasty courtship, his wedded life proved happy. His writings throw some light upon the subsequent relations of the pair, and indicate that dame Elizabeth soothed her husband's damaged pride, making the shepherd's cot and lot more attractive.[7]

The following year was long remembered by the Willoughbys, the Hutchinsons, and other gentlemen farmers. A drought descended upon the countryside, laying waste all the crops. In the meantime the chaplain had left the parched plain of the Derwent and traveled down to Cambridge. The commons records indicate

[5] See Clark's "Note on a Poem by Phineas Fletcher," *The Reliquary*, April, 1869. Clark was the first to solve the identity of Nicaea. Fletcher's eclogue contains the following dark passage:
"The rock that bears her name, breeds that hard stone
With goats bloud onely softned."
Piscatorie Eclogs, V, st. 10.
Clark suggested that Fletcher was referring to St. Vincent's Rocks at Clifton, which produce the so-called Bristol diamonds. Later discoveries have fully corroborated his clever conjecture.
[6] See Hartopp's *Index to the Wills of Leicestershire* and his *Leicester Marriages*. No similar record is available for Derbyshire, but presumably the family was scattered through that county as well.
[7] "To my onely chosen Valentine and wife," "To Mr. Jo. Tomkins," and *A Father's Testament*.

that he occupied his old place at table from June 15 to July 7, and again from July 23 to August 11. Because of his marriage, the college payment which fell due on the following Lady Day was his last. With his fellowship on the point of lapsing, there were formalities to be attended to and stipends to be collected. The curious sixteen-day interruption of the business, however, thrusts us into a major and still unsolved mystery of Fletcher's life.

Dated July 17, 1616, and classified as a marriage, this entry is found in the Wilne register: "Francis Flecher & Elzabeth Vincet." One's inclination is to regard the matter as a coincidence until one remembers that "Feneas," an unusual name, whereas "Francis" was common about Risley, might easily be misrepresented as such by a careless copyist. Furthermore Phineas was the only Fletcher, and Elizabeth the only Vincent, whose names were recorded separately or jointly throughout one hundred years of Wilne baptisms, marriages, and deaths. Finally the date, July 17, occurs exactly midway between the poet's sudden departure from King's College and his return, while the sixteen-day interval gave him just enough time to travel to and from Risley. There is no escaping the conclusion that "Francis Flecher" and "Elzabeth Vincet" are Willoughby's chaplain and his bride of eleven months. It has been suggested that difficulties over his King's College fellowship forced Fletcher into a second marriage ceremony. Since his admission of marriage cost him all his privileges and stipend, what reason had the collegiate authorities for investigating the statement? The very lapse of those perquisites in 1616 is itself a proof that the officials were aware of the 1615 ceremony and accepted it at face value.

The second register entry, misguiding as it is, contains elaborate hints as to its true meaning. The person who set it down wrote "Francis" for "Feneas," an error that could only arise in transcription from a written record, because, although the two might look alike, they are not similar in sound. In addition to his first error, the copyist rendered "Vincent" as "Vincet" and "Elizabeth" as "Elzabeth," achieving three blunders in the course of four words. He must have been the most scatterbrained of clerks, and consequently the chances were even that he would make an error by labeling the entry "marriage" if it should have read "baptism." Such carelessness was not unusual during these years. For example, the Cranbrook register twice buries John Fletcher, the vicar's own child, once on October 14, 1566, and again on January 28. The first was obviously intended as a baptismal date. The problem is clarified once and for all by the poet's will, where the testator mentions his children individually. The first name on the list was that of Anne, whom he calls his daughter. The christenings of his numerous offspring were recorded in the Hilgay register, all except that of Anne. Because her name heads the roll, she must have been the eldest and must have been born at Risley. Since there is no reference to her in the Wilne register, the entry of July 17, 1616, seems to be an erroneous registration of her baptism.

It is strange, then, that the young husband should have gone off to Cambridge when he did. Perhaps he received an imperative summons from the authorities of his foundation, perhaps he intended to conclude his business more rapidly than proved possible, or perhaps the delivery came earlier than was expected. Whatever the situation, he showed his solicitude for his wife if he made a flying trip from the fenlands to Derbyshire and back again.

Both Giles Fletcher and John Tomkins were still at Cambridge to welcome the loved one who had returned. Neither the author of *Christs Victorie and Triumph* nor the organist was to remain at the university much longer. Phineas Fletcher's departure made college life less pleasant for each. Furthermore, the patron of the younger brother, Thomas Neville, never recovered from the illness which kept him bedridden during the royal visitation, and he died on May 2 of that year. At the time Giles Fletcher was rising in college affairs, but thereafter matters went less smoothly. Apparently, without Neville's backing, he was succeeding no better than his brother had, and he became restless for outside preferment. He petitioned Sir Roger Townshend, a friend and patron of Phineas Fletcher. Although well disposed toward his supplicant, Townshend was unable to offer anything material. He had, however, an influential uncle whom he proposed to interest in the poet. That uncle was Sir Francis Bacon, who owned the rights to more than one living and who proved receptive to his nephew's mediation, the more so because the needy divine was a son of his brother's one-time aide and comrade. Spedding offers the following important note:

By the copy of a letter of the Lord Chancellor Bacon, 24 Apr. 1617, to the Bp. of Norwich, it appears that his Lp. had presented Mr. Gyles Fletcher of Trin: Coll: Camb. to the rectory of Helmingham in Suffolk.
Bacon's Life and Letters, VI, 172.

Giles Fletcher left Cambridge early in 1617 to enter upon his new duties. He found himself in a situation similar in many respects to his brother's at Risley. The Suffolk hamlet was altogether as small and almost as remote. The Church of St. Mary, little more than a chapel of the great Tollemachie family, stood but a few steps from Helmingham Hall. Resident there were Sir Lionel Tollemachie, the head of the family; his wife, Elizabeth, the daughter of Lord Stanhope; his brothers, Robert and Edward; and his sisters, Susan, Mary, and Catherine. The youthful Sir Lionel had succeeded to his title only two years earlier. Whereas Phineas Fletcher and the Willoughbys were on affectionate terms, there is no indication that the Tollemachies were even friendly to their new rector. If such a coolness did exist, there would be no living in a Helmingham dominated by this one family. Such a state of affairs is suggested by Giles Fletcher's activities, for he was restless and within less than a year had abandoned his benefice. The Helmingham register is extant for the period of Fletcher's incumbency. Written in Latin and very meager, it yields no information concerning the newcomer, although it probably provides the one known sample of his autograph. A visit to the Church of St. Mary at Helmingham has thrown new light upon the young man's life. For instance the building has a plaque and upon it is engraved a list of the rectors, which reads in part:

1576	Thom. Wilkenson
1617	Egid. Fletcher
	Will. Ashton
1633	Joes. Vincent

The hiatus, marking the year when Fletcher left and Ashton succeeded, is eloquent concerning the difficulties that arose as a result of his hasty and informal departure.

Evidently the young clergyman returned to Trinity College, because the university records state that he was appointed Lector Graecae Linguae in 1618 and that he proceeded to his B.D. in the following year. During the same months he negotiated for an exchange of livings,[8] securing Alderton in Suffolk. The philosopher seems to have again been active in his behalf, making the exchange possible. Fletcher dedicated his last work, a prose treatise entitled *The Reward of the Faithfull,* to Townshend. The epistle dedicatory, written shortly before 1623, refers to Bacon:

> Your most noble and learned Uncle, the Right Honorable Francis Lord Verulam, Viscount Saint Albones my free and very Honourable Benefactor, whose Gift, as it was worthy his bestowing, so was it speedily sent, and not tediously sued for; Honourably given, not bought with shame, to one whom he never knew or saw, but only heard kindly slaundered with a good report of others, and opinion conceived by himselfe or sufficiencie and worth. For by your Favours I confesse, my estate is something, but the sence of my povertie much more increased.

Since at the moment the author's estate was the rectory of Alderton and since Lord Verulam owned the rights to that living,[9] there can be little doubt concerning the nature of the "Gift."

At about the same time the younger Giles Fletcher married a certain Anne, whose surname is still unknown. Although his new rectory temporarily satisfied him, it proved to be no Promised Land, and he lived to regret bitterly the move he had made.

Presumably the chaplain of Risley Hall learned by letter of these critical happenings in the life of his brother. He also had news concerning his bosom friend, Tomkins, but in this case the subject matter was more happy. In 1619 Thomalin left Cambridge to become organist of St. Paul's Cathedral, setting out upon a career which was to make him one of England's famous musicians. He was succeeded at King's College by Matthew Barton, who, some five years later, gave way to another Tomkins brother, Giles. Phineas Fletcher celebrated his friend's preferment to St. Paul's by composing "To Mr. Jo. Tomkins." The author was compelled to contrast his humble lot with the other's triumph, but the poem reveals the serenity which, like a shining mantle, had fallen upon him.

During the same year, one other piece of intelligence, melancholy enough, found its way to Risley. The Edmund Cook of

[8] Fuller's *Worthies,* II, 380-81.

[9] I came upon a manuscript in the church at Alderton which indicated that Sir James Bacon bought the rights to the living of Alderton from a Sir John Soame or Soane, in 1589.

King's College days had gone off on a voyage to Algiers, presumably having recovered his reason. During his travels, he succumbed to a tropical fever and died. The object of Fletcher's brief but heartfelt epitaph, "On my friends picture, who died in travel," has long remained unknown. There can be little doubt that it mourned Edmund Cook, the youth once referred to as the poet's "sonne by the University."

Such, then, was Fletcher's life at Risley—as quiet as the waterways and leas of the countryside which sustained him. The discordant notes all came from an outer and distant world. His six years in Derbyshire were happy, but they brought slight accomplishment by which he might be remembered, and Fletcher could not look forward to a lifetime in the Risley chaplaincy. Even though his ambitions had crumbled, he was too capable a man for so poor a living. His patron owned the rights to Hilgay; probably it had long been promised to the poet. On June 11, 1621, James Williams, the incumbent, was buried, and five months later he was succeeded by Fletcher. No explanation for the interval between Williams' passing and his successor's arrival offers itself, unless perhaps the poet was detained in Derbyshire by the nuptial revelry at Risley Hall. At an unknown date Lady Elizabeth Willoughby had died, and in 1621 her lord took to himself a second wife, Lettice, the daughter of Sir Francis Darcy. At any rate, the new rector was installed and had entered upon his pastoral duties by November 1, 1621.

VII

HARVEST TIDE AT HILGAY
1621-50

H AD Fletcher been a man of ordinary gifts, Hilgay would have made for him an ideal be-all and end-all. Its richest land-owner, though in absence, was Willoughby, a patron of stubborn loyalty whose dependent need have no misgivings for the future. Friendships begun eight years before had been lying fallow, ready for renewal. All Saints' Church was a substantial structure that has been largely altered since the poet's day. The village itself, bound by both the Ouse and the Wissey, lies in the very heart of the fen country. The situation must have been peculiarly gratifying to Fletcher, after his exile in Derbyshire. Cambridge, where many of his old comrades were still in residence, was twenty-five miles to the southwest, and the historic towns of Ely and King's Lynn lay scarcely ten miles distant. From the first, Fletcher accepted the new living as his ultimate destiny, cheerfully throwing all his energies into its ministry. But what had Hilgay to satisfy the intellectual curiosity that produced *The Purple Island,* the delicate sense of rhythm which made music in the *Piscatorie Eclogs,* or the vigor that intensified *The Apollyonists?*

Although the new rector had dawdled about at Risley and al-though even now he shrank from answering his real calling, he entered upon his duties with zeal. The register, which has proved an invaluable source of information concerning the poet's life, is a sample of his industry. Written in Fletcher's own delicate hand, it preserves the vital statistics of thirty years with unusual neatness and accuracy. There are, however, other and larger evidences of the earnestness with which he set about, maintained, and concluded his task at Hilgay.

Fletcher's prose treatise, *The Way to Blessednes,* was the fruit of ten years of pastoral labor. By the good effect of his preaching upon his parishioners, he was induced to seek a wider ministry through the printing press. Unlike many clergymen who have been similarly persuaded, he refrained from publishing his sermons in an undigested mass. Instead, he drew the best from them, from his studies, and from his practical experiences, amalgamating all into one living exhortation which is somewhat autobiographical. The clergyman's first concern should be himself:

> Art thou a Minister of the word? then hast thou this precept from *God, give attendance to reading: take heed unto learning and continue therein.*
>
> The Way to Blessednes, p. 11.

The works written by Fletcher at Hilgay are replete with evidence that he continued his reading in Boethius, Aristotle, and the scholiasts. After the pastor has enriched and purified his own spirit, he is ready to be active among his flock. Speaking directly to his congregation, Fletcher wrote:

> I never spared any paines for your profit, either publike or private, but by prayer for you, and preaching to you, have laboured with all, nay above my strength, to bring you to that true knowledge of God.
>
> The Way to Blessednes, "Address to Parishioners."

Nor was Hilgay without need of prayer and preaching. The fenland folk were equally robust in work and in sin, delighting in the time-honored vices of drunkenness and profanity. Their new rector, on the other hand, was a man who loved a fight for what he conceived to be righteousness—witness *The Apollyonists.* Such enthusiasm pleased certain of his flock poorly, and he complains of the "opposition of some instruments of Satan." Yet these children of darkness were a small minority, and Fletcher was able to write, "Surely there is a wonderfull love betweene a faithfull Pastor and his faithfull people." The remark reminds one of George Herbert's beautiful ministry at Bemerton. For the most part, however, Fletcher's practicality as a workman kept him from rising to the ethereal mysticism of the author of *The Temple.* The priestly occupation stirred his energy, courage, intellect, and even anger, but rarely did it inspire him.

Typical of the man's pragmatism was the careful organization of his preaching. At the outset of his ministry, he plotted a logical ten-year plan to which he adhered scrupulously. It is an indication that even in 1621 Fletcher looked forward to no advancement beyond Hilgay. He proposed to bisect the decade. During the first five years his sermons were to deal with "the more contemplative, and doctrinall parts of Scripture," for this was to be a campaign of sustained persuasion which would bring his heathen to see the light. The second five were set aside for "the practicall . . . how to do that, which they have there learnt must be done." Whether or not it be effective pedagogy to forestall the practical with the contemplative, is of no present importance. It is notable, however, that here was a village clergyman who projected a long term of strategy in sermonizing. Such conscientiousness was rare in that day of "blind mouths."

Although these conceptions of a rector's duties were not set down in writing until ten years after the poet came to Hilgay, they were well founded within his mind on November 1, 1621, when he began his work. Meanwhile Giles Fletcher was getting started upon a similar undertaking some sixty miles off, in Suffolk. The distance was too great to admit of frequent intercourse between the brothers, but the news that came from Alderton was never good and grew worse constantly. Little more than a year after Phineas Fletcher had established himself, it announced a catastrophe. Giles and Phineas Fletcher, with parallel careers, provide an interesting study of dissimilarity foiled against similarity. Since they were remarkably alike in so many respects, the shades of difference in personality and character are accentuated. The younger brother's leisurely methods of composition and the other's feverish haste, the one's long-enduring contentment at Trinity College and the other's struggle for preferment in or out of King's, the almost feminine delicacy of *Christs Victorie and Triumph* and the virility of *Locustae,* all contrast; but even more than these, Phineas Fletcher's three decades of happy, purposeful activity at Hilgay, and Giles' repining at Alderton, the three years of agony that led to his death.

Undoubtedly the physical variations between Alderton and Hilgay must be reckoned with. The Suffolk hamlet was a coastal village, isolated upon a seaboard that stretched out barren and flat. To this day the natives are a people who talk gloomily of tidal waves that rush in and devour sections of their country, of towns, even cities, that have vanished overnight with nothing more than a bit of church spire rising above the waves to mark the site. Then again Giles Fletcher seems to have owned a less robust physique than his brother, a fact that may account for his more delicate nature. For the most part his tragedy at Alderton came from within his being. It was the struggle of a gentle spirit chained to a crude and revolting task.[1] In his *Reward of the Faithfull,* the author devotes an entire chapter to the difficulties of his ministry—to the "Country-Divels of drunkenness, Blasphemy, Gaming, Lying, and Queaning." Despite the fire and brimstone which the elder brother hurled down upon these rural sins, apparently they were his breath of life. The poet of *Christs Victorie and Triumph* found them to be a deadly fume which he lacked the vitality to combat, and in 1623 he died.[2] Some years later his widow married a Mr. Ramsay, incumbent of Rougham, Norfolk. Since this village and Hilgay were no more than twenty miles distant, Phineas Fletcher may have had some converse with the two.

In addition to his flock, the Hilgay rector had two dynamic interests—his family and his friendships. During the first five years of her marriage, Elizabeth bore only Anne, but after 1621 she enjoyed greater increase. Her husband had been installed at the rectory a month when she was delivered of a second daughter, Elizabeth, and two years later she had her first son, Edmund. As for the other source of stimulation, fellowship with sympathetic men became possible largely because Hilgay was so near King's Lynn and Cambridge. Fletcher's stanchest comrade of the university days had gone off to London, but there is proof that he maintained contact with Tomkins at least until 1624. Close to that year the organist married Margaret, daughter of Dr. Sylvanus Griffiths, Dean of Hereford. The earlier version of a piscatory eclogue [3] alludes to Tomkins' ladylove as Stella; but in the quarto of 1633 she becomes Melite. Evidently the change was made to fit the new development in the musician's life, concerning which Fletcher had kept himself

---

[1] The Alderton register casts no light upon Giles Fletcher's life, because all sections earlier than 1674 have been lost.

[2] Fuller attributes his death to his sufferings over the sinfulness and boorishness of his parishioners. Giles Fletcher's *Reward of the Faithfull* entirely substantiates this explanation.

[3] See *Piscatorie Eclog* VI, in the Sion College MS.

informed. With the passing of the years Tomkins rose in fame, becoming organist to the Chapel Royal and later to Charles, on his 1633 progress into Scotland, while the understanding between him and the insignificant country priest lessened and lessened. He died in 1638; William Lawes mourned his passing in an elegy, and old St. Paul's erected a monument bearing this informative eulogy:

Johannes Tomkins, Musicae Baccalaureus Organista sui temporis ;eleberrimus, postquam Capellae regali, per annos duodecim, huic autem Ecclesiae per novem decem sedulo inserviisset, ad coelestem chorum migravit, Septembrio 27, Anno Domini, 1638, Aetatis suae 52.

In the very year of his decease, the musician was presented with a son, Thomas, who lived to sign the imprimatur upon the first edition of *Paradise Lost*.

Although Thomalin had receded from Fletcher's life, there were other men, many of them of considerable literary distinction, who drew increasingly closer. One of the figures in Quarles' *Emblemes* depicts a globe, supposedly the world. Upon it are inscribed the names of only four places: London, Finchfield (*sic*), Roxwell, and Hilgay. They seem to be points of significance in the author's life; for example, Roxwell in Essex was the haven to which Quarles retired about 1635. How could he have known Hilgay hamlet without entering into some association with its rector, whose *Purple Island* he admired so excessively? Perhaps Quarles met Fletcher at Cambridge before 1613, but it is certain that he knew the clergyman at some time during his Norfolk residence.[4] The younger poet led a mobile existence, giving his biographers a merry chase and often eluding them. As far as can be determined, he was in Germany, Ireland, and Scotland from 1613 to 1621. In 1629 he again voyaged to Ireland, where he stayed for some five years, returning to England, and dying in 1644. His visits to Hilgay—and probably Fletcher was the attraction—must have occurred during the 1620's.[5]

Several other attachments, which also do not admit of a precise dating, belong to the rector's thirty years at Hilgay. Izaak Walton

[4] "Francis Quarles . . . was bred up in the University of Cambridge, where he became intimately acquainted with Mr. Edward Benlowes, and Mr. Phineas Fletcher," Winstanley's *Lives*, pp. 155-56.

[5] Of course Quarles may have visited Hilgay between 1635 and 1644, but his *Emblemes*, with the significant *orbis terrarum*, was published in 1635.

was a reliable judge of men, and therefore the most convincing tribute to Fletcher, not as a writer, but as a living human being, is found in *The Compleat Angler*:

Phineas Fletcher, an excellent divine, and an excellent angler; and the author of excellent Piscatory Eclogues, in which you shall see the picture of this good man's mind: and I wish mine to be like it.

Compleat Angler, pp. 175-76.

The graceful and warm eulogy seems to permit two conclusions: first that its author had personal knowledge of his subject, and secondly that their friendship followed Fletcher's taking of the cassock. If Walton was familiar with the poet, it is not surprising that he came into possession of a variant manuscript of *The Purple Island,* from which he quoted in his discourse of fish and fishing.

John Arrowsmith, Puritan divine, wrote a complimentary poem on *A Father's Testament* many years before the book was published.[6] Arrowsmith was probably an intimate, because this work long remained in the bosom of the Hilgay family. In 1631 he was incumbent of St. Nicholas' Chapel at King's Lynn, and thus was almost a neighbor to the Hilgay rector. Twenty years later he was elected master of Trinity College, the office once occupied by Thomas Neville. As we follow Fletcher's history chronologically, the years will produce other friends, some of whom, if less distinguished than Quarles or Wotton, were still more devoted. The pent-up poetic intellect, which would have atrophied for want of employment in Fletcher's daily work, evidently found release in such relationships.

[6] Several other complimentary addresses, also printed with *The Purple Island,* suggest additional acquaintances. A brief panegyric, "On The Most Accurate Poem, Inscribed The Purple Island," bears the initials "A. C." The name of Abraham Cowley immediately presents itself, and the poem is in his manner. If he was its author, there would be even greater reason for marveling at the boy's precocity. The panegyric must have been written before 1633. Cowley was born in 1618, and in 1632 he was attending Westminster School, and in the following year he published his *Poeticall Blossomes.*

Dr. Daniel Fairclough (commonly called Featley) was the author of a prose panegyric which was likewise printed with *The Purple Island.* Fairclough, born in Oxfordshire in 1582, and thus a coeval of Fletcher, entered Corpus Christi College at Oxford and later went to France as chaplain to the English ambassador, Thomas Edmunds. After a variety of ecclesiastical employment, he became the third provost of Chelsea College. He retired to Kennington in 1625, and died at about the time of the Restoration. What acquaintance he had with the poet is unknown. They may have met in London, where the provost was famous for his anti-papist disputations. At least the two had a common enthusiasm.

Much of that which galvanized life for the Hilgay rector seems to have come from the world beyond his parish: occasional intelligence from London concerning the exploits of Tomkins, a message from Alderton announcing the death of Giles, or the men who visited him, Quarles, for instance, with his news of France and Ireland. At rare intervals, however, absorbing events transpired in Fletcher's Hilgay. In May, 1626, he was called upon to bury Henry Pappen of Stoke, who had been drowned. In the springtime the Ouse and the Wissey changed from leisurely waterways into dark torrents that were a daily menace to the lives of the field workers. Again the humdrum of country existence was broken by repeated additions to the rectory family. Phineas was born on September 3, 1626, William, two years later, and a daughter, Frances, in 1631.

The circle of infant faces was Fletcher's crown of joy, and of his children he wrote:

> I have ever esteemed you the special blessing which God hath given me upon earth.
>
> *A Father's Testament,* p. 2.

The man undertook his paternal duties with an intensity of affection and an unselfishness which now seem the most admirable phases of his character. Nor did his unusual devotion lead to any weak-kneed indulgence. In *The Way to Blessednes* the author places emphasis upon the text:

> With-hold not correction from the childe, if thou smite him with the rodde, hee shall not dye: Thou shall smite him with the rodde, and shalt deliver his soule from hell.
>
> *The Way to Blessednes,* p. 164.

Fortunate for the world that Fletcher's noblest trait crystallized into a book, and that *A Father's Testament* found its way into print, despite the author's intention to have it perish with him! [7]

For the most part it was written in prose, but each chapter concludes with a poem, meager stanzas which constitute both a joy and a regret. They are the clearest indication of the greatness their author could have achieved, had he not become the victim

---

[7] See *A Father's Testament,* "The Publisher to the Reader," where it is stated that the author wrote the book, not for publication, but to be read by his own children and relatives.

of the *Sicelides* disappointment. They appeal to me as his best poetry, and *A Father's Testament* might be regarded as his supreme accomplishment in letters and in life. The book was not written for publication, nor even to be disseminated among his friends. *Locustae* and *Sicelides* were the products of an author whose mind seems to have dwelt largely upon the patronage to be won by his work. The *Testament,* on the other hand, grew directly from his love for his offspring and for literature. Is there any wonder that the work has a freedom from affectation, a lyricism, and an idealism that are somewhat lacking in the poet's other writings?

Fletcher kept in touch with Sir Walter Robarts, the chief landowner of Cranbrook, at least until 1628. The contact was no thin formality, but real enough to lead the rector to write a tract, *Joy in Tribulation.* A Cranbrook tombstone fixes the composition of this work between the years 1628 and 1632. The occasion which called it forth is suggested in the dedication, addressed to Robarts and his wife, where the author wishes Sir Walter "everlasting Consolations of the Eternall Comforter." Obviously the Kentish squire had suffered a bereavement, and we learn that his distinguished father, Sir Thomas, died on February 21, 1627/8, aged sixty-seven. Four years later the poet published his manuscript, because "God hath blessed his little treatise to some in private." It may be unfair to Fletcher, and yet one cannot help sensing in his excessive and prompt sympathy for Robarts a requickening of the eagerness for preferment. Perhaps he found a certain unholy joy in tribulation, a dim hope that his old friend, having fallen into his heritage, might open to him avenues of advancement. If Fletcher's ambitions returned to life, they seem to have been stillborn and nothing came of them. The old man's principal bequest to his son was a burden of indebtedness. During this same year of sorrow Robarts was made sheriff of Kent, and he lived to distinguish himself upon several occasions. He went to London, where he became commissioner of sewers and, assisted by Sir Edward Stradling, undertook the construction of an aqueduct to convey water from Hoddesden to the metropolis.[8] At the time of the Kentish Petition, he was in Cranbrook where he drew considerable attention to himself by securing

[8] *Calendar of State Papers, 1638-39.*

a trumpet from a certain army officer, blowing repeatedly upon it, and shouting his loyalty to King Charles.[9] Perhaps faint sounds of the picks and mattocks at Hoddesden, and of a trumpet at Cranbrook, reached Hilgay.

Phineas Fletcher lost John Tomkins when he abandoned Cambridge for Risley. Yet with human shortsightedness he persisted in placing the responsibility upon the musician, maintaining that Thomalin broke their friendship several years later when he went off to London.[10] The two had been Jonathan and David, and Tomkins left a void in his comrade's world that never could be quite filled. Their attachment had grown out of the optimism of youth, which had vanished like the snows of yesteryear. Along in the 1620 decade, Edward Benlowes came into Fletcher's life to occupy, so far as was possible, the place Tomkins had left.

Fletcher's poetry is rich in allusions to his friends, but the name of Benlowes appears everywhere with an impertinent prominence, even overshadowing that of the organist. Both *The Purple Island* and *Sylva Poetica* were dedicated to him. Three copperplate engravings were bound in the first edition of the anatomical poem, bearing verse anagrams: "Edward Benlowes, Sun-warde beloved"; "Edovardus Benlowes, Durus, a Deo Benevolus"; while the third featured the arms of Fletcher—an azure cross patonce set in a sable field between four escallops—joined with those of Benlowes, beneath which was the following Senecan maxim: "Benevolo coniunctio Animi maxima est Cognatio." The British Museum owns a *Purple Island,* a presentation copy to Benlowes, which contains in the author's own hand: "Benevolus esse suj voluit monumentu et pignus Amoris."

Undoubtedly Benevolus makes a much finer showing in the pages of Fletcher's poetry than Thomalin. He is praised, however, in engravings, dedicatory addresses, and autograph inscriptions, which, after all, are excrescences. Tomkins, on the other hand, appears as one of the *dramatis personae* in some poems and as the inspiration of others. Fletcher's 1633 publications suggest that the organist enjoyed the poet's spontaneous love, but that Benlowes

[9] *Calendars of the Committee for Compounding,* IV, 2602.
[10] "To Mr. Jo. Tomkins."

sought out the rector at a time when his affections were largely absorbed by a wife and numerous children. Fletcher wished to install the newcomer as a bosom comrade, went through all the gestures of Platonic friendship, but never got entirely away from gestures.

Although Edward Benlowes failed to succeed Tomkins, he was the clergyman's warmest friend during his Hilgay residence. Benlowes, who was more than twenty years Fletcher's junior, was the son of Andrew, lord of Brent Hall in Essex. He proceeded to St. John's College on April 8, 1620. After his matriculation at Cambridge, an acquaintance with Fletcher became possible, geographically speaking. Yet Benlowes was a mere boy, and could hardly have won the other's esteem for several years. He is supposed to have been a Papist during his youth; but later he recanted, becoming a bitter anti-Romanist—another reason for setting the date of his familiarity with the author of *Locustae* closer to 1630 than to 1620. Upon his father's death, the young man fell heir to Brent Hall and to an annual income that ranged between seven hundred and one thousand pounds. Is it hypercynical to observe that various literary men—like Quarles, D'Avenant, and Fletcher—discovered what they called Benlowes' unparagoned genius only after prosperity had smiled upon him?

Exact information upon the when and the where of the poet's consorting with this rich youth is wanting. Indeed Benlowes is almost as elusive as his friend Quarles. For some five years after 1620, he remained at Cambridge, and in 1634 and 1636 he was at Cressing Temple, near Braintree in Essex. Probably Fletcher became acquainted with him during his late academic years. The meeting may have taken place in the town of Cambridge; on the other hand it seems more probable that the young man made a literary pilgrimage to Hilgay, escorted perhaps by Quarles, who was a mutual comrade. Among their other common acquaintances was William Neville, and to him Benlowes dedicated his *Sphinx Theologica*. Neville was the brother of Thomas, Giles Fletcher's erstwhile patron, and he was probably a distant relative of the poet. One of the panegyrics prefixed to *The Purple Island* was signed with the name of William Benlowes, evidently a kinsman of the heir to Brent Hall and by him introduced to Fletcher. Little is known about this second Benlowes,[11] but he was the author of the familiar epigrammatic couplet on Fletcher:

> For thou art Poet born; who know thee, know it:
> Thy brother, sire, thy very name's a Poet.
> "To the Learned Authour," lines 18-19.

Whether at Cambridge or at Hilgay, the Edward Benlowes-Phineas Fletcher attachment began about 1625, was strongest in 1633, and survived to an unknown date. The younger man's *Theophila,* issued in 1652, was graced with an extravagant Fletcherian encomium which hailed the author as a rival of Sophocles. Despite its late appearance, the panegyric may have been written long before its publication.

Benlowes' life was that of a meteorite; he shone brightly but briefly. After inheriting his patrimony, he became a lavish contributor to arts and letters. He enriched the library of St. John's College with books,[12] and a swarm of literary men with money. His *Theophila* is a convincing token of the reputation he had achieved as a patron, being adorned with encomiums by no less than sixteen different authors, including Fletcher. Even in Caroline England, an income of one thousand pounds did not warrant expenditure, well-intentioned as it was, upon so grandiose a scale. Benlowes' resources sank lower and lower. Evidently the young man had fancied himself a Maecenas of the North and, when he saw that his wealth was not inexhaustible, he was too proud to retract, and kept on spending to the last penny. There was a dramatic quality about Benlowes' career which was not without its tragic dénouement. Shortly before his death, in 1676, he was seen wandering the streets in rags. The Hilgay rector was spared any knowledge of his friend's sad fate.

Fletcher's poetry is littered with gramercies and thanksgivings, almost all of which are addressed to Benlowes and not a one to Willoughby. Yet he owed the Hilgay rectory and his very bread and butter to the lord of Risley Hall. Although it is likely that

---

[11] No information can be obtained concerning William Benlowes other than the following irrelevant and fragmentary notice. On January 28, 1637/8, Joseph Neal brought action against William Benlowes, Jr., who had so far escaped suit on permission granted him by Sir John Lenthall (*Calendar of State Papers,* 1637/38).

[12] Baker's *History of the College of St. John,* p. 340.

poetic tributes were not welcomed by Willoughby, we must still regard the poet's gratitude to Benlowes as inordinate, in comparison with that rendered to the first patron. We know of no benefice or worldly preferment received from the younger man. In dedicating his *Sylva Poetica* to the Maecenas, the author wrote:

> Tu faveas, primoque adsis, Edovarde, labori,
> Quem teneras subter vites salicesque recurvas
> Ignoti Chamo cecinit nova fistula vatis.
> *Sylva Poetica,* dedicatory address, lines 25-27.

Since Benlowes supported the labors rather than the singer, it becomes understandable why so many expressions of obligation are found in the poems—not that the author owed more to his new patron than to any other man, but his poems did.

There is no evidence that Willoughby ever took an atom of interest in his dependent's versifying; on the other hand, Benlowes was an impassioned littérateur. In the "Manuductio" of his *Sphinx Theologica* and elsewhere, he praised Fletcher's genius in extravagant terms. Probably he was the most appreciative admirer that the poet ever had known, and his enthusiasm came at a time when Fletcher would find it peculiarly welcome. *The Purple Island* and *The Apollyonists* had long ceased to be seventh wonders. Whereas their author was once accustomed to being hailed as Cambridge's laureate, of late people had begun to greet him as the rector of Hilgay. When he felt that the world had forgotten his literary achievements, this youth arrived shouting paeans of praise. Such fervent encouragement was almost enough to stir up the sense of obligation, which lavished acknowledgments. Benlowes' share, however, in the Fletcher poems could not have ended with sentences of wordy commendation.

The better part of twenty years had passed since the Hilgay rector had given over serious versification, and during that long interval he had made no visible move toward preserving his many manuscripts. The causes for this apathy are obvious. The longing for an immortality in print, so common with literary artists, was lacking in Fletcher—even in the Cantabrigian poet of 1610. He wrote to provide courteous little offerings to his friends, to gain the respect of his university associates, and to better his academic position. Since the audience which he addressed was small, all these ends could be achieved by the circulation of his manuscripts, and hence the printing press had little allurement. At Cambridge he had had a very honest pride in his work, but at Hilgay he became unduly modest about it. As he grew more and more of a clergyman, there developed within him an abhorrence for the vanities of the world, and poetry was of these.[13] Had he been allowed to keep the even tenor of his way, he might never have published. The world would have known *Sicelides* and *Locustae,* because they are still extant in manuscript form. Perhaps *The Purple Island,* the *Piscatorie Eclogs,* and *The Apollyonists* would have been turned into print by the same mysterious agencies which carried *A Father's Testament* to the press of Henry Mortlock many years after the author's death; or perhaps they would have gone to the limbo of oblivion, where the nameless drama of 1606 now resides. Posterity is indebted to the power which exploded his indifference and drove him to the publishing houses.

During the exact years when Fletcher was friendly with Benlowes, the presses of London and Cambridge commenced to turn out his works, one after another, in a steady stream: *Locustae* and *The Apollyonists* in 1627; *Brittain's Ida* in 1628; *Sicelides* in 1631; *Joy in Tribulation* and *The Way to Blessednes* in 1632; and *The Purple Island, Piscatorie Eclogs, Poeticall Miscellanies,* and *Sylva Poetica* in 1633. Was it a mere coincidence that the poet's desire to publish and his acquaintance with his admirer were coetaneous? In dedicating *The Purple Island* to the virtuoso, he wrote:

> But since you please to have them see more *Day* than their credit can well endure, marvel not if they flie under your *Shadow.* . . . In letting them abroad I desire onely to testifie, how much I preferre your desires before mine own, etc.
>
> *The Purple Island,* dedicatory address.

Benlowes persuaded Fletcher to let his works see daylight. A Maecenas would not stop with exhortation, but would certainly lend physical and material aid to the project for which he was responsible. Possibly he acted as intermediary between the author and his agents, and probably he subsidized the undertaking whenever money was needed. The precise nature of the young man's assistance can only be conjectured.

[13] The well-known closing of "To Mr. Jo. Tomkins" expresses scorn for poetry.

The six years of negotiation with printers form a chapter in Fletcher's history that is as important as it is dark. Its opening and closing pages are more or less legible: in the neighborhood of 1627, the patron seems to have induced the poet to publish; and by 1633, the title-pages of Fletcher's various works had established when and where they were published. The interim—devoted to the preparation of manuscripts; business trips between Hilgay, London, and Cambridge; the drawing of contracts; the dispatch of letters, packages, emissaries; and the other miscellaneous activities necessary to transpose seven volumes from autograph to printer's ink—all these are clouded with obscurity. We can be almost surer of Benlowes' rôle in the undertaking than of the author's. Fletcher, convinced of the vanity of poetry and sensitive about sullying his cloth, set his writings before the public, but at the same time acted as a man of mystery, resorting more than once to extraordinary deceptions.

The first Fletcherian poetry was published in 1603, and then twenty-four years rolled by before *Locustae* and *The Apollyonists* were issued at Cambridge by Thomas and John Bucke, printers to the university. The entire procedure was open and aboveboard, each poem bearing the signature, Phineas Fletcher of King's College. Apparently the author regarded these as his supreme achievements, because he published them first and was proud to acknowledge them. They were the only major poetic works that he ever publicly recognized as his own. The text of each contains elaborate evidence that Fletcher had gone to some trouble in revising his manuscript before sending it to the Bucke brothers.[14]

In the following year there appeared the amorous stanzas composed in honor of Lady Colepeper and called *Venus and Anchises* at the time of writing. Issued at London by Thomas Walkley, anonymous, supplied with the strange title of *Brittain's Ida,* and fortified with the publisher's suggestion that Edmund Spenser was its author, the work stood little chance of being attributed to the rector of Hilgay. Events proved the disguise, whether intentional or accidental, to be well designed. Through two centuries the somewhat lurid cantos were included in the Spenserian canon; and

---

[14] Among these indications of revision, are the differences between the Harleian *Locustae* and the printed version; the *Apollyonists* marginal, which alludes to Hutchinson's library; and the compliment to Charles at the close of the same poem.

even after they had been rejected, it was long before anyone suspected their true parentage. Then upon internal evidence they were assigned to one of the Fletchers, and finally to Phineas. The Hilgay rector, however, was past caring whether or not his child had been restored.

Everyone assumed that Walkley had pirated the edition—everyone except perhaps Miss Ethel Seaton. She discovered the manuscript of *Venus and Anchises* in the Sion College Library, and suspected the real significance of her find. Miss Seaton, however, was overcautious, because the manuscript proves that all the mysterious circumstances connected with *Brittain's Ida* form one complicated and successful hoax, involving Fletcher, Walkley, and possibly Benlowes. The early or manuscript version had undergone three changes before being set into print: it was divided into cantos and the arguments were added; four of its stanzas were deleted; and its title was changed. Variations of the first type have no meaning, being those which a publisher would regard as necessary improvements. The omissions and the new title, on the other hand, are unmistakably significant. One of the deleted strophes is the lewdest portion of a free poem, while two others contain references to the author in the course of which he calls himself Thirsil and alludes to his residence on the banks of the Cam. These three would have promptly solved the mystery of the origin of the poem, and at the same time would have convicted the originator of immodesty. The character of the suppressions is such that there can be no doubt concerning their intentionality and the identity of their perpetrator, who must have been Fletcher himself. If *Brittain's Ida* were actually pirated, what reason would Walkley have had for cutting out the Thirsil stanzas? The name meant nothing to him. Furthermore, the publisher of *A King and No King, Philaster, Othello,* and *Thierry and Theodore,* instead of being squeamish about Fletcher's voluptuous lines, would cherish them.

Thus it is no longer a strange coincidence that *Brittain's Ida* should have been issued in 1628, during the very six-year period when the poet was conscientiously publishing almost every known line of poetry he had ever written. Since *Brittain's Ida* followed close upon the heels of *Locustae* and *The Apollyonists,* there is a possibility that the author valued it as his second-best creation.

The trickery to which he resorted in order to put it forward, indicates, on the one hand, how timid he was lest he be identified with its eroticism, and, on the other, how he prized the work as a piece of artistry. Whether it was Fletcher, Benlowes, or Walkley who conceived the last refinement of the deception, the assigning of the poem to Spenser, is in doubt. We shall find that Fletcher believed imitation and unacknowledged borrowing to be the best ways of expressing admiration for an earlier writer, and that he at the same time was an undisguised worshiper of Colin Clout. He would regard the deceit as ethical. On the other hand, the ascription of *Brittain's Ida* to Spenser was an excellent device for promoting its sale, and may have originated in Walkley's commercial instinct. There is no specific mention of Benlowes' name in the records of these proceedings. Nevertheless he turned his friend to the printing press, and in this, Fletcher's most difficult publishing venture, the young patron may well have played an important, perhaps a major rôle. If the rector had taken leave of his Hilgay duties and gone to London to make the arrangements with Walkley, the register would betray the fact, as it does several years later when he seems to have traveled to Cambridge upon a similar errand. Therefore an intermediary between the publisher and the author was required, and who more eligible for the post than the young enthusiast? Whereas the remainder of Fletcher's non-dramatic poetry was issued at Cambridge, *Brittain's Ida* was sent to London, probably to conceal its source and also because Walkley had a reputation for marketing the lighter effervescings of the literary art.[15]

There never has been the least doubt that the next publication, *Sicelides,* was pirated. The *Stationers' Register* provides the bare facts: "25 Aprilis, 1631—William Sheeres—Entred for his Copie under the handes of Sir Henry Herbert and Master Kingston warden a play called Sicelides acted at Cambridge." Sheares, not so successful as Walkley, was a printer of miscellaneous works, with a preference for the less circumspect variety. The text of *Sicelides,* unlike *Brittain's Ida* with its almost perfect typography, is cankered with errors. After familiarity with the evidence concerning *Venus*

---

[15] It may be significant that Walkley was John Fletcher's publisher. On the other hand we have noticed evidence of ill feeling between the children of Richard Fletcher and their Cambridge cousins.

and *Anchises,* there is reason to suspect that Sheares' edition of the piscatory drama was likewise authorized. It appeared in London midway during the period in which four Fletcherian works were issued at the metropolis. Since the author had labored to make the play a dazzling achievement, it is not strange that it should have been third in order of publication. Although *Sicelides* bore no signature, it is just a little less immodest than *Brittain's Ida,* and was a work its author would never have acknowledged after taking the cloth. The one argument to support the theory of piracy is the corruption of the text, which might have been the result of circumstances other than the publisher's theft. For instance, the blunders could indicate that the Hilgay rector or his deputy was so occupied with the beautiful text of *The Purple Island* and other poems issued at Cambridge in 1633 that he gave insufficient time to the proof reading of *Sicelides.* If the piscatory drama, like its predecessor, was sent abroad under disguise, the deception was successful, at least with the general public. Anthony à Wood wrote: [16]

> In 1631 was published in qu. a book entit. *Sicelides, a Piscatory,* several times acted in King's coll. in Cambr. and therefore, I presume, 'twas made by one of that house.
>
> *Athenae Oxoniensis,* II, 675.

On November 10 of the same year, "Master Boler entred for his Copy under the handes of Master Austen and Master Islip warden a booke called A treatise or Comentary on the first Psalme by Phinies Ffletcher Bachelor in Divinity." Boler made a similar application on March 9 for "a booke called Christian Consolacion applyed to the afflicted spirritt." These were Fletcher's two devotional tracts which saw the light in 1632, *The Way to Blessednes* and *Joy in Tribulation,* the title having been changed in each case. James Boler, of London, a publisher of religious and scientific books, was a logical agent to handle the pious treatises. In these works the author made no effort to cozen the reading public, nor was there any reason for so doing. *The Way to Blessednes* was dedicated to Fletcher's "most honored, free, and bountiful patron, Sir Henry Willoughby, Baronet."

[16] If *Sicelides* had been enacted more than once, it would be interesting, but probably Wood was inaccurate.

The following year must ever be regarded as the essential harvest time of Fletcher's life. Midway in 1633, the "Printers to the Universitie of Cambridge" brought out two volumes: the first, in quarto, was *The Purple Island, or the Isle of Man: together with Piscatorie Eclogs and other Poeticall Miscellanies;* the second, in octavo, *Sylva Poetica* and *De literis antiquae Britanniae.* The poet seems to have prized at least two or three of his accomplishments before the anatomical poem, and consequently published it last. On the other hand there was considerable labor attached to the preparation of these final collections, and that might account for the delay in their publication. Whatever the author's private opinion, his reputation with the reading public has rested primarily upon *The Purple Island.* Furthermore, most of the information which makes possible a biography of Phineas Fletcher has been provided by the *Piscatorie Eclogs, Poeticall Miscellanies,* and *Sylva Poetica.* Having returned to lighter literature, Fletcher again sought refuge in anonymity or semi-anonymity. The first volume he signed "P. F., Hilgay." *Sylva Poetica* received like treatment, but *De literis antiquae Britanniae,* Dr. Giles Fletcher's poem which Phineas edited and then added to his own Latin collection, bore the full signatures of both father and son. With the quarto and the octavo, the disguise was so thin that it could have taken in only the unknowing.

The volumes of 1633 boast an excellence of typography that reflects the care of both printers and author. The Hilgay register reveals that twice during this important year a strange hand made the entries: from April 5 to May 20, and again from October 5 to October 31. The two periods suggest activities connected with the quarto and the octavo, which might well have been separated by five months. Since it was the first time in his Hilgay career that the author had sought a substitute to carry on his tasks, he must have regarded the occasion as important. Possibly he went to Cambridge, took up residence, and read proof. Although the dedication of *The Purple Island* was dated "May 1, 1633, Hilgay," this last chore before publication could have been written at Cambridge.

In 1632, at the very time when the poet was laboring most heavily beneath these various burdens, Francis Green issued a second edition of *Christs Victorie and Triumph.* The first had contained a commendatory poem from the older brother, "Fond Ladds, That

Spend So Fast Your Poasting Time." The same encomium reappeared in the *Poeticall Miscellanies* of 1633, and also in the second edition of *Christs Victorie and Triumph,* but in the last instance, and in that alone, it had acquired a new couplet entitled *"Defuncto fratri"*:

> Think (if thou canst) how mounted on his spheare,
> In heaven now he sings: thus sung he here.

It is obvious that Phineas Fletcher had interrupted his busy life to cast this flower upon the grave of his brother. Although there is no proof that he had anything more to do with the book, a new edition of *Christs Victorie and Triumph* may have been a part of the publishing campaign which included all of his own prose and verse and also his father's *De literis antiquae Britanniae.*[17]

Late in 1633 Fletcher was able to sink back into comparative leisure while he enjoyed the sense of a task well done. So far as we know, life at Hilgay ran on more or less uneventfully for the next five years. During the summer of 1634, the poet baptized his fourth son, Edward, who, some two years later, was followed by a girl, Sarah. She was Elizabeth Fletcher's eighth and last child. In the spring of 1635, the rector recorded the burial of a man whom he could not identify. The entry has about it a suggestion of the sinister, because seldom did Hilgay harbor utter strangers. Was the unknown some unemployed wayfarer who grew weary of plodding and lay down to die in the village? Or does the notation suggest an event still more dramatic?

From 1638 on, peace abandoned the Norfolk hamlet, never to return again, that is, for Fletcher. At the outset of this latter era, the man's serenity was disturbed by private tragedies, but hard on their heels arrived those of a more public character. First came the passing of Lady Elizabeth Colepeper, the Fusca of the golden years at King's College. Thirsil had long outlived the day when Fusca

[17] A third edition of *Christs Victorie and Triumph* appeared during Phineas Fletcher's lifetime. This 1640 reprint was brought out at Cambridge by Roger Daniel for Richard Royston. It is enriched by seven charming engravings, each of which is set off by a verse. Because the Hilgay rector had some part, although it may have been extremely small, in the 1632 *Christs Victorie and Triumph,* it is possible that he was the author of these seven verses. The strongest argument to the contrary is the mediocrity of the couplets in question. It would be unfair to foist such bungling upon Phineas Fletcher without much surer proof of his authorship.

could cause him any deep-seated sorrow, but her death would not leave him unaffected. On September 14 of the same year, he buried fifteen-year old Edmund, his eldest son. The tenderness that inspired *A Father's Testament* gives some measure of the grief he must have known at this time. Finally during the same autumn and thereafter, unpleasant events occurred at Risley.

The poet's patron, Sir Henry Willoughby, was ambitious for the office of high sheriff of Derbyshire. On November 27, Lord Keeper Coventry wrote to Secretary Windebank concerning Willoughby's aspirations.[18] Though admitting the baronet's great wealth to be a recommendation, he counseled against the appointment because Willoughby had incurred the disfavor of Charles. The king had sponsored the union of Anne Willoughby and Sir John Suckling, but the girl's father had opposed the match. His obstinacy, dubbed "indiscreet" by Coventry, was undoubtedly sagacious. Suckling would have lost little time in melting down the Risley Hall plate, cumbersome as it was. Evidently affected by his disgrace and disappointment, Sir Henry went mad. Thenceforth the poet could no longer hope for the benefits of his wisdom or generosity. Fortunately he had somewhat repaid his benefactor's kindness by dedicating to him and to Lady Lettice Willoughby *The Way to Blessedness*. That Fletcher was allowed to mention the baronet's name only in his most pious work is significant of the older man's modesty and seriousness.

In the meantime Anne had married her first husband, Sir Thomas Aston. In 1640/1 he brought suit "for the custody of the body and government of the estate" of his father-in-law, "who hath been for divers months past visited with great weakness and distraction of mind and sense."[19] The patron, who to all practical purposes departed the poet's life before 1640, actually outlived Fletcher. He was buried at Risley on November 22, 1653.

Thus for Fletcher the times were evil. Once again death and decay ravaged his intimates and, as in the era of 1610, he suffered frequent and sad blows. By 1641, however, English horizons were widening, and private sorrows rapidly gave way before the ava-

---

[18] *Calendar of State Papers,* 1638-39.
[19] *Ibid.,* 1640-41.

lanche of national misfortunes. During that winter the rector recorded the drowning at Hilgay of Rolf Cutting and John Cook, an
event which might have caused greater sensation in other years. In
the meantime Strafford had been arrested and at St. Stephen's the
Long Parliament had gone into session, the last Fletcher was to
know. One of its lesser members, who wore a plain cloth suit and
linen none too clean, was destined to dominate his party and country. This man, Oliver Cromwell, sat for Cambridge, and had come
from his residence at Ely, both towns close to Hilgay. His views
were those of his district, and the Royalist cause was eventually
broken by the people of Fletcher's own East Country.

No record of the poet's attitude upon the great political and religious questions has been handed down. The very absence of evidence implies that he was disinclined to enter the dispute or to take
a strong position concerning it. There were several reasons for such
apathy. His earlier writings and associations suggest the emotions
he must have felt when king and Commons were at one another's
throats. Almost certainly he was torn between two loyalties and
knew not whither to turn, suffering an internal conflict which even
a younger and more vigorous man could scarcely have endured.

The reader of *The Purple Island* must become aware of the author's penchant for preaching to the profligates of his day. The
latter half of the poem narrates an epic battle, where Satan has enlisted an army of vices. The *dramatis personae* of many a contemporary work included vices, but they were generally bloodless ab-
stractions. Here each is a lively representation, and at the same
time a condemnation, of a lecherous courtier, a vinous clergyman,
or some such Jacobean worldling. A like didacticism is found in
Fletcher's devotional treatises, and to an exaggerated degree. Thus
he possessed at least a portion of the self-righteousness which was
the stock in trade of a large group of Caroline Englishmen. There
are numerous additional evidences of Fletcher's leaning toward
Puritanism in religious and political belief. His *Joy in Tribulation*
inculcates the doctrine of predestination [20] and various other Gene-
van tenets, all of which prove him to have been an orthodox Calvinist. Fletcher's politics and theology were faithful patterns of his

[20] *Joy in Tribulation*, pp. 217-18.

home and academic training. Cambridge University had been a rallying point for Calvinistic divines, almost a transplanted Geneva. The poet's grandfather and father had always been vigorous servants and occasional champions of the Puritan party of their own generations. His uncle, the erstwhile Bishop of London, was held responsible for the Calvinistic tone of the Lambeth Articles, and it led him to break with his queen.

The Puritanism of 1645, of the Independents, of Cromwell, of Milton, had traveled many a league from the Calvinism of the 1590's. Only once did Fletcher show that he had even an inkling of the new insistence upon freedom of worship. In *The Way to Blessednes* he unexpectedly sets out to defend the Puritan from the catcalls of schism and heresy.[21] For the rest, his doctrines were of an older vintage, those of the vicar, Bishop Richard Fletcher, and Dr. Giles Fletcher. It seems as if the poet had never realized that the day of the Marian persecutions was over and, like a Don Quixote, he fought Romanism to the end of his life. The poems of his university years, *Locustae, The Apollyonists,* and *The Purple Island,*[22] the shorter leaves from *Sylva Poetica,* "In imaginem Christi a Papista cultam" and "Gladio Pontificio vita principis non permissa," are bitter attacks upon the Vulgate, the communion service, holy relics, celibacy, popes, monks, friars, and Jesuits. Even late in his Hilgay period, when other Puritans were concerned with Arminianism and Laud, Fletcher had not given over the old hostilities. He gloried in a controversy with a Catholic priest, who had asserted to him that "the Scripture was not written by the command of *God,* nor of set purpose, but by chance." Furthermore, his *Way to Blessednes,* though written twenty years after *The Apollyonists,* was equally rabid in its Protestantism.[23]

One of the key articles in this 1590 creed, to which Fletcher still adhered after forty years, was an intense nationalism. His poems are as patriotic as they are Puritan.[24] During Elizabethan days, the Calvinist Essex party rallied to defend the queen from the influence of Roman Catholic diplomats and from her own ministers. The poet's Puritanism was founded not only upon Calvinism and anti-

[21] *The Way to Blessednes,* p. 83.
[22] *The Purple Island,* VII, st. 29-30, 44, 61-65.
[23] *The Way to Blessednes,* pp. 39-40, 52-54, 85-86, 214, 245-47.
[24] *E.g., The Apollyonists,* II, st. 14; V, st. 38-40.

Romanism, but also upon royalism. His references to James, Prince Henry, and above all to Charles, were not only complimentary but adulatory. In addition to the political traditions of his family, there were other bonds that drew him to the Stuart cause. Tomkins, the closest comrade he ever knew, had been Charles' private servant and organist; and in 1642, his other friends, almost without exception, declared themselves Cavaliers.

We can understand the Hilgay rector's dilemma when King Charles raised the royal standard at Nottingham in 1642. His allegiances drew him irresistibly and simultaneously in opposite directions. A third-generation Puritan, a resident in a Parliamentarian country, and a loyalist to the core, he was called upon to choose sides. The division in the nation was the result of advances in religious and political theory, which he was asked to evaluate. As a boy he had accepted his views blindly; he clung to them tenaciously through mature life, and never learned habits of rationalization in either theology or political philosophy. The crisis found him an old man with failing health, and it left him stunned and apathetic. Outwardly he was probably a lukewarm Royalist, but inwardly, confusion personified.

The meager records of the rector's last years at Hilgay confirm the theory that he took no vigorous stand against the Presbyterians or the Independents. While many a Cavalier parson was suffering for his loyalty, Fletcher held his living. He continued in Norfolk throughout the Civil War and into the Commonwealth. On June 24, 1645, his boy William matriculated at St. John's College, Cambridge, after preparing at Ely. The poet's oldest son, Edmund, had died, and the fate of the youngest, Edward, is unknown. His name went unmentioned in his father's will, a fairly certain indication that he was no longer of this world. Possibly he went off to Ely, like William, where he did not live long enough to enter the university. The fourth son, Phineas, also seems to have been denied an academic career, but he flourished for long years.

The poet's gradual but inevitable descent, his temporary illness, a brief recovery, and finally his mortal sickness, can be plainly seen in his Hilgay register. The firm hand that traced a clear and beautiful penmanship across the pages of twenty-five years, gave over in November, 1645. It resumed in March, 1647, but it wrote a wavering and uncertain script. Fletcher made his last entry on the second day after Christmas of 1648, and thenceforward, until the year of his death, several different persons performed the task. On June 21, 1649, he drew up his will, a grimmer *Father's Testament,* which was witnessed by John Lamb and William Lite. By this document he left the pitiful sum of twenty shillings to each of his children, and the remainder of the estate to Elizabeth, his wife. Whatever life had given him, it had never satisfied the feverish ambition of the King's College fellow for the things of this world. He died in 1650, aged sixty-eight, and was buried in his own churchyard, although the site of his grave is unknown. The will was probated on December 13 of the same year. That no record of the burial was made in the register is an indication of how his successors failed to meet the standards of industry and regularity which he had set.

The remainder of the story can be told in a few words. Arthur Towers succeeded Fletcher at Hilgay. The times were stormy and he seems to have run into difficulties about his tenure. For some years he was forced to sign the records as clerk, and it was not until 1660 that he could call himself rector. The poet's widow, the Nicaea of a gayer day on the Derwent, survived her husband by only a few years. Towers buried her in the churchyard on November 6, 1654. Fletcher's last and noblest work, *A Father's Testament,* Henry Mortlock published in 1670. Possibly the manuscript was conveyed to the printer by the author's son Phineas, who was described at this time as "a worthy citizen of London." He it was who arranged with Samuel Lee for the publication of his grandfather's *Israel Redux* in 1677. His brother William, after graduating from St. John's, settled down at Hilgay, married Katherine Carter, and was interred at Hilgay on December 14, 1695.

A century later a Fletcher Dearsley was laid to rest beside the same church. The inscription over his grave read in part:

> He was Grandson of Phineas Fletcher—sometime
> Rector of This Parish.

Thus any traditions left behind by the poet-pastor had evaporated, and he was no more than a name. Today the village has forgotten him utterly, and yet there are Dearsleys, Phineas Fletcher's direct descendants, still alive in Hilgay.

VIII

FOREIGN ECONOMY

READINGS AND IMITATIONS

PHINEAS FLETCHER's biography, his external life, has been considerably better known than the inner, the history of his mental
development. Between 1627 and 1633, some seven volumes of prose
and verse traveled from the Hilgay rectory to the bookshops, along
channels more or less devious. Within them they carried a burden
of material, curious for both its dependence and its lack of dependence. The ensuing chapters will be devoted to untwining the
original from the unoriginal and identifying each. The poet's borrowing falls into two divisions of equal importance: literature
other than Edmund Spenser's works, and Spenser's works. The
former, as a field of inquiry, is still a *terra incognita* whose borders
have been infrequently crossed. Fletcher's dependence upon Spenser has been more fully investigated, but never thoroughly.

Fletcher had three vocations, for he was a teacher, a clergyman,
a poet; and we shall later discover that he added to these three an
avocation, his experimental research in physiology. The tutor's
reading embraced standard works of information; the Bachelor
of Divinity's was directed toward securing a foundation in theology; the scientist pored over the human body more often than
over books, but he was familiar with a few scientific treatises; and
the poet went to ancient and modern, foreign and English versi-
fiers, among whom he schooled himself in his art. Our principal
interest lies with the last, and yet Plato affected the philosophy of
Sicelides and the Romanism of Sir Thomas Hutchinson's book on
the martyrs stirred up some of the scorn of *The Apollyonists,* so
that it will be necessary to note Fletcher's reactions to his reading
of the philosophers, scientists, and religious controversialists, in
addition to his levies upon the poets.

A limiting and defining element in a man's studies is his language equipment. Like any other well-trained university fellow of

the day, Fletcher was as much at ease in Latin as in English. His occasional use of Greek words, in the dedication of the 1627 *Locustae*, for instance, and again the *Purple Island* marginal, "Gustus, or the taste is in the palate, which in the Greek is called the heaven," [1] prove that he knew something of that language and literature, which of course was taught at Cambridge in the poet's time. So, too, was Hebrew, and with it Fletcher may have been familiar, though he leaves no indication of the fact. It seems that he was not acquainted with any Continental speech, French, or Italian, or Spanish.[2] Here was an extraordinary failing in the son of Dr. Giles Fletcher, that traveler of travelers.

In his use of the books he conned, Fletcher differed from his contemporaries in several respects. The average Jacobean prose writer "bumbasted," to use Thirsil's own phrase, "his pages with a multiplicitie of references to give a flavor of deepe-learning," while his brother, the poet, ransacked the cantos of other poems for words and lines with never an intimation of his borrowing. It would be unsafe to presume that the former was profoundly versed in all the books he mentioned, whereas seeking the sources of the latter could only be a game of blindman's buff. As a prose writer, Fletcher is no "bumbaster" except in his multitudinous biblical and Aristotelian references,[3] while he is strikingly modern in his conscientiousness about naming the writers he imitates. In consequence we meet with a considerable number of allusions to authors read, a few prose writers (and it can be safely stated that with these he was well acquainted) and a large company of poets whom, by his own confession, he admired and copied. To these I have added a smaller group of poets that Fletcher evidently knew and assimilated, and yet whose names he left unmentioned.

[1] *The Purple Island*, V, st. 54, marg. z.

[2] An author's familiarity with a language is likely to leave traces in his writings, and such was particularly true during the seventeenth century, with its pedantic tendency. Fletcher gives no hint that he was acquainted with any modern European language. As will be noted, the available evidence all points in the other direction. As Upham observed in his *French Influence in English Literature*, Fletcher's imitation of Du Bartas' *Semaines* regularly echoes Sylvester, rather than the original author. Furthermore, in imitating Tasso and Ariosto, Fletcher gives no indication that he is following the originals rather than the translators.

[3] Biblical allusions are a characteristic of the age. For the artificiality of the Aristotelian references, see Chapters XI and XII below.

Our first and less important concern is with the prose writers—classical, medieval, and Renaissance—to which the poet alludes. They affected his thinking in his own prose works and had some influence upon the notions developed in his poetry. For the most part, however, they exerted their control in ways that are too subtle for recognition. These authorities fall into two further classes, the divine and the secular. Since almost all of the references to the former are found in Fletcher's prose works—*Joy in Tribulation, The Way to Blessednes,* and *A Father's.Testament*—it might be assumed that the studies of his later years were entirely pious and those of his youth and university career worldly. There is some justice in such a distinction, but it must not be drawn too finely, because the young man preparing for the divinity degree and the author of *Locustae* must have known the theologians well.

Scattered throughout the prose and poetic works of Phineas Fletcher are references to Plato and Pliny and, preëminently, to Aristotle. The allusions to Plato are interesting, for in *Sicelides* we encounter the professor of love, a love which commands fire, water, earth, and air, and *The Purple Island* finds its climax in the great Idea of beauty and wisdom, all expressions of the Renaissance Platonism to which Thirsil subscribed. These matters belong to our study of the Spenser-Fletcher relations, since the poet imbibed most of his Platonism from *The Fowre Hymnes.* It is important, however, if he knew the great origins of this philosophical system at first hand.[4] That would be to Fletcher's credit and so, too, was his sanely critical reading of Pliny.[5] The new and the old, the Renaissance and the medieval, merge in a baffling juxtaposition in the Fletcherian poems. On the one hand, we have this Platonism and also the poet's refusal to repeat Pliny's vulgar errors about natural phenomena. In physiology, in all science, as we shall find, he was a Baconian and was in advance of the average contemporary writer. On the other hand, a marked medieval strain winds through the very work that is most regenerate in its enthusiasm for the inductive

[4] References to Plato occur in the following places: *The Purple Island,* III, 10, marg. h; IV, 11, marg. f; V, 24, marg. x. Although Fletcher's allusions to Plato never specify work and chapter like those to Aristotle, one of them is sufficiently detailed to suggest that he had actually read Plato: "Plato affirmed them [the eyes] lighted up with heavenly fire not burning, but shining" (*The Purple Island,* V, 24, marg. x).
[5] *The Way to Blessednes,* p. 128.

method. The occasional harking back to the Middle Ages is a con-
comitant of Fletcher's conservatism and is particularly evident in
his many references to Aristotle. He pretends that the Stagirite was
his chief authority, which, as I have said, was not at all the case, the
Aristotelian citations being true "bumbastings."

In his three prose works Fletcher occasionally expresses his opinions about the patristic writings, and more often quotes from the
Fathers—from Gregory Nazianzus, Chrysostom, Hilary, Tertullian,
Augustine, and Tyrannius Rufinus. He makes it plain that he
holds Augustine to be the most dependable of them all; [6] nor, in his
opinion, is the Bishop of Hippo, and certainly none of the rest, to
be relied upon indiscriminately.[7] Here is a normal seventeenth-
century attitude to the Church Fathers, for those mentioned were
the patrologic authors most commonly read during the Jacobean
era, particularly among Church of England clergymen. About this
time less conservative scholars were turning to the Pseudo-Diony-
sius, but not Fletcher. This last was one phase of a general movement toward eccentric literary adventure, on the part of many of
the poet's coevals; but the books he admired were almost exclu-
sively the standard classics of his day. In his reading Phineas
Fletcher was a Tory.

One is reminded of the medieval strain in *The Purple Island*
when the author, elsewhere in his works, cites Bernard, Vincent of
Beauvais, and Antoninus, three writers of the Middle Ages who
were still known widely. Saint Bernard, the Abbot of Clairvaux,
was an illustrious preacher and writer of the medieval world; Vincent was the author of the great compendium of all knowledge,
Speculum majus; and Saint Antoninus, or Antonio Pierozzi, wrote
the famous *Summa theologica moralis.*

Fletcher's ventures into contemporary prose were almost entirely
directed by an interest in religious controversy, more particularly
in Calvinism and its struggle with Romanism. We are temporarily
bewildered as we find the stern Protestant of *The Apollyonists*
demonstrating his familiarity with the writings of Paul the Fourth
(Giovanni Pietro Caraffa), one of the most notorious of the Renaissance popes; Roberto Francesco Romolo Bellarmino, the Jesuit

[6] *Ibid.*, pp. 156, 177, 244; *Joy in Tribulation*, pp. 125, 148, 183.
[7] *The Way to Blessednes*, p. 216.

champion of the papacy; and Cardinal Caesar Baronius, compiler of *Annales ecclesiastici,* a Church history with a controversial purpose.[8] Can it be that he who called upon the Lord to swim his snowy steed in the blood of the Purple Whore had read Bellarmino and Baronius in a fit of modern broad-mindedness? Desiring to be fair above all things, had he given the paladins of the papacy a chance to defend their cause? These are pleasant but futile conjectures, for we have to do with a man of 1610 whose religious code had been cast for him by Richard Fletcher, the vicar, during the dark years of the Marian persecutions, and had been tempered when Essex's head fell beneath the ax. He went to Caraffa and the *Annales ecclesiastici* that he might obtain ammunition for his own attacks on the papacy; in order to gather, at first hand, evidence about "the cannibal priests who grew fat on the flesh of their Maker," and he found what he sought.

The remaining contemporary prose writers on the poet's list were warriors of the opposite camp, the protagonists of strict Protestantism: James the First, King of England and Scotland, monarch of learned letters and of anti-Romanism; William Perkins, lecturer of Great St. Andrews, most popular preacher of Cambridge at the opening of the century, an unflinching Calvinist reputed to be only slightly inferior to Calvin or Hooker as a theological authority; Robert Bolton of Oxford, another rigid Puritan, whose works had a wide and sustained popularity; Jacob Andreae, or Schmidtlein, opposed to Calvinism, but the promoter of the Reformation throughout Württemberg; and Dr. Playfere, Lady Margaret Professor in Divinity and chaplain to King James. These names, with the exception of that of the pedantic monarch whose present fame is political, come like strangers out of oblivion, but in the first decade of the seventeenth century they were well known, indeed they appeared on the title-pages of the best sellers of Fletcher's time.

These were the prose writers read by Fletcher—we can state that because he himself asserts it—and yet they influenced the Fletcherian poems only in more general and less definable ways. Exactly

---

[8] Another Romanist book read by Fletcher is one which he describes as "Sir Thomas Hutchinson's account of the Roman Catholic Martyrs." This, of course, was some work he had come upon in Hutchinson's library at Owthorpe, the literary oasis in the Derbyshire desert.

opposite is the case of those works from which the poet paraphrased or translated—the Psalms, Boethius' *De consolatione philosophiae,* and the poems of "Mr. H. S."—for the paraphrastic rendering or translation is the most precise kind of literary heritage.

One's first impression upon reading Fletcher is that he derived more material from the Roman philosopher than from any other writer. There are no fewer than thirteen translations from *De consolatione* scattered throughout his pages. Nine of these occur in his latest book, *A Father's Testament,* while the remaining four,[9] found at widely separated intervals in the earlier works, suggest that this solace of his autumnal years was the culmination of an interest begun in youth.

It is extraordinary that four of the thirteen are variant renditions of the single passage in the third book of the Latin classic which tells the story of Orpheus and his half-regained Eurydice.[10] Apparently Fletcher's intense interest in the theme—though we have no less than Milton's *L'Allegro* and *Lycidas* to testify to its more widespread popularity during this era—was founded upon the Christian allegory which he read into it. With but one exception, all his versions emphasize the moral of the story: if the man who strives to bring his dead soul to Heaven turn his yielding eye to Hell again, his sore will grow more desperate, deep, and deadly than before. The younger Giles Fletcher paid tribute to the obscure fables of the Gentiles, foreshadowing biblical episodes—the accounts of Deucalion, Nisus, Phaethon—but above all these he set the Orpheus story, which, as he said, "typed" the climax of the New Testament, Christ's triumph over death.[11]

Fletcher's dependence on Boethius proves to be more apparent than actual. Despite his thirteen translations from *De consolatione,* despite the absence in his work of translations from Vergil, Ovid, Sannazaro, Tasso, or Ariosto, each of the foregoing (to say nothing of Spenser and Sylvester) will prove to have a greater ascendancy in

[9] The nine translations of passages from Boethius in *A Father's Testament* are reprinted by Boas, II, 333-39. The four in the earlier poems are to be found in the following locations: *The Purple Island,* V, st. 61-68; *Poeticall Miscellanies,* pp. 243-45; *Sicelides,* IV, chorus.

[10] *The Purple Island,* V, st. 61-68; *Poeticall Miscellanies,* Boas, II, 243-45; *Sicelides,* IV, chorus; *A Father's Testament,* pp. 62-64.

[11] "Christs Triumph over Death," st. 7-8.

the Fletcherian poems than Boethius. A reading of *De consolatione* has revealed no phrasings or thoughts which the poet carried over into his own work, to compare with those found repeatedly from the *Aeneid,* the *Metamorphoses,* or *Orlando Furioso.* Considering that Fletcher was highly susceptible to literary influence, it is astonishing that the Roman philosopher should have exercised at one and the same time so great and so small an authority upon his admirer. The second writer translated by Fletcher is even less of a factor in his craftsmanship than the philosopher of the prison cell, but his identity offers a mystery.

The *Poeticall Miscellanies* contains a slight piece entitled "These Asclepiads of Mr. H. S. translated and enlarged," with the four lines of Asclepiadean verse, followed by a paraphrastic translation of twenty-four lines. I have not succeeded in locating the short Latin stanza in its original publication, but can say with a fair assurance that the author was a Henry Smith who was born in 1550 and who died in 1591. No other composer of Latin poetry whose initials were "H. S." is known to have been alive during the Elizabethan or Jacobean years. Like almost all of the contemporary writers read by Phineas Fletcher, Smith was a distinguished clergyman who published abundant sermons and Latin verse, the latter amazingly various in its meters and stanzas. Sylvester's *Du Bartas* translates not only the *Semaines* but the works of miscellaneous writers, among them Henry Smith's *Micro-cosmo-graphia: The Little-Worlds Description: or, The Map of Man (from Latin Saphiks of that Famous, late, Preacher in London, Mr. Henry Smith).* Although *Micro-cosmo-graphia,* itself, bears no resemblance to *The Purple Island,* the title is strongly suggestive of Fletcher's masterpiece; there must at least have been a sympathy of taste and idea shared by the London clergyman and our geographical-anatomical poet. Since Sylvester found it desirable to translate Smith's Saphics (we shall learn that Fletcher was a follower of the translator of Du Bartas), it is less surprising that Thirsil should have done the same for the Asclepiads. It is also significant that certain of Smith's Latin epigrams, similarly rendered by Sylvester, are very like in style to the four lines of Asclepiadean verse. His work is everywhere distinguished by its wordplay and antithesis. There was no reason why Fletcher should have concealed his source, and he was not doing so if the initials, "H. S.," were famous in 1610. Such seems to have been the case, for Smith does not feel the necessity of printing out his name in full.

In his excursions into the prose works of the ages, in his lifelong veneration for *De consolatione philosophiae,* and in his translating of the Asclepiads, the poet of the Cam has avoided any real borrowing. Now, however, a formidable company comes under the leadership of its co-captains, Vergil and Spenser, followed by Du Bartas, Sylvester, the younger Giles Fletcher, Sannazaro, Ovid, Homer, Euripides, Seneca, Daniel, Ariosto, Tasso, Marlowe, and Sidney. Phineas Fletcher imitated most of them. They haunt the lines of *The Purple Island, The Apollyonists,* and the other poems, in character, theme, idea, stylistic shading, phraseology, word, philosophy—in short, in every conceivable aspect of the poetic art. At one moment the echoes are heard but faintly, as if from a great distance, and at the next the voice of Ovid or of Tasso rings out almost as clearly as in the *Metamorphoses* or *Jerusalem Delivered* themselves. Then again one of Fletcher's phrases is plainly derived from Spenser alone, but in another Colin Clout, Tasso, Vergil, and Sylvester may all be jumbled together in a welter of coalescing influence. It is as if memory in the writer had struck every ivory of the keyboard simultaneously, or perhaps it is simply that one Renaissance poet passed an idea or phrase, first gleaned from the classics, around a circle of fellow authors. Thus the original of an idea or a figure of speech in *Sicelides* may be found not only in Ariosto, but also in Vergil and Spenser. In such a case it is difficult to determine from which of the three Fletcher had it, for there is proof that he imitated and studied the work of each.[12]

If Thirsil differed from his coevals in any respect, it was that he was unusually careful about acknowledging his sources: he admits his relationship, either directly or by inference, to most of the poets I have mentioned. He made four such statements about his dependence upon Spenser, and on one or more occasions alluded to Vergil, Du Bartas, Sylvester, the younger Giles Fletcher, Sannazaro, Ovid, Homer, Euripides, Seneca, and Daniel. Fletcher conceded his imitation of these authorities, and them we shall consider first,

---

[12] Appendix B below consists of a tabulation of the various possible sources of ideas and phrases in Fletcher's poetry.

postponing the inquiry into his connection with others like Ariosto and Tasso, whom he did not acknowledge.

The poet of the Cam approached *The Shepheardes Calender,* *The Faerie Queene,* and the *Complaints* with the reverence of a disciple, and there he learned a lesson that was so large a factor in his own writing that consideration of it must be consigned to a subsequent chapter. The second of the co-captains was Vergil. To Fletcher, Maro was the "celebratus," the high-towering swain, the never-equalled, and the first enrolled in the shrine of memory. Homer had sung the fires of Troy, but the muse of slow Mincius sang them twice better. Thirsil worshiped Vergil as the god of poetry and confessed his faith upon at least six different occasions.[13] He tells of how he and his dear Willy (who, we have found, was probably William Cappell) went down to the bank of the yellow Cam, where they selected a spot shaded from the summer sun, and there they read the *Bucolics*.[14] Less romantic but more pertinent to our investigation is his explicit account of how he paid his devotions to his deity in his poetizing: it was, he said, "all his prides aspiring to lackey" the Vergilian works.[15]

These acknowledgments suggest that Fletcher's poetry contains abundant reminiscences of the Mantuan's lines. Comparison of the master's work with the pupil's yields prompt confirmation. Curiously, the one investigation into their relationship was restricted to the *Piscatorie Eclogs*,[16] a work which has relatively few of these echoes; for it is in *The Purple Island, The Apollyonists,* and *Locustae* that the "lackeying" is most thoroughly achieved. There the imitations are to be found in the large and the small, in mood, manner, incident, and phrase.

Thirsil and Willy may have read the *Bucolics* amid the lush peacefulness of the Backs, but it is the *Aeneid* and the *Georgics* that resound through the pages of Fletcherian poetry. In the former, Vergil describes the gate of Hell, "Vestibulum ante ipsum primisque in faucibus Orci," where a dismal allegorical society con-

[13] *The Purple Island,* I, st. 11; VI, st. 5, 51-52; *Sylva Poetica,* the dedication, line 9; "To my beloved Thenot," lines 17-24; "To Master W. C.," lines 20-21.

[14] "To Master W. C.," lines 20-21.

[15] *The Purple Island,* VI, st. 5.

[16] The editor of the *Piscatory Eclogues* (Edinburgh, 1771) points out what he considers to be parallels between Vergil's and Fletcher's eclogues. Most of these are not sufficiently close to justify mention.

sort—"Luctus," "Cura," "Morbus," "Senectus," "Metus," "Fames," "Egestas," "Sopor," "Discordia," and "Letum." [17] In a general way these lines, with their personification, inspired a body of Renaissance poetry, including *The Faerie Queene* and the entire latter half of *The Purple Island*. From a more restricted point of view, the same *Aeneid* passage laid the foundations of a structure that was to rise with grandeur in *Paradise Lost*—the nine gates of brass, iron, and adamantine rock, impaled with circling fire. There can be little doubt that certain of the details of Milton's Hell-Gate came to him from Vergil, and also that some entered *Paradise Lost* by way of *The Apollyonists*, which, in turn, was motivated by the Vergilian scene. Fletcher wrote, translating his original with almost literal exactitude,

> In th' entrance Sicknes, and faint Languor dwelt,
> Who with sad grones tolle out their passing knell, etc.[18]

The Vergilian account of the speech-making in the council hall of the Latin peoples, bears precisely the same relationship to the Satanic councils of *The Apollyonists* and *Paradise Lost*.[19] Prototypes of Fletcher's characters are often found in the *Aeneid:* Camilla, for instance, is the progenitress of those lovely, fearful Amazons of Ariosto and Spenser, and of Parthenia of *The Purple Island*.[20] Although the *Piscatorie Eclogs* were primarily inspired by Sannazaro, it is worth noting that Vergil gave Fletcher a precedent in this form, since both the *Aeneid* and the *Georgics* present Father Neptune with his entourage.[21] These are a few of the broader Vergilian themes copied by Fletcher. The rest I have relegated to the appendices, along with the list of passages which reveal verbal identity, for a full accounting of either would be tedious. The most extraordinary of the latter is found in the chorus of the second act of *Sicelides*, some twenty lines of which constitute a careful and unacknowledged translation from the *Georgics*.[22]

Fletcher left Joshua Sylvester distinctly "uncelebratus," nor did he enroll him in the shrine of memory; and yet Fletcher owed al-

[17] *Aeneid*, VI, lines 273-81.
[18] *The Apollyonists*, I, st. 16. For the entire scene, see st. 9-16.
[19] *Aeneid*, VI.
[20] *Ibid.*, VI.
[21] *Ibid.*, V, lines 816-26; *Georgics*, IV, lines 334-547.
[22] *Sicelides*, II, chorus, lines 13-31; *Georgics*, II, lines 475-86.

most as much to the translator as to Vergil. The fact that Thirsil
never lauded Sylvester in words, but in practice was a tireless imitator, provides a mystery rendered the more impenetrable by investigation. The author of *The Purple Island* can scarcely find super-
latives to meet Du Bartas' deserts:

> And that *French* Muses eagle eye and wing
> Hath soar'd to heav'n, and there hath learn'd the art
> To frame Angelick strains, and canzons sing
> Too high and deep for every shallow heart,
> Ah blessed soul! in those celestiall rayes,
> Which gave thee light these lower works to blaze,
> Thou sitt'st emparadis'd, and chaunt'st eternall layes.
>
> *The Purple Island,* I, st. 14.

Since Fletcher probably had no French, his acquaintance with the
"strains" and "canzons" must have been by way of Sylvester. Sub-
stantiation is found in the derivative passages which regularly bear
the marks of Sylvester, rather than of Du Bartas.[23] Nevertheless,
though Fletcher showers blessings, emparadisings, and angelizings
upon the Frenchman, he does not offer one poor monosyllable to
the translator.

The culminating circumstance of the perplexity lies in the
personal bond between the two English poets, for the importance
of kinship and loyalties in Fletcher's life and writing has been
brought out repeatedly in the preceding chapters. Joshua Sylvester
was related to the Nevilles through his mother's brother, who
married a daughter of Sir Thomas Neville. Thus he belongs to that
numerous Neville-Molyneux-Willoughby-Fletcher kindred and
was probably a distant relative of the poet. In addition, he was
steward to the Earl of Essex at Lamborne, and therefore was a comrade in service of the elder Giles Fletcher. Finally, both the poet's
father and Sylvester were friends of Anthony Bacon.[24] Phineas
Fletcher may have had some strong notion about the self-obliter-
ating function of the translator—perhaps that it was his glory to
submerge himself in the elevation of a great foreign writer—which
persuaded him to leave Sylvester's name unheralded, even unmentioned.

[23] Upham's *French Influence in English Literature,* "Appendix B."
[24] Sylvester dedicated his *Second Week* to Anthony Bacon and gave him credit
for "first inflaming" the prosecution of his sacred argument (Sylvester, p. 78).

With *The Divine Weekes* we are plunged into that welter of coalescing influence, for the blisses of "the thrice happie shepherds life and state" are enumerated not only by Sylvester [25] and Fletcher, but also by Spenser and other Renaissance poets. The same company, possibly inspired by Ovid, often warn their readers of the destructive lure of gold, a common theme of *The Purple Island* and of the *Piscatorie Eclogs,* which is also treated by Sylvester.[26] The "huntie, puntie ork" that sweeps through the five acts of *Sicelides* almost certainly swam over from the seas of *Orlando Furioso,* but it is interesting that the interpreter of Du Bartas refers to the ork.[27] Like Vergil, the translator has a council-hall scene, a parliament of the Israelites under Samuel with speech-making [28] that presages the oratory of Lucifer and Apollyon. Others of these broader resemblances in Fletcher's work can be more surely and directly traced to *The Divine Weekes.* The invocation to God which opens the translation is like an address in *The Purple Island.*[29] Sylvester and Fletcher share an unusual interest in the internal affairs of remote nations, such as Russia and Turkey.[30] Although the ladies of *The Apollyonists,* Sin and the Whore of Rome, are for the most part modeled upon Spenser's Duessa, some of their features appear to be derived from Death, of *The Divine Weekes.*[31] Once again relegating the complete accounting of the verbal similarities to the appendices, I quote the following as a sample of this type of influence:

> For, as a stone, that midst a Pond ye fling,
> About his fall first forms a little ring,
> Wherein new Circles one another growing
>
> . . .
>
> Still one the other more and more compell.
> Sylvester, *The Divine Weekes,* p. 130.

> As when a stone, troubling the quiet waters,
> Prints in the angry stream a wrinkle round,
> Which soon another and another scatters,
> Till all the lake with circles now is crown'd.
> *The Purple Island,* V, st. 47.

[25] Sylvester's *Divine Weekes,* pp. 29-39.
[26] *Ibid.,* p. 45.   [27] *Ibid.,* p. 40.   [28] *Ibid.,* p. 187.
[29] *The Purple Island,* I, st. 32-33.
[30] Sylvester's *Divine Weekes,* pp. 3, 13, 16. As I have previously indicated, Fletcher's interest in remote nations was more hereditary than literary.
[31] *Ibid.,* p. 97.

The two major themes of the Fletcherian poems, the Gunpowder Plot and the allegorical conception of the human body, are both found in *The Divine Weekes*,[32] and in each case there is verbal identity, proving that Fletcher had read *The Divine Weekes* before composing his own poems. In his physiological allegory, Sylvester describes the eyes, nose, cheeks, teeth, stomach, joints, brain, lungs, and intestines in language that presents many striking parallels with the first half of *The Purple Island*. The situation is complicated in an extraordinary way, for Spenser's "House of Alma" is really another translation of the same Du Bartas passage. A. H. Upham has untangled these intermeshed influences and has arrived at the following conclusions: Spenser translated Du Bartas; Sylvester did likewise, but at the same time imitated Spenser's "House of Alma"; and Phineas Fletcher copied both *The Divine Weekes* and *The Faerie Queene*.[33] The great importance of this part of Sylvester's work in connection with Fletcher is that it involves the entire first half of *The Purple Island*. We shall bid the matter a farewell that is only temporary, for we shall later find in it the most significant heritage Fletcher received from Spenser. In general, Spenser, Sylvester, and Fletcher shared a considerable amount of poetic material. Although our poet owed most of his portion to the author of *The Faerie Queene,* there is a residue which can be indisputably traced to Joshua Sylvester.

In turning from the riddle of a Sylvester imitated but unmentioned, to the poetic relations of Giles and Phineas Fletcher, we escape from one difficulty to find another. The annals of literary history can present few pairs of collaborators so intricately bound as they are. Most brothers commune and thus influence one another, but we have Phineas' own statement to prove his exceptional intimacy with Giles:

> Among the rout they take two gentle swains,
> Whose sprouting youth did now but greenly bud:
> Well could they pipe and sing; but yet their strains
> Were only known unto the silent wood:
> Their nearest bloud from self-same fountains flow,

[32] Sylvester's discussion of the Gunpowder Plot is to be found on page 189 of *The Divine Weekes*. For the passage on the human body, see pages 53-55.

[33] Upham's *French Influence in English Literature*, pp. 169-71, 199-201, and Appendix B.

> Their souls self-same in nearer love did grow:
> So seem'd two joyn'd in one, or one disjoyn'd in two.
> *The Purple Island*, I, st. 3.

It is to be expected that these "self-same" souls, these two joined in one, should prove to have been united in a relationship that was literary as well as personal. There is particular reason for anticipating such a relationship, since the above lines describe the affiliation which existed during the productive seasons of both poets, periods which were coterminous. Our other investigations into Fletcher's lackeyings involve combinations of giver and receiver that are one-half solidified, that is, where it is possible to comprehend absolutely the Vergil or the Spenser that Fletcher knew—the unchanging poetic text. Now we meet with two intelligences, quickened by ambition, genius, the sheer vitality of young manhood, two minds constantly at play with each other. There is no adequate method for measuring the transfer of thought as the brothers philosophized on literature, criticized each other's writing, rewrote, reëxchanged, and recriticized. Our one recourse is to determine the parallelism between the published works of each. The similarities, having been detected, will be of dubious value, because there is little to indicate the originator, whether Giles or Phineas.

The interchange of poetic compliments provides the last solid ground from which we can view the situation. In "Christs Triumph after Death" Giles Fletcher wrote:

> But let the Kentish lad, that lately taught
> His oaten reed the trumpets silver sound,
> Young Thyrsilis, and for his musique brought
> The willing sphears from heav'n, to lead a round
> Of dauncing Nymphs, and Heards, that sung, and crown'd
> Ecléctas hymen with ten thousand flowrs
> Of choycest prayse, and hung her heav'nly bow'rs
> With saffron garlands, drest for Nuptiall Paramours.

> Let his shrill trumpet, with her silver blast,
> Of faire Eclecta, and her Spousall bed,
> Be the sweet pipe, the smooth Encomiast:
> But my greene Muse, hiding her younger head
> Under old Chamus flaggy banks, that spread
> Their willough locks abroad, and all the day

With their owne watry shadowes wanton play,
Dares not those high amours, and love-sick songs assay.
"Christs Triumph after Death," st. 49-50.

Phineas, the Kentish lad, lifts his reed to pipe the praises of Giles on five different occasions,[34] the most important being the following, from *The Purple Island:*

Heard you not late with what loud trumpet sound
Her breath awak'd her fathers sleeping ire?

. . .

Who then those sugred strains can understand,
Which calm'd thy father, and our desp'rate fears;
And charm'd the nimble lightning in his hand,
That all unwares it dropt in melting tears?
Then thou deare swain, thy heav'nly load unfraught;
For she her self hath thee her speeches taught;
So neare her heav'n they be, so farre from humane thought.
The Purple Island, VI, st. 14-19.

Was Giles' or Phineas' the dominant influence? The foregoing adulatory lines, inspired by unusual fraternal affection and, to no little extent, by contemporary fashions in encomiastic verse, are a slight help in answering that question. Since Eclecta, her locks garlanded with stars, joined her spouse in the twelfth canto of *The Purple Island,* the anatomical poem apparently was completed before *Christs Victorie and Triumph.* Similarly Mercy pleaded for mankind in the opening stanzas of the younger brother's work, and Phineas Fletcher's sixth-canto reference to the scene might indicate that *Christs Victorie and Triumph* was barely under way when the other poem had reached the midway mark. These are possibilities rather than certainties, for there is no assurance that either was composed in the sequence in which it was published.[35] I believe I can detect slightly more reverence in the younger brother's apology for his own "greene Muse, hiding her younger head," and then Giles was the junior. If either had a dominant influence, it was probably Phineas.

[34] Additional references by Phineas Fletcher to his brother are to be found in the following places: "Upon my brother, Mr. G. F. his book entituled *Christs Victorie and Triumph,*" "Upon my brothers book called, *The grounds, labour, and reward of faith*" (both included in the *Poeticall Miscellanies*) ; the closing sentence of the dedication of *Locustae* to Roger Townshend, and "Charissimo fratri Aegidio."

[35] There is reason for thinking that *The Purple Island* was not composed in its final sequence. See above, p. 52.

A striking similarity of technic and of idea has led to the brothers' names being coupled in criticism and to their works being published in a perpetual conjunction. Both were sacred poets, both were Spenserians who embellished the matter and manner of their teacher with a certain sugared Italianism and, after taking orders, both were writers of devotional prose. Giles' lines had a romantic grace that Phineas' lacked, but the latter compensated for this failing with forcefulness.

Numerous minor correspondences come to light when the texts of each are compared. Like his brother, the author of *Christs Victorie and Triumph* revered Boethius and ornamented his prose work, *The Reward of the Faithfull,* with three translations from *De consolatione philosophiae.* Most of the senior poet's Boethian renderings also appeared in a prose work, *A Father's Testament.* Both were intrigued by the paradoxes of Christianity, and praised God in literary conceits. Phineas took delight in increasing and elaborating the contradictions of Christ's nature and his birth of a virgin, calling him an immortal father of his mortal mother, the child of his younger brothers, the brother of his children, an eternal being who was born and who died, creator of himself, etc.[36] Thus he toiled to bring forth cobwebs. It is one of the more noticeable weaknesses of *Christs Victorie and Triumph* that its opening stanza should be in the same empty vein:

> The birth of him that no beginning knewe,
> Yet gives beginning to all that are borne,
> And how the Infinite farre greater grewe,
> By growing lesse, and how the rising Morne,
> That shot from heav'n, did backe to heaven retourne,
> The obsequies of him that could not die,
> And death of life, ende of eternitie,
> How worthily he died, that died unworthily.
>> "Christs Victorie in Heaven," st. 1.

The bowers of the Garden of Delight in *Brittain's Ida* are laid out on the plans followed by Pangloretta of "Christs Victorie on Earth" in setting forth the trees and flowers of her Garden of Vain Delight. Possibly Edmund Spenser was the master gardener who came to instruct each poet separately. The Circe-and-enchanted-beast image of *Locustae* was reëmployed in "Christs Victorie on

[36] *The Purple Island,* VI, st. 72.

Earth." [37] Parallelisms of phrase are fairly frequent in the works of Giles and Phineas Fletcher, two instances of which I quote, the first for its unusual closeness:

> How may a worme, that crawles along the dust,
> Clamber the azure mountaines, thrown so high,
> And fetch from thence thy faire Idea just,
> That in those sunny courts doth hidden lie,
> Cloath'd with such light, as blinds the Angels eye;
> How may weake mortall ever hope to file
> His unsmooth tongue, and his deprostrate stile?
> O raise thou from his corse, thy now entomb'd exile.
>
> "Christs Victorie in Heaven," st. 43.

> How shall a worm, on dust that crawls and feeds,
> Climbe to th' empyreall court, where these states reign,
> And there take view of what heav'ns self exceeds?
> The Sunne lesse starres, these lights the Sunne distain:
> Their beams divine, and beauties do excell
> What here on earth, in aire, or heav'n do dwell:
> Such never eye yet saw, such never tongue can tell.
>
> *The Purple Island,* VI, st. 9.

The second is perhaps the most curious of these verbal correspondences because Giles Fletcher's version is in English, while Phineas' appears in Latin:

> Thear lies the captive soule . . .
> Reck'ning a thousand yeares since her first bands,
>
> . . .
>
> But tells to them the starres, and heapes the sands,
> And now the stars are told, and sands are runne.
>
> "Christs Triumph over Death," st. 43.

> Cum vero nullum moriendi conscia finem
> Mens reputat, cum mille annis mille addidit annos,
> Praeteritumque nihil venturo detrahit aevum,
> Mox etiam stellas, etiam superaddit arenas,
> Jamque etiam stellas, etiam numeravit arenas.
>
> *Locustae,* p. 104.

To Jacopo Sannazaro, Fletcher was indebted for all that makes the *Piscatorie Eclogs* an unusual, if not a unique, outcropping of English poetry. There are passages in both Vergil and Spenser that

---

[37] *Locustae,* p. 110; "Christs Victorie on Earth," st. 49.

have about them a suggestion of the piscatory, and these may have instilled in the Jacobean fisher boy a taste for the form. His eclogues, however, were frank and thorough imitations of Sanna-zaro, a circumstance not at all displeasing to Izaak Walton, who praised Fletcher for the honor he conferred upon the brotherhood of anglers. A few of the poet's compatriots made sporadic attempts to write this variation of the pastoral: for instance, John Donne composed a piscine adaptation of Marlowe's *Passionate Sheepheard* and the sixth nymphal of Drayton's *Muses Elysium* blossoms into a debate betwen Silvius, Melanthus, and Halcius, a fisher swain who haunts the pearl-paved fords and blue-eyed deeps.

Although he never acknowledges his imitation in so many words, Fletcher gives a reader an inescapable hint:

> And now of late th' Italian fisher-swain
> Sits on the shore to watch his trembling line;
> There teaches rocks and prouder seas to plain
> By *Nesis* fair, and fairer *Mergiline:*
> While his thinne net, upon his oars twin'd,
> With wanton strife catches the Sunne, and winde,
> Which still do slip away, and still remain behinde.
> *The Purple Island*, I, st. 13.

It is a curious commentary upon the poet's methods that a measure in the very strophe which pays tribute to the Italian "fisher-swain" should itself be a literal translation of a Sannazaro line:

> Raraque per longos pendebant retia remos.
> *Piscatory Eclogues*, III, l. 10.

In his *Piscatory Eclogues of Jacopo Sannazaro,* Mustard has efficiently analyzed Fletcher's borrowings from the Italian pastoral-ist. It is worth noticing, however, that the Englishman's piscatories are not his sole catch from the Neapolitan fishing banks: one finds unmistakable evidence of the same foreign original in the "Lusus Ecloga" and particularly in the "Myrtillus Ecloga" of the *Sylva Poetica.*

Perhaps Sir Philip Sidney is out of place among the group of poets whom Fletcher imitated and acknowledged, for his name is left unmentioned in the pages of Fletcherian poetry. On the other hand, the younger poet quoted a couplet from the fifty-fourth sonnet of *Astrophel and Stella* as the opening for his "Non invisa cano," and to a Jacobean this served as a notice of relationship between the two works. "Non invisa cano" was the most important part of the Sion College Manuscript discovered by Miss Ethel Seaton, who has called attention to the present connection. In copying the English Bayard, Phineas Fletcher was again true to his family loyalties. His father had been an admirer of Sidney and had written an elegy on his death which he contributed to the collection, *Academiae Cantabrigiensis lacrymae*. Although his son, the eulogist of the grave and sacred poets, had repeatedly denounced the fond lads who turned out sonnets, one chorus of *Sicelides* [38] and most of *Brittain's Ida* are in the general manner of Sidney and the other love sonneteers. Thus Fletcher was led into inconsistencies by fidelity to his father.

Miss Seaton went on to single out the *Astrophel and Stella* echoes in Fletcher's poems, but there has been no recognition of the enormous dependence of *Sicelides* on *Arcadia*. Despite the differences in type—the former being a piscatory drama, and the latter a pastoral romance—the two are like father and son. The paternal likeness is undisguised in the following parallelism:

> Who sowes the sea, or plowes the easy shore?
> Yet I, fond I, more fond, and sencelesse more:
> Who strives in nets to prison in the winde?
> Yet I in love a woman thought to bind.
> > *Sicelides*, II, 2, lines 1-4.
>
> Hee water plowes and soweth in the sande,
> And hopes the flickering wynde with nett to holde
> Who hathe his hopes layde up in womans hande.
> > *Arcadia*, p. 69.

Other similarities inhere more in the structure of *Sicelides*, in character and incident. Two gentle fisher boys, Perindus and Thalander, are bound in a love, like in its constancy to that which ties Musidorus and Pyrocles of *Arcadia*. The base fishermen, Scrocca and Cancrone, are blood brethren to Dametas, the shepherd. A mad wag called Pas runs riot through Sidney's romance, and bursts through its covers into *Sicelides*, where he finds a renewed life. The element of disguise dominates each plot, with Thalander masquerading as Atyches, in the one; while Musidorus and Pyrocles, who pose as girls, break a masculine heart in the other. *Sicelides*

[38] *Sicelides*, III.

reëmploys the device, for Conchylio, in his mistress' apparel, incites Rimbombo, son of the one-eyed Polyphemus, to an impassioned love. The two narratives are mutually complicated by the equivocations of oracles and by the extraordinary statutes of mythical states. The Arcadian bear terrifies Dametas, while the Sicilian "ork" makes cravens of Cancrone and Scrocca. In the romance, Cleophila, by a pretense of indifference, torments Philoclea, and Sicilian Glaucilla suffers the like at the hands of Perindus. Fletcher casts the same Perindus from a cliff top—to certain death, which in the event proves less certain—that Olinda might be saved from the law to which she was an innocent victim. Pyrocles, too, attempts suicide to rescue Philoclea from a similarly obnoxious statute. The mighty Duke of Arcadia, Basilius, is poisoned, is lamented as dead, and then revives; and Olinda experiences the identical sequence of events. Persons who unexpectedly arrive from oversea solve both agonizing plots. Many of these details—the disguises, monsters, human sacrifices, oracles, and such—were the stock in trade of Greek and Renaissance romance; but although Fletcher's *Sicelides* may have uncles and godfathers without end, there can be little doubt of its essential parentage.

Though Ovid's influence on Fletcher's work be considerable, precise measurement is difficult because of the pervasiveness of Ovidian ideas and sentences throughout Renaissance literature in England. Thus most of the echoes can be traced not only to Ovid, but also to one or more native poets; and what is more perplexing, many Ovidian themes are Vergilian. The following excerpts, dealing with a kind of devaluation of the gold standard, are typical of these complicated radiations of influence:

> Who was it first, that from thy deepest cell,
> With so much costly toil and painfull sweat
> Durst rob thy palace, bord'ring next to hell?
> Well mayst thou come from that infernall seat;
> Thou all the world with hell-black deeps dost fill.
> Fond men, that with such pain do wooe your ill!
> Needlesse to send for grief, for he is next us still.
> *The Purple Island*, VIII, st. 28.

> nëc tantum segetes alimenta debita dives
> poscebatur humus, sed itum est in viscera terrae,

quasque recondiderat Stygiisque admoverat umbris,
effodiuntur opes, inritamenta malorum.

Metamorphoses, I, lines 137-40.

Identical ideas couched in much the same phraseology are to be
found in Sylvester's translation of Du Bartas [39] and again in *The
Faerie Queene*,[40] so that it is impossible for us—and probably it was
for Fletcher as well—to discern whom the poet is following here.
There are, however, enough of the Ovidian echoes, which have no
counterparts either in Vergil or in the English poets, to establish
Fletcher's first-hand imitation of the *Metamorphoses*.[41]

Fletcher would have us believe that his dramatic training, which
bore fruit in *Sicelides*, had been confined to the schools of the
ancient and classical masters, for Seneca and Euripides are the
only playwrights to whom he refers:

> Who ha's not seen upon the mourning stage
> Dire *Atreus* feast, and wrong'd *Medea's* rage,
> Marching in tragick state, and buskin'd equipage?
>
> *The Purple Island*, I, st. 12.

No one can be duped by this ingenious guile, since Fletcher's comedy is obviously Elizabethan in its coarse buffoonery and complex
love tangles. Probably the author of *Sicelides* had read or seen the
entertainments of the commercial stage, but guarded against acknowledging a familiarity with the non-academic drama, which was
in bad odor at Calvinistic Cambridge. Accordingly his allusions to
Seneca and Euripides, who really had little or no influence upon
Sicelides, were largely an affectation of scholarly sobriety, and the
same may be said of the reference to Homer contained in the following lines:

> Who ha's not often read *Troyes* twice-sung fires,
> And at the second time twice better sung?
>
> *The Purple Island*, I, st. 11.

The one Homeric trace in Fletcher's work is the story of Venus
and Anchises as related in *Brittain's Ida*, an incident which was

---

[39] *Divine Weekes*, p. 45.
[40] *Faerie Queene*, II, vii, st. 17.
[41] See Appendix B below.

ultimately derived from the Homeric *Hymn to Aphrodite*. Samuel Daniel is the last of the poets named by Fletcher:

> Such was that *Woodstock* cave, where *Rosamand*,
> Fair *Rosamand*, fled jealous *Ellenore;*
> Whom late a shepherd taught to weep so sore,
> That woods and hardest rocks her harder fate deplore.
> *The Purple Island*, I, st. 11.

Rosamand's shepherd made only the slightest contributions, if any, to the Fletcherian poems.[42]

Having concluded the study of Fletcher's imitation of his acknowledged poetic sources—Spenser always excepted—we have very nearly finished with the entire burden of his dependence on poets. There remain Tasso and Ariosto, from whom he borrowed rather heavily without a vestige of admission; and Marlowe, whom he copied slightly. As for the former, Fletcher's extraordinary scruples about acknowledging the English and classic poets possibly were relaxed when he utilized Italians. Furthermore, much of the *Orlando Furioso* and *Jerusalem Delivered* influence seems to have entered Fletcher's cantos by way of the Spenserian land of Faërie, another reason why Fletcher should have felt himself free to slight these foreign romancers when parceling out credit. There is, however, abundant proof that the poet knew Tasso and Ariosto with as much intimacy as was possible when his approach was, as appears

---

[42] The following passages from Daniel and Fletcher may be remotely related:

> "Opprest with griefe, his passions had no bound:
> Striving to tell his woes, words would not come;
> For light cares speake, when mightie griefes are dombe."
> "Complaynt of Rosamond," lines 796-98.

> *"Light grief floats on the tongue; but heavie smart*
> *Sinks down, and deeply lies in centre of the heart."*
> *The Purple Island*, XII, st. 43.

The same idea is repeated by Fletcher in "Elisa" (I, st. 45) and *Brittain's Ida* (VI, st. 10).

Many brief passages in Fletcher's works, like the foregoing, are italicized. Some of these are borrowings. *"Like to his like will move"* (*The Purple Island*, I, st. 18), and *"How soon prospers the vicious weed!"* (*The Purple Island*, VII, st. 42), have proved almost identical with two proverbs of Heywood's *Proverbs* (Part I, Chap. IV; Part I, Chap. X). A fourth, *"Sweet are stoln waters"* (*The Purple Island*, VII, st. 18), is derived from the Bible (*Proverbs* 9 : 17). The large residue, however, are original with Fletcher. The italicization had nothing to do with the borrowing, but apparently was intended to emphasize phrases which the author regarded as epigrammatic. The custom of so indicating aphorisms was general in the poet's day. It is a distinctive characteristic of the *Purple Island* stanza that it frequently closes with a maxim.

evident, restricted to the avenues of the translators, to Edward Fairfax, Richard Carew, and Sir John Harington.

Fletcher's relationship with Tasso has been treated by E. Koeppel,[43] whose discussion is mainly concerned with *Brittain's Ida*. He
overlooked other and more important echoes, such as the following
four lines from *Sicelides:* Sophronia and Olinda of *Jerusalem Delivered* are struggling in a mutual endeavor to assume the death
penalty, which must fall to the lot of one or the other. It is a situation where romance carries heroism to the apex of exaggeration:

> Thus spake the nymph, yet spoke but to the wind.
> She could not alter his well-settled thought:
> O miracle! o strife of wondrous kind!
> Where love and virtue such contention wrought,
> Where death the victor had for meed assigned.
> *Jerusalem Delivered*, p. 29.

Sicilian Perindus and Glaucilla wrestled in precisely the same kind
of contest:

> But briefe to give their words in short contracted,
> Was never part of love more lovely acted:
> Both loath to live, and both contend to die,
> Where only death strove for the victory.
> *Sicelides*, V, 5, lines 62-65.

The largest levy Fletcher made upon both Tasso and Ariosto is
as immeasurable as it is important—the Italianate embroidery
which distinguishes his style from Spenser's, Sidney's, Daniel's,
indeed from almost every other English poet's with the notable
exception of his own brother, Giles Fletcher's, whose manner is
even more exuberant in its Italianism. It is equally impossible to
compute accurately Fletcher's more superficial borrowings from
Tasso's miscellaneous collection of female warriors, shields that
paralyzed whole armies by their sunlike rays, eulogies of the pastoral life, and similar Renaissance matter, because these materials
are omnipresent in *Orlando Furioso, The Divine Weekes,* the
Faerie Queene, and other works, as well as in *Jerusalem Delivered.*
There are additional minor correspondences between Tasso's masterpiece and the Fletcherian poems, particularly *Brittain's Ida,* but
a major analogy remains.

[43] E. Koeppel, "Der Englischen Tasso-Ubersetzungen," *Anglia,* XI, 33 ff.

To the historian of English literature, the most important passages in all Fletcher's works are the Satanic council scenes of *The Apollyonists* and *Locustae*. Lines of influence from Italy and France, from pre-Christian Rome and from the sixteenth century, from Vergil, Du Bartas, Sylvester, and Tasso, all converge toward these several vivid pages of Fletcherian verse where they are gathered together and projected upon *Paradise Lost*. Tasso's portrayal of Satan and his followers,[44] half classical and half biblical in its details, is frequently analogous to the same conception in *The Apollyonists, Locustae,* and *Paradise Lost*. The great commander addresses his fallen legions, chides them for lying in idleness about Tartarus, and reminds them of their former glory. He suggests that man is fast fulfilling his holy destiny as he converts wider and wider tracts of the earth to the kingdom of God. Mankind's latest advance has been the carrying of Christianity into Asia. Satan urges his followers to oppose the Crusades with force or guile. Coming events—the composition of *The Apollyonists* and *Paradise Lost*—cast their shadows before.

Ariosto, Spenser, and Fletcher are joined in a triple suzerainty over a considerable stretch of poetic territory. Fletcher certainly acquired his share from one of the other two, but there is no telling from which. The following samples of interdependence are typical. Although *Orlando Furioso* is primarily a romance, while the latter half of *The Purple Island* is a moral allegory, Ariosto's work anticipates, in a condensed form, the entire theme of that latter half, with a battle between the virtues, led by Logistilla, and the vices, misled by Alcina.[45] She, Alcina, in rendering her garden of love seductive,[46] employed the same horticultural devices as did Venus of *Brittain's Ida*. The Gryll of *Orlando Furioso,* a swinish French warrior,[47] appears in *The Purple Island,* although he has undergone an Ovidian metamorphosis and has become a hog. Each of these somewhat distinctive details is present in *The Faerie Queene*.

The human-sacrifice incident of *Sicelides,* the crux of the plot, came directly to Fletcher from Ariosto, with no possibility of a Spenserian intermediation. Although Faërie-land is pleasingly free of

---

[44] *Jerusalem Delivered,* IV.
[46] *Ibid.,* VII.

[45] *Orlando Furioso,* X.
[47] *Ibid.,* XVIII, st. 176.

orks, the monsters are present in Elizabethan drama,[48] but nowhere do they appear in situations exactly like those of *Orlando Furioso* and *Sicelides*. Plainly Fletcher's ork is Ariosto's. The sea monster is first described in the eighth book of *Orlando Furioso,* where mention is made of Proteus' law condemning a damsel a day to his maw. In *Sicelides,* Neptune has decreed that he who eats of the Hesperian fruit must pay by offering himself as fodder for the ork. Subsequently Angelica, of the Italian romance, is chained naked to a rock to await her dismal fate, but Rogero rescues the beauty by slaying the monster.[49] Sicilian Olinda was chained half-naked to a rock, and was saved by Thalander, who for the second time slew the phoenixlike ork.

Bush, in his *Mythology and the Renaissance Tradition in English Poetry,* presented indisputable evidence that *Brittain's Ida* was slightly dependent upon Marlowe's *Hero and Leander.*[50] A careful search through the ill-fated dramatist's other work has produced nothing additional, and I have undertaken several other quests that have proved equally futile. Theocritus, Drayton, Montemayor, and Sackville have been credited with exerting much influence upon the Fletcherian poems. If the poet had ever read Drayton or Montemayor, he was supremely cautious in avoiding indication of it in his writing. I suppose Theocritus is thrust into Fletcherian criticism because he was the remote originator of the piscatory. Since this type of the pastoral has so limited a company of exponents, it is natural to assume that they all recognized one another as kinsmen. Actually, there are no convincing similarities between the Greek idylls and Fletcher's piscatories. Theocritus' fifth, like the later poet's seventh, describes a poetic contest in the course of which the rivals vie in promising gifts to their loved ones; but gentle struggles of the same nature may be found in almost any collection of Renaissance pastorals. Greg has stated that the twenty-first idyll of Theocritus suggested Cancrone and Scrocca to the author of *Sicelides*. Asphalion, of the ancient poem, is a boorish, amusing fisherman, but Theocritus was by no means the last poet

---

[48] *E.g.,* Jonson's *Masque of Neptune* and Massinger's *Roman Actor,* V, 1.

[49] *Orlando Furioso,* X, st. 92 ff.

[50] *Brittain's Ida,* I, st. 2; II, st. 3; VI, st. 6-7; *Hero and Leander,* I, lines 88-89; I, lines 191-93; II, lines 61-69, respectively.

to obtain comic effects from the ignorance and ill manners of the humble class.[51] The relation between Sackville and Fletcher is of the same nebulous character. It is true that the allegorical figures of *The Purple Island* are similar in a general way to the impersonations of Sackville's "Induction"; yet they more surely resemble the personifications of Spenser, Vergil, and Ovid. Other than this, there are no bonds between Fletcher and Sackville.

Such is Phineas Fletcher's dependence upon writers other than his master, Spenser. His personality is repeatedly submerged in the conscious and unconscious imitation of his predecessors, and the same may be said of almost all the contemporary poets. Fletcher, however, has his own peculiarities at the very instant of submergence: conservatism is evident in all his reading and copying, for the medieval and Renaissance prose writers he mentioned, and the poets he imitated, were the popular authors of the first decade of the seventeenth century. Although Fletcher's references to Seneca, Euripides, and Homer were pedantic affectations, those to other classic authors prove to be confessions of heavy borrowing. Ovid and Vergil *per se*, and Ovid and Vergil in Spenser, rule with mighty sway throughout the Fletcherian poetry. One of the important distinctions between the work of the poet of the Cam and that of his master, Spenser, is this increased dependence upon Roman authors. It is obviously dangerous to draw overfine distinctions between the so-called classic poets and the Spenserians of the Jacobean era. The length of the foregoing account is somewhat unfair to Fletcher, for it gives his dependences an undue prominence. How Fletcher reconciled himself to conscious borrowing is a matter of some interest, but belongs to our consideration of his relations with Edmund Spenser. For the present it is enough to say that he regarded the practice as being doubly blessed, for it served not only to grace his own writing but also paid honor to the great geniuses whom he copied.

[51] Drayton's definition of the piscatory yields further proof that the writers of this time did not go to Theocritus for their piscatorial inspiration:

> "This [the pastoral], as all other formes of Poesie (excepting perhaps the admirable Latine Piscatories of that noble Neapolitan, Sanazara) hath beene received from the Greekes, and as at the second hand, from the Romanes."
>
> *Works*, "To the Reader," VII, 517.

If Drayton thought that the piscatory originated at Naples and not in Greece, it is possible that Fletcher thought the same.

IX

THE MASTER AND THE APPRENTICE

PHINEAS FLETCHER's dependence upon Spenser is no news. Francis Quarles referred to the author of *The Purple Island* as the "Spencer of this age," in his verses prefixed to that poem, while another contemporary anagrammatized his name in these somewhat unequivocal lines:

> Hath Spencer life?
> Or Spencer hath life.
> That Spencer liveth, none can ignorant be,
> That reads his works (Fletcher) or knoweth thee.
> *Witts Recreations*, No. 200.

Little was written about the minor poets of the seventeenth century until the Romantic era, but the nineteenth-century critics were prompt in finding this feature of Fletcher's work. Firing critical broadsides, Henry Headley and George Macdonald sailed into action against *The Purple Island,* condemning the author as "a vulgar imitator." Alexander Grosart rallied to the defense with more gallantry than judgment, for he strove to deny the evidences of influence brought forward by Macdonald and Headley; and, where denial was impossible, he argued that Fletcher had "improved" Spenser. Grosart was foolish to allow himself to be stung by the catcalls of plagiarism, because, whatever may be the relation of Fletcher and Spenser, it is not plagiaristic. From Grosart's day to the present, almost every writer on the literature of the seventeenth century has remarked upon this Fletcherian dependence, the best recent studies being those of Traugott Boehme and Karl Weibel.

Since "none can be ignorant that Spenser has life in Fletcher's poetry"—there may be those of the opinion that Spenser would have gone on living without it—what is the value of proceeding with a new treatment of the matter? A comparison of the work of the two poets has shown that Spenser's influence upon his follower was even greater than previous students have indicated. Actually he dictated

the style, the imagery, the philosophy, the vocabulary, the subject
matter, the character portrayal, the prosody, and the wording, of
parts of almost every Fletcherian poem. The word "Spenserian" has
been used somewhat freely to describe the Fletchers, Drummond,
Wither, Browne, Davies, Greville, and Wotton, but the present
study will demonstrate how full an implication the term can have.

Even if Fletcher were a modern poet, he could scarcely be accused of plagiarism, because he made four important statements in
which he frankly set forth his dependence upon Spenser. One of
these occurs at the beginning of *The Purple Island,* two more in
the middle, and a fourth in the *Poeticall Miscellanies,* locations
which seem to have been chosen so that no reader could be unaware
of the author's attitude. The first is a glowing tribute to Spenser,
the man and the poet:

> Witnesse our *Colin;* whom though all the Graces,
> And all the Muses nurst; whose well taught song
> *Parnassus* self, and *Glorian* embraces,
> And all the learn'd, and all the shepherds throng;
> Yet all his hopes were crost, all suits deni'd;
> Discourag'd, scorn'd, his writings vilifi'd:
> Poorly (poore man) he liv'd; poorly (poore man) he di'd.
>
> And had not that great *Hart,* (whose honour'd head
> Ah lies full low) piti'd thy wofull plight;
> There hadst thou lien unwept, unburied,
> Unblest, nor grac't with any common rite:
> Yet shalt thou live, when thy great foe shall sink
> Beneath his mountain tombe, whose fame shall stink;
> And time his blacker name shall blurre with blackest ink.
>
> *The Purple Island,* I, st. 19-20.

The "Hart" is the Earl of Essex, while the "great foe," denounced
in Fletcher's most astounding thunder, is Burghley. The passage is
a revelation of the author's principal reasons for imitating and celebrating Spenser, both to be achieved at one and the same time.

The second statement assigns the creator of *The Faerie Queene*
to his place in Eumnestes' Hall of Fame. It is self-evident that this,
unlike most of the contemporary encomiastic poetry, is a sincere
appraisal of Spenser's standing among the poets of the world. In
addition, the passage proves its author to have that un-Jacobean

and almost modern scrupulousness about calling attention to his sources, for it refers the reader to the "House of Alma" section of *The Faerie Queene,* which was the origin of the entire *Purple Island:*

> For these three late a gentle shepherd-swain
> Most sweetly sung, as he before had seen
> In *Alma's* house: his memorie yet green
> Lives in his well-tun'd songs, whose leaves immortall been.
>
> Nor can I guesse, whether his Muse divine
> Or gives to those, or takes from them his grace;
> Therefore *Eumnestes* in his lasting shrine
> Hath justly him enroll'd in second place:
> Next to our *Mantuan* poet doth he rest;
> There shall our *Colin* live for ever blest,
> Spite of those thousand spites, which living him opprest.
> *The Purple Island,* VI, st. 51-52.

The final *Purple Island* passage completes the author's admission, for here he acknowledges his sources and describes his method of imitation:

> Two shepherds most I love with just adoring;
> That *Mantuan* swain, who chang'd his slender reed
> To trumpets martiall voice, and warres loud roaring,
> From *Corydon* to *Turnus* derring-deed;
> And next our home-bred Colins sweetest firing;
> Their steps not following close, but farre admiring:
> To lackey one of these is all my prides aspiring.
> *The Purple Island,* VI, st. 5.

The *Poeticall Miscellanies* statement is a careful reëmphasis of much that had been said previously, but it also provides an interesting bit of seventeenth-century poetic criticism:

> Two shepherds I adore with humble love;
> Th' high-towring swain, that by slow *Mincius* waves
> His well-grown wings at first did lowly prove,
> Where *Corydon's* sick love full sweetly raves;
> But after sung bold *Turnus* daring braves:
> And next our nearer *Colin's* sweetest strain;
> Most, where he most his *Rosalind* doth plain.
> Well may I after look, but follow all in vain.
> "To my beloved Thenot," lines 17-24.

Spenser "plains" his Rosalind in the January and June eclogues of *The Shepheardes Calender;* evidently Fletcher preferred *The Shepheardes Calender* to *The Faerie Queene.*[1]

It must be admitted that Phineas Fletcher was entirely candid about his dependence upon Spenser. As a commentary upon the seventeenth-century attitude toward plagiarism, the sequence rivals Milton's sentence about borrowing being bettered by the borrower. Fletcher's pride aspired no higher than to "lackey" one of the immortals, and he made no pretense about bettering what he borrowed. It was left to Grosart to say that he "improved" the poetry of *The Faerie Queene.*

The reasons why Fletcher was persuaded to imitate Spenser, thereby offering his humble sacrifice at the shrine, form a gloss upon his character. When he began his *Purple Island,* the last book of *The Faerie Queene* had been off the press for some ten years, and Spenser dead for a mere six or seven. Colin Clout was still the great innovator, and Fletcher went to his cause with the vigor of a young man who enlists under the banner of a persecuted prophet. This noble action implied poetic discrimination; it meant that he recognized the well-tuned songs and sweet strains of *The Faerie Queene* and *The Shepheardes Calender.* In addition, there were political and family reasons for the poet's action. Like Spenser, the elder Giles Fletcher had nearly all of his hopes crossed and nearly all of his suits denied, was oppressed by a thousand spites, lived poorly and died poorly. Burghley, the man who lay below the mountain tomb, had been Dr. Fletcher's great foe as well as Spenser's. Some of the father's suits were rewarded because the great "Hart," Essex, pitied his plight. Possibly Dr. Fletcher and Spenser were personally acquainted, for they were coevals at Cambridge and each was in Essex's service. We know that Phineas Fletcher subscribed completely to his father's politics, which were the same as Spenser's. His political creed had much weight in the formulation of his poetical creed, as is evident in the prominence given to party matters in the four statements. Then Spenser was a son of the

[1] Possibly Fletcher's preference for *The Shepheardes Calender* was shared by his contemporaries. Edward P. Morton, in his article, "The Spenserian Stanza before 1700" (*Modern Philology,* May, 1907), states that the political interest of *The Shepheardes Calender* was the reason why the Jacobeans admired the poem more than *The Faerie Queene.*

yellow sands and green cells of Chamus, and Fletcher was the poet of the Cam. But I think that the most important reason for Fletcher's poetic allegiance was his patriotism. The Spenserians—Drummond, Wither, Browne, the Fletchers—might have elected to follow French, Italian, or classic influences, but they turned away to walk in the footsteps of the great Englishman, the Apollo of "this blessed plot, this England."

If *The Purple Island* were not provided with the three statements, its casual references to Spenser's poems would indicate that the author's mind was seldom playing truant to the school of Colin Clout. We have in these an evidence of his fondness for, as well as familiarity with, the master's work. They are in no sense a form of imitation. Thus Fletcher's "Gluttonie," [2] with the gouty limbs, lugged a shield on which he had emblazoned "old Gryll." And lovely Voletta,[3] whose radiance would dim the silver cheek of Cynthia, was unparagoned, outdazzling even "that great Soveraigne of the Fayrie land." With Elizabeth dead, Fletcher was safe enough in discriminating. The allusions to Eumnestes and the "House of Alma" have already been noted. Finally the following lines, used to attack Burghley and taken bodily from "The Ruines of Time," [4] were served up to the reader as an undisguised quotation: [5]

> O may that man that hath the Muses scorn'd,
> Alive, nor dead, be ever of a Muse adorn'd!
> *The Purple Island,* I, st. 21.

[2] *The Purple Island,* VII, st. 83.   [3] *Ibid.,* VI, st. 58.
[4] "Ruines of Time," lines 454-55.
[5] There can be no doubt that Fletcher intended his readers to recognize this couplet as a quotation, but his italicizing was not for that purpose (see above, p. 126, n. 42). The same lines set up a second problem, never before noticed; for their wording, as quoted by Fletcher, differs from that of any edition of Spenser's *Complaints.* Professor Boas suggested to me, with characteristic sagacity, that Fletcher might have altered Spenser's lines to fit his own metrical or rhyme scheme. Upon returning to the lines in question, I found that the exigencies of meter and rhyme had been completely satisfied by the introduction of the word "ever," and hence the suggestion did not explain the numerous additional changes. There is one other quotation in Fletcher's poetic writings (see pp. 122-23 above); it is a couplet from Sidney's *Astrophel and Stella* (sonnet 54). Fletcher used it at the beginning of his "Non invisa cano." The quotation differs from the known Sidney texts, as does that from "The Ruines of Time." It seems to be a problem which never will be completely solved, but in my opinion the solution narrows down to one of two possibilities: either Fletcher was quoting from an imperfect memory or else he came into possession of variant Sidney and Spenser manuscripts.

For one undisguised quotation, Fletcher's poetry provides us with some 103 that were unacknowledged, and concealed both by the completeness with which they were woven into the weft of his own verse and by the changes the weaving necessitated.[6] It is typical of the poet's method that in the very passage where he professes his imitation,

> Their steps not following close, but farre admiring:
> To lackey one of these is all my prides aspiring.
> *The Purple Island*, VI, st. 5.

his pride is aspiring with considerable success. Those lines "lackey" the word and spirit of Spenser, who paid this tribute to Chaucer:

> I follow here the footing of thy feete,
> That with thy meaning so I may the rather meete.
> *The Faerie Queene*, IV, ii, st. 34.

There follow examples of Fletcher's indebtedness, and in these, however small in number, the alchemy of poetic borrowing is at work. The witch abandoning her pursuit of the Redcross Knight through Faërie, darkens the seven hills of Rome. A sun ascending from the oriental gate of Gloriana's realm, swoops cometlike and banishes the night shades of a purple isle. Soft music that graced an Irish wedding floats out over the Bay of Youghal, across the remorseless deep, to accompany an English bride to a Kentish altar. A menagerie of historical animals, Arlo Hill, and a curious philosophical disputation, all are transmuted to other times and other scenes.

A few passages may serve their purpose as proof of the verbal borrowing, but they can never descend upon the reader with the conviction to be attained by running the entire gamut of the 103 "lackeyings." I have, however, selected illustrations of the particular types of Spenserian passages from which Fletcher borrowed most regularly. They fall into two broad divisions: those which proved attractive because of their style, and those which drew attention because of their content. The reader must realize that taking

---

[6] See Appendix B below. I have omitted thirty-three parallels listed by Weibel because the correspondences did not seem sufficiently close to justify inclusion. Of course there is reason for asserting that every Fletcherian passage even remotely resembling a Spenserian one was inspired by it.

excerpts from their separate contexts is an artificial performance, serving to throw differences rather than similarities into relief. It would be more natural and more convincing if we might read through the entire texts of Edmund Spenser and Phineas Fletcher and search for the immortal footprints across the tracts of Faërie-land and the purple isle. That being impossible, I shall assay some scattered flakes of that golden dust blown from Faërie-land and showered upon the isle.[7]

A Fletcherian stylistic device, particularly evident in *The Apollyonists*, is the use of brutal Anglo-Saxonisms that were more at home on peasant than on gentle lips. I mean expressions like "frie," "hizze," "chewe," "feede," "rotten," "nayles," and the "maw" of the following quotation, terms frequently lifted directly from the master. This shift, taught by Chaucer to Spenser, was studied by Fletcher, and it lent him a vigor of manner which is one of his most commendable characteristics:

> Else his own maw doth eat with spitefull will
> *The Purple Island,* VII, st. 66.

is the painful disease of "squint-eyed Envie," very evidently contracted from the "Envie" of another island kingdom:

> But inwardly he chawed his owne maw.
> *The Faerie Queene,* I, iv, st. 30.

Here is a fresh addition to the categories of contagious maladies.

Similar to the foregoing is Fletcher's emphasis upon loathsome details, by means of which he puts vigor into his poetry. His Whore of Rome is scarcely an Amaryllis or Neaera:

> Her putride pendant bagges, her mouth that sents
> As this of hell, her hands with scabbes array'd,
> Her pust'led skin with ulcer'd excrements.
> *The Apollyonists,* II, st. 29.

[7] Many of the passages which Fletcher borrowed from Spenser may also have been affected by other writers (see Appendix B below). In the preceding chapter we have noticed how frequently the influence of Vergil, Ovid, Tasso, and other authors converges upon a single stanza of Fletcher. Whenever Spenser is involved in such confusion, I believe that it is safe to regard his as the effective influence. In nearly all such cases, there is exact verbal identity to indicate that Fletcher is following Spenser closely and the other writer or writers either unconsciously or more remotely. Perhaps Fletcher, without realizing it, sometimes imitated that in Spenser which was already secondhand.

She is twin to Duessa, of equally endearing charms whose

> . . . dried dugs, lyke bladders lacking wind,
> Hong downe, and filthy matter from them weld;
> Her wrizled skin, as rough as maple rind,
> So scabby was.
> *The Faerie Queene*, I, viii, st. 47.

The sun of the purple island scatters ten thousand flowers, dapples Aurora's horses with roses, invests the spangled heavens in golden robes, for it is a third Fletcherian idiosyncrasy, more familiar in the work of the younger Giles, to deal profusely in ornate nature similes. On one bright morning the star of the day rose in this manner:

> He shook his sparkling locks, head lively rouz'd.
> *The Purple Island*, IX, st. 1.

Another sun, rolling up over that happy land of Faërie—

> Came dauncing forth, shaking his deawie hayre
> *The Faerie Queene*, I, v, st. 2.

and one suspects that the two suns are the same; in like manner, much of Fletcher's nature imagery reveals verbal borrowings from Spenser.

Perhaps the most convincing example of Fletcher's imitation of Colin's rhetorical sleight of hand is found in the following line:

> In *Ida* Vale (who knowes not *Ida* Vale?)
> *Brittain's Ida*, I, st. 1.

which duplicates—

> Of Arlo-hill (who knowes not Arlo-hill?)
> *The Faerie Queene*, VII, vi, st. 36.

The melody, the winding bouts and linked sweetnesses of Thirsil's occasional verse, particularly of his epithalamiums, was often attuned to Colin Clout's. Certainly the following couplets strike similar pitches:

> While the woods back their bounding Echo fling,
> *Hymen*, come holy *Hymen; Hymen* lowd they sing.
> "An Hymen," lines 13-14.

And evermore they "Hymen, Hymen" sing,
That al the woods them answer, and theyr eccho ring.
"Epithalamion," lines 145-46.

Other imitations result more from the attractions of thought and idea. Like the circus returning to town, Spenser's animalian conception of ancient history came to life again in Fletcher's work:

What nowe is of th' Assyrian Lyonesse,
Of whome no footing now on earth appeares?
What of the Persian Beares outragiousnesse,
Whose memorie is quite worne out with yeares?
Who of the Grecian Libbard now ought heares,
That overran the East with greedie powre,
And left his whelpes their Kingdomes to devoure?
And where is that same great seven headed beast,
That made all nations vassals of her pride?
"Ruines of Time," lines 64-72.

On two different occasions the lioness, bear, leopard, and dragon went footing through the stanzas of *The Purple Island* and *The Apollyonists*. One example will suffice: [8]

Th' Assyrian Lyon deck't in golden hide,
Once grasp't the Nations in his Lordly paw:
But him the Persian silver Beare defi'd,
Tore, kill'd, and swallowed up with ravenous jaw;
Whom that Greeke Leopard no sooner spi'de,
But slue, devour'd, and fill'd his empty maw:

.   .   .

Meane time in Tybris fen a dreadfull Beast
With monstrous breadth, and length seven hills o're-spreads.
The Apollyonists, III, st. 18-19.

Fletcher delighted in poetic excursions into natural history, some mineralogical, some meteorological, and so on, but the wording of such passages frequently is dictated by Spenser:

Then gan a cursed hand the quiet wombe
Of his great grandmother with steele to wound,
And the hid treasures in her sacred tombe
With sacriledge to dig.
The Faerie Queene, II, vii, st. 17.

[8] The passage is substantially repeated by Fletcher in *The Purple Island*, VII, st. 4-6.

Set alongside this the following:

> Oh hungrie metall, false deceitfull ray,
> Well laid'st thou dark, prest in th' earths hidden wombe;
> Yet through our mothers entrails cutting way,
> We dragge thy buried coarse from hellish tombe.
> *The Purple Island,* VIII, st. 27.

The philosophical sallies in *The Faerie Queene* reëcho word by word through the pages of the Cambridge poet's work. The discordant unity of nature and art, a paradox that enthralled seventeenth-century wits, passes from Spenser to Fletcher:

> One would have thought, (so cunningly the rude
> And scorned partes were mingled with the fine,)
> That Nature had for wantonesse ensude
> Art, and that Art at Nature did repine;
> So striving each th' other to undermine,
> Each did the others worke more beautify;
> So diff'ring both in willes agreed in fine:
> So all agreed through sweete diversity,
> This gardin to adorne with all variety.
> *The Faërie Queene,* II, xii, st. 59.

> And as he goes, he markes how well agree
> Nature and arte in discord unity:
> Each striving who should best performe his part,
> Yet arte helping nature; nature arte.
> *Brittain's Ida,* II, st. 6.

Thus early did Spenser become a poet's poet, and the foregoing parallels are representative of the entire 103 which I have located in Fletcher's pages. A study of the complete group leads to these conclusions: the borrowings are more frequent in *Brittain's Ida,* the *Piscatorie Eclogs, The Apollyonists,* and *The Purple Island,* but they are most frequent in the latter or allegorical cantos of *The Purple Island,* which are drenched in a flood tide of verbal influence. Furthermore, in imitating the earlier poet, Fletcher tended to contract rather than to expand his original, usually boiling down several of Spenser's stanzas into one or two lines. Did Fletcher thumb his volume of Spenser through and through, to lift deliberately word, phrase, and line; or was it all the unconscious reminiscing of a poet who had lost half of his individuality in a blind literary adoration? Though a definitive answer is impossible, we can strike sufficiently near to the truth.

Many of Thirsil's borrowings are so close that they are almost transcriptions; of these he must have been fully conscious, for no one knew his Spenser better than the poet of the Cam. When Fletcher confessed to "lackeying" and "after-looking," I might better say boasted, he was thinking partly of such conscious imitations. Of this nature are all or nearly all of the foregoing examples; on the other hand, his pages are crowded with phrases so turned because of involuntary Spenserian imitation, phrases which I have not included among the 103 parallels. Unconscious reminiscence is more or less a feature of every poet's workmanship. As for the conscious, the man gloried in it; it was "all his prides aspiring." He believed that here was the correct way of blessing and gracing the unblest and ungraced shepherd swain. Such was Phineas Fletcher's major indebtedness, and it constitutes an aspect of his technic which is of no little significance.

In our consideration of verbal influence, we have studied Fletcher's primary debt to Spenser, for the fundamental character of a poem rests in its individual words and phrases. Colin Clout's dominance, however, worked on his successor in other and broader ways. There is Fletcher's addiction to similes, repetition, and above all, to archaisms.[9] Fletcherian terms like "lozel," "herie," "yfere," and "tine" were not seventeenth or even sixteenth-century words, but ghosts from the Middle Ages, raised by Spenser in his efforts to be antique. Cautioned, perhaps, by Sidney's denunciation of Spenserian archaism, Fletcher never went the full way in imitation, not even in his "Verses of Mourning and Joy" in 1603, where the obsolescences come closest to that Tower of Babel, *The Shepheardes Calender*. As time went by, he gradually abandoned the use of antique words, and practically none are found in the poetry of his Hilgay years, published in *A Father's Testament*.

[9] Professor Greg takes what I think is an untenable position: he states that Phineas Fletcher does not imitate Spenser's archaism. Greg was thinking particularly of *Sicelides* and *Piscatorie Eclogs,* which are less archaic, especially the former, than some of the other Fletcherian poems. Still such words as "loaden," "liefest," "faitour," and "lozel" are to be found in the *Piscatorie Eclogs*. Of course there can be no comparison between any Fletcher poem and *The Shepheardes Calender* with respect to the proportion of obsolete words.

Fletcher's poems, one after the other, fall into the genres prescribed by Spenser. The *Piscatorie Eclogs* are analogous to *The Shepheardes Calender*. "E.K." divided Spenser's eclogues into these four classes: plaintive, recreative, commendatory of special persons, moral-satirical; and he could have catalogued the piscatory eclogues similarly.[10] Spenser's various complaints have their counterparts in several of these piscatories, and Spenser even gives Fletcher some precedent for the distinctive quality of his eclogues. Book III of *The Faerie Queene* tells the story of Florimell, imprisoned in the submarine bower of Proteus, carrying with it much of the fishy apparatus of the piscatory convention. Fletcher's hymens are analogous to Spenser's "Epithalamion," and "Elisa" to "Daphnaida," with a more striking resemblance between the latter two elegies, since in each case the assumed narrator is the one in mourning. "The Hymne of Heavenly Love" finds a counterpart in Fletcher's religious poetry of *A Father's Testament,* while at the other extreme is the boisterous comedy of *Sicelides* involving the low characters, Scrocca and Cancrone. Similar comedy is to be found in the account of Malbecco and his dame in *The Faerie Queene*.[11] *The Purple Island* itself was more or less modeled on that work, since Spenser's vast plans for his poem, as set forth in his letter to Sir Walter Raleigh, may have been one of the reasons why Fletcher plotted songs adventurous in scope. The result was *The Purple Island,* although, as the younger Giles stated, his brother projected an even longer poem. Finally there is Fletcher's *Brittain's Ida,* which is the nearest thing to an *Amoretti,* an *Astrophel and Stella,* or a *Diana* that could be achieved by any poem comprised of octonaries rather than sonnets.

The progeny of Spenserian characters throng Fletcher's pages. With a curious lack of prejudice, he arranges for the procreation of Spenser's Idleness, Gluttony, Lust, Avarice, Envy, Fear and then of Faith, Hope, Contemplation, Justice, and Mercy. Duessa is couched with a monstrous delivery of triplets—Fletcher's Caro, Sin, and

---

[10] *Piscatorie Eclog* I, plaintive and commendatory of special persons; II, the same; III, recreative; IV, moral-satirical; V, recreative; VI, moral-satirical; and VII, recreative.

[11] *The Faerie Queene,* III, x, st. 48 ff.

Hamartia; while Belphoebe and Britomart of Faërie-land can only manage a single offspring, the glorious Parthenia. Thirsil was too much interested in reviving the allegory of *The Faerie Queene,* and quite guiltless of recapturing its romantic charm.   .

Somewhat related to this process of reincarnation was Fletcher's use of names derived from Spenser's poems and particularly from *The Shepheardes Calender.* These names were reëmployed to cloak real persons in the *Piscatorie Eclogs,* and thereby to provide modern students with annoying detective work. The March eclogue has a Thomalin, and the April eclogue, a Thenot. Spenser's poetry throws informative light upon one hitherto mysterious figure of Fletcher's *Piscatorie Eclogs,* the Tryphon who appears in several of the sections. He is more particularly mentioned in the fifth piscatory eclogue, where he seems to be a real personage, and as such, he complicates the interpretation of the entire eclogue. He seems to be some Derbyshire curer, either spiritual or medical. *The Faerie Queene* suggests that Fletcher shadowed no real person under this name, but was enlisting old Tryphon in a new service,

> For Tryphon of sea gods the soveraine leach is hight.
> *The Faerie Queene,* III, iv, st. 43.

Tryphon was drafted to increase the piscatory atmosphere, and probably for no other purpose.

Another phase of Spenserian influence, broad in scope, is found in the large motivating ideas that stimulated Fletcher to poetic composition, the recurrent themes of his work. Joy in the humble life of the shepherd swain, his country cell, his untainted breast, his quiet spirit, and his sweet ditties, is one of the most important of these.[12] Spenser expressed the same views,[13] and with both poets, each disappointed in his worldly ambitions, it was largely a defense mechanism. The master provided the follower with most of his arguments in favor of the life of the shepherd, himself as innocent as his simple sheep:[14]

[12] *The Purple Island,* XII, st. 1-7; *Sicelides,* II, chorus; and "To Mr. Jo. Tomkins," lines 28-60.

[13] "Virgils Gnat," lines 89-152; *The Faerie Queene,* VI, ix, st. 19-25.

[14] I have rearranged the order of the lines in each passage so that the two may correspond.

Thrice, oh thrice happie shepherds life and state,

. . .

But sweet content exiles both miserie and spite.

. . .

His lambes warm fleece well fits his little need,

. . .

His life is neither tost in boist'rous seas
Of troublous world, nor lost in slothfull ease.

The Purple Island, XII, st. 2-5.

"How much," sayd he, "more happie is the state,"

. . .

But doe my selfe, with that I have, content;

. . .

The fields my food, my flocks my rayment breed;

. . .

Leading a life so free and fortunate
From all the tempests of these worldly seas,
Which tosse the rest in daungerous disease.

The Faerie Queene, VI, ix, st. 19-20.

Thirsil commanded aged Charon to ferry Orpheus across the
Stygian flood, not only in *The Purple Island* but in three additional works.[15] The fable had a strange appeal for Fletcher so that,
like the humble shepherd's life, it can be considered as one of his
major themes, and it is a legend with which Spenser had previously
dealt.[16] Fletcher's many apostrophes to the waters and temples of
learned Cam won him the title, poet of the Cam. Colin Clout addresses the university in a passage that is all the more interesting
because it is echoed in *The Apollyonists:*

He Patron to my Mother Cambridge, where
Thousand sweet Muses, thousand Graces dwell.

The Apollyonists, V, st. 14.

My mother Cambridge . . .
                . . . and is adorn'd of it
With many a gentle muse.

The Faerie Queene, IV, xi, st. 34.

The two dominant Fletcherian motivations are religion and
science, a strangely modern juxtaposition. *The Apollyonists* and

---

[15] *The Purple Island,* V, st. 61-68; *Poeticall Miscellanies,* "A translation of
Boethius"; *Sicelides,* IV, chorus; *A Father's Testament,* pp. 62-64.
[16] "Virgils Gnat," lines 433-80.

Locustae flame with a violent anti-Romanism, a fire which is burning less wildly, but burning none the less, in the first book of *The Faerie Queene* and in the May eclogue of *The Shepheardes Calender*. Of course Protestant zeal was an important part of the political creed which Spenser, the elder Giles, the Earl of Essex, and Phineas Fletcher shared.

Readers can glide through Spenserian poetry without observing the expressions of scientific interest, which are positive enough, though not dominant like those of *The Purple Island*. It is probably more than coincidental that Spenser, like Fletcher, should have borrowed from the *Georgics* the passage about pallid Cynthia and astronomical studies; [17] and here again the fact that it is really little more than a translation detracts from its weight as evidence of Spenser's scientific interest.[18] The discussions of the cosmos in the mutability cantos of *The Faerie Queene* and in *The Fowre Hymnes* do not have any such imitative weaknesses. A consideration of the origins of life enters the former poem [19] with the conception of the twins, Belphoebe and Amoretta, with their birth from the womb of morning dew, and with their upbringing in the Garden of Adonis, all of which has a certain bearing upon *Paradise Lost* as well. It is important that Spenser's footsteps led the way down each of these paths, and Fletcher was ever on the lookout for the Spenserian footprint.

The mark of Edmund Spenser dots the pages of Fletcherian poetry. We have traced it in word and phrase, melody and idea, personification and method, genre and theme. At one point, however, it struck deeper than ever before or ever after. The Pegasus of the fable lashed out with fetlock of fire against Mount Helicon, to bring forth the Hippocrene fountain; and Spenser's influence burst into Fletcher's poetic consciousness, at one stroke opening the way for the entire *Purple Island*. The "House of Alma" passage of *The Faerie Queene* [20] is the very seed and root of Fletcher's poem, and to it Fletcher owed his conception.

We have seen that this situation is complicated by the fact that Spenser took his "House of Alma" from Du Bartas, that Sylvester used Spenser's passage in translating this section of the *Semaines*,

---

[17] *The Shepheardes Calender*, December, lines 83-84.
[18] See above, p. 114, n. 22. [19] *The Faerie Queene*, III, vi. [20] *Ibid.*, II, ix-xi.

and that the poet of the Cam was indebted to both Spenser and Sylvester.[21] There can be little doubt, however, that in Fletcher's case Spenser, and not Sylvester, was the prime mover in a confusion of influence as complex as a Newtonian problem in celestial mechanics.

Spenser's "House of Alma" is an allegorical presentation of the human body, which is described as a house, or more properly, as a castle. The disciple enlarged his master's conception by treating the body as an island, but the difference between the two is not so great as might be expected. Spenser allegorizes the skin and flesh as the castle wall, the mouth as a gate, the lips as a portcullis, the teeth as warders, and the stomach as the kitchen, in the right *Purple Island* manner, extending his allegory to embrace practically all of the bodily functions later treated by Fletcher. In the eleventh canto of this same book of *The Faerie Queene* is to be found the origin of the second half of the isle-of-man poem. Here are narrated the events of an allegorical battle between virtues and vices, when a monstrous rabblement of foul misshapen wights attack the various senses of the body and are eventually dispersed and slain by Prince Arthur and Sir Guyon.

"The House of Alma" episode, then, is like a topical outline for the much longer *Purple Island;* but so, too, is Sylvester's passage. As I have hinted, however, there are several proofs that he went first to Colin Clout's "Alma" for his plan. The *Purple Island* stanzas, already quoted in part,[22] with their extended allusions to Eumnestes and Phantastes, are indicative of how this section of *The Faerie Queene* haunted Fletcher's consciousness. More important than this is the reëchoing of "House of Alma" phrases from the first to the fifth cantos of the later poem. The wide distribution of the following *Purple Island* quotations is to be contrasted with the concentration of those from *The Faerie Queene:*

The Purple Island

For close within he sets twice sixteen guarders.

V, st. 59.

The Islands common Cook, Concoction.

II, st. 33.

---

[21] See above, p. 117.
[22] *The Purple Island*, VI, st. 46-53.

There many a groom the busie Cook attends
In under offices, and severall place:
This gathers up the scumme, and thence it sends
To be cast out; another liquours base.

> II, st. 36.

The last down-right falls to port Esquiline.

> II, st. 43.

That Trine-one . . .
     . . . purple dust takes from the new-born earth;
Part circular, and part triang'lar fits.

> I, st. 44.

The Faerie Queene

Twise sixteene warders satt.

> II, ix, st. 26.

The maister cooke was cald Concoction.

> II, ix, st. 31.

The rest had severall offices assynd:
Some to remove the scum, as it did rise;
Others to beare the same away did mynd.

> II, ix, st. 31.

That cleped was Port Esquiline.

> II, ix, st. 32.

The frame thereof seemd partly circulare,
And part triangulare: O worke divine!

> II, ix, st. 22.

It is significant that the "House of Alma" conception, and hence the plan of *The Purple Island,* are offshoots of the Renaissance Platonism which impregnates Fletcher's writings. He took both the scheme for his major poem and his philosophy from his master. *The Purple Island* presents the human body as an index which should impart the sum of all, a little world in every particular analogous to the great world. Plato himself would scarcely have recognized this child of his, and yet the poet frequently and carefully relates it to one of the fundamental concepts of the *Phaedo*—that the cosmos is the shadow of the great Idea. Divine Plato spoke through the mouth of Phineas Fletcher, but a considerable chain of intermediaries relayed the message down to him—Plotinus, Ficino, Du Bartas, and above all, Edmund Spenser. It is no wonder that the tidings became somewhat garbled during transmission.

One of the fairer glories of the *Phaedo* is the description of the other world, where the colors

are brighter far and clearer than ours; there is a purple of wonderful luster, also the radiance of gold, and the white which is in the earth (that other earth) is whiter than any chalk or snow. . . . And in this fair region everything that grows—trees, and flowers, and fruits—is in a like degree fairer than any here; and there are hills, and stones in them in a like degree smoother, and more transparent, and fairer in color than our highly valued emeralds and sardonyxes and jaspers.[23]

Plotinus interprets this vision in more practical terms: "For since we say that this All is framed after the Yonder, as after a pattern, the All must first exist yonder as a living entity, an animal; and since its idea is complete, everything must exist yonder." [24]

It would be difficult and perhaps impossible to prove that Du Bartas derived his conception of man's body from the foregoing. Instead of being Platonic, his ideas probably came to him from the medieval theory that man, the microcosm, was made in the image of the universe, the macrocosm. Even Spenser may not have regarded his "House of Alma" passage as Platonic. Perhaps Fletcher was not aware of the specific passages wherein Plato described his world of purple and gold and Plotinus expounded his All and Yonder, but he certainly knew that his own Man of *The Purple Island,* a part of the whole and yet the whole,[25] was a Platonic creature. He relates his idea with the Platonic, by explanations set at strategic intervals:

> For as this Isle is a short summarie
> Of all that in this All is wide dispread;
> So th' Islands face is th' Isles Epitomie.
> *The Purple Island,* V, st. 8.

> That mighty hand in these dissected wreathes,
> (Where moves our Sunne) his thrones fair picture gives;
> The pattern breathlesse, but the picture breathes;
> His highest heav'n is dead, our low heav'n lives.
> *The Purple Island,* IV, st. 9.

Plainly such elucidations were conceived after familiarity with the Platonic World Idea, shaper of the world of fact. Fletcher comes remarkably close to the Plato of the *Dialogues* in his "Vast Ocean

---

[23] Jowett, p. 135.   [24] *Enneads,* VI, vii, 12.   [25] *The Purple Island,* I, st. 43.

Of Light, Whose Rayes Surround," which I regard as his finest poem:

> Our Seas (a drop of thine) with arms dispread
> Through all the earth make drunk the thirsty plains;
> Our Sun (a spark of thine) dark shadows drains, *etc.*
>> *A Father's Testament,* pp. 91-92.

Love and beauty are the great themes of Renaissance Platonism, of Spenser's *Hymnes,* and of at least a third of Fletcher's composition. Most of his treatment was dictated by *The Fowre Hymnes.* Thalander of *Sicelides* is a professor of love and a graduate of the school of experience, for he has been tortured on all the racks that Cupid and Olinda can invent. Alcippus, a mere freshman in love, conceives the emotion to be but a passionate affection for one of the opposite sex and to be founded, more or less, on physical attraction. He has never succumbed to the sweet agony of an Olinda; the professor, somewhat scornful of the boy's ignorance, teaches him:

> True, true Alcippus, love is of the fairest,
> And therefore never tyed unto the body:
> Which if compared unto the mindes faire graces,
> Seemes like the blocke that Lunaes face defaces;
> But grounded on the mind, whose vertuous parts
> And living beauties are loves surest darts.
>> *Sicelides,* V, 1, lines 19-24.

Thalander had conned his lesson presumably from Cupid and Olinda but actually from "The Hymne in Honour of Beautie," where Spenser excoriates the heresy that love is naught else but the outward show of things, preaching that the exterior is a transparency through which the beauty of the soul shines.

With the Platonists, love transcends the bond between man and woman, for it is the generic principle of all life, indeed of all creation, animate and inanimate. "Love is the creator and preserver of all things," Ficino observed upon *The Symposium,* and "The Hymne in Honour of Love" sings the same tune:

> The earth, the ayre, the water, and the fyre,
> Then gan to raunge them selves in huge array,
> And with contrary forces to conspyre
>
>   .   .   .
>
> Till Love relented their rebellious yre.

He then them tooke, and tempering goodly well
Their contrary dislikes with loved meanes,
Did place them all in order, *etc.*
    "The Hymne in Honour of Love," lines 78-87.

In no other particular of his Platonizing is Fletcher's source any clearer, for in this he follows his master word for word:

Fire, Water, Earth, and Aire (that fiercely strove)
His soveraigne hand in strong alliance ti'd,
Binding their deadly hate in constant love:
So that great Wisdome temper'd all their pride,
(Commanding strife and love should never cease)
That by their peacefull fight, and fighting peace,
The world might die to live, and lessen to increase.
    The Purple Island, I, st. 41.

Love, that fire commanding the world's wide regiment, as a conception, commanded Fletcher's thinking and writing, for he dwells upon it frequently.[26]

Since love is a vast principle of which the inclination of male for female, even the Olinda and Thalander situation, is but an elementary expression, so that kind of love is an introduction which should lead the enamored into the more ethereal realms of the passion. "Plato taught that in love the mind should pass from a sight of the objects of beauty through ever widening circles of abstraction to the contemplation of absolute beauty in its idea." [27] Love, then, in the Spenserian *Hymnes* is like an eagle that soars from a crag and circles upward in huge gyrations until he is lost to sight in the pure sunlight of heaven. Fletcher was infatuated with this concept, too, and never tires of expounding it.[28] It is the theme of his sixth piscatory, wherein Thirsil, here the professor of love but more skilled than Professor Thalander, urges upon Thomalin that love is born of fire and fitted with mounting wings, that at his highest he may wind himself higher, an eagle on pinions of flame. In the opening stanzas, he makes it clear that new light hath brought new love; new love, new life hath brought. It was the greater love which inspired *The Purple Island,* and those lightning wings flap through every canto of the poem.

[26] *Sicelides,* III, chorus, lines 1-4; *The Purple Island,* IX, st. 32 ff.; X, st. 4-5.
[27] Harrison's *Platonism in English Poetry,* p. 95.
[28] *Piscatorie Eclogs,* VI; "A vow," lines 15-17; *The Purple Island,* I, st. 6-7; VI, st. 75.

The eagle was lost to mortal eyes in the sun, but whither was he bound, what was the high goal of his winding? With Thirsil and with Colin Clout the destination is the same, a participation in Christ; whereas Plato taught that the ultimate objective was contemplation of absolute beauty and absolute wisdom. Fletcher almost founders his ship on pagan rocks when he creates Understanding as the sovereign of the island, but he hastily saves himself by submitting Understanding to a league of suzerain lords, Eclecta, Spiritto, Urania, and above all Christ, and a love to him to whom all loves are wedded.[29] Parthenia, whose adoration brightens her beauty until it is like a taper burning in a clear crystal, has reached the great objective and lives a maiden wife, a wifely maid, wedded to a heavenly spouse.[30]

At the close of *The Purple Island,* Fletcher allegorizes this culmination in the magnificent pomp of a marriage ceremony that unites Christ and Eclecta. For such an allegory the poet found no authority in Spenser, and his curious fusing of Renaissance hymeneal and Renaissance Platonism is perhaps his one original contribution to the philosophy of love and beauty.

In the foregoing pages the question—what is a Spenserian?—has been so answered that it leaves one wondering why our Spenserian is not a second Spenser. Since Fletcher imitated his master, often word for word, in phase after phase of the poetic art, why do not the stanzas of *The Purple Island* or the *Piscatorie Eclogs* have the genuine savor of *The Faerie Queene* or *The Shepheardes Calender?* No one can read the account of the isle of man and, napping, fall into the deception that he is reading Spenser. An inferior genius and the lapse of years have created the subtle yet unescapable differences. In the Louvre I have seen a painter daubing at his copy of the Mona Lisa, and while the imitation was mathematically accurate in detail and shading, it was as though this breathing artist were dead, while Leonardo still lived. Fletcher's lines and phrases in simulation of Spenser's are also lusterless, but happily there are large sections of his work which have little to do with his master, preëminently the science of his anatomical cantos. *The Faerie Queene* has captured the sunset glow of the Middle Ages,

[29] "A vow," lines 15-17; *The Purple Island,* I, st. 6-7.
[30] *The Purple Island,* X, st. 38-40.

in colors that were perhaps lovelier than those of the noontide, but by Fletcher's day that sun had stretched out all the hills and dropped into the western bay, and another sun had risen. Thirsil's work is lighted by the new sunrise, despite all his theories and efforts toward "far admiring," "after looking," and "lackeying."

X

ANOTHER POETICAL MISCELLANY

THE new sunrise, if such it may be called, was the inductive science which was to revolutionize human existence. Sympathy for this movement was Phineas Fletcher's great originality, but there are other unusual aspects of his writings. For after the influence of Vergil, Sylvester, Spenser, and the other poets has been reckoned with, the remaining peculiarities of Fletcher's craftsmanship are his own. Not all of these were to his credit. Most important are his willingness to repeat himself and to revise his work, his shiftings from Latin to English, his innovations in the pastoral conventions, and his flair for prosodic variations.

The queerest characteristic of Fletcher's workmanship is his habit of self-repetition, a peculiarity which caught the attention of both Grosart and Boas. The parallel passages are not partially similar, or alike in theme and idea only, but are often word for word duplications. There can be little doubt that the large majority were intentional labor-saving devices, and constitute transcription from an earlier poem for the purpose of decorating a later. The total number of such instances, so far as I have been able to ascertain it, reaches the unusual sum of 215.[1] The reproductions vary in length from phrases of 2 or 3 words to passages of some 60 lines. There are instances of Fletcher's translating parts of his Latin poems and using them to increase his English verses. He even turned several lines of poetry into prose, and reëmployed their words and thoughts in his devotional treatises. Because of its prevalence, this reproduction, to be found in a small measure in the works of almost every writer, becomes almost a kind of self-plagiarism.

The variations on the Orpheus and Eurydice theme are the longest and most hydra-headed instance of the habit. There are four different treatments of the myth, and in each the poet consumes

[1] See Appendix A below, where the passages are tabulated.

some sixty-five lines in developing his narrative. The passages vary slightly, just as do all the parallels, but more about the variations later. What seems to be the parent, may be found in the *Poeticall Miscellanies,* where it is entitled "A translation of Boethius, the Third Book" and last verse. The legend was next used in *The Purple Island* as an illustration that has about it an air of having been lugged in. It served for an entire chorus in *Sicelides,* and many years later cropped up as one of the verses adorning the prose of *A Father's Testament.*

Every major poem is thoroughly inoculated with the virus of repetition. Indeed the same is true of very nearly all of the minor poems as well, for there are only a few of these that are entirely without it. *The Apollyonists,* with thirty-seven stanzas (or one-fifth of the total) which are entirely or partly the duplicates of passages in other poems, is the most affected. That does not mean that all the reproduction occurred in the writing of this work, since some of the stanzas may have been first composed for *The Apollyonists* and then re-used in a subsequent undertaking. The difficulty of ascertaining the dates of the poems frequently makes it impossible to determine the direction of the repetition, that is, to distinguish the first use of a phrase or stanza from the second. We can, of course, be sure that a figure of speech shared by *The Purple Island* and *Sicelides* was originally composed for the former and was then reënlisted some five years later to decorate the drama. On the other hand, what can be said for all those passages common to the *Piscatorie Eclogs* and *The Purple Island,* when it is not known whether the eclogues were written before or after the anatomical poem?

The bulk of Fletcher's poetry was completed within the space of four years. It seems likely that the author wrote several works simultaneously, and it is more likely that he altered and polished earlier poems while he was busy with later projects. The whole of Fletcher's writing is small, in comparison with Spenser's or Drayton's, but it looms large when measured by the number of years he gave to intensive versifying. For a certain time he must have turned out meters and rhymes with all the systematized economy of factory production. These machinelike methods evidently included a stock of standardized phrases, similes, and anecdotes, to be used for recurring situations. The repetitious material is almost always found among the decorative stuff, the pretty trimmings, of the work in question. *Sicelides* carries a heavy burden of booty from earlier productions, but little of it is present in the drama proper, the author having largely confined it to the choruses. Although *The Purple Island* is shot through with repetition, the second and third cantos, which deal with pure anatomy, are practically unmarked. Thus whenever a major work departs into its peculiar subject matter, the echoes die away.

The number of similar passages in Fletcher's poetry is astonishing, but equally so is the presence of numerous minute dissimilarities between repetitious stanzas or groups of stanzas. We have noticed that the four treatments of the Orpheus and Eurydice legend were almost identical, but only almost, because of the minor variations. The outstanding example of these dissimilarities among similarities is found in "Upon my brother, Mr. G.F. his book entituled *Christs Victorie and Triumph*" (*Poeticall Miscellanies,* 1633) and "Fond Ladds, That Spend So Fast Your Poasting Time" (the same piece prefixed to *Christs Victorie and Triumph,* 1610). These cannot be regarded as reproductions, because they are one poem—Fletcher has exercised the right, possessed by all authors, of reprinting an earlier publication in his collected works—and yet they best exemplify the differences which are found between the repetitious passages. In these two twenty-four-line versions, there are twenty-eight changes in spelling, sixteen in punctuation, and four in wording. Obviously the alterations are of two types: the mechanical kind of spelling and punctuation on the one hand, and the stylistic or verbal on the other. When the repetitious passages are compared, differences of spelling, punctuation, and wording will appear; but the last will be proportionately more numerous than in the present case.

There is nothing extraordinary in the cropping up of such mechanical changes to differentiate the 1610 and 1633 editions of a poem, although there is some wonder in their abundancy, for they teem like the very locusts of *The Apollyonists.* One is inclined to attribute them to the divergent canons of two printers, until he discovers that each issue was the work of the Cambridge Press. A change of personnel took place among the university printers during the twenty-three-year lapse, Thomas Buck and Roger Daniel replacing Cantrell Legge; but it is unlikely that the successors threw over the standards to the extent of making forty-four alterations in a brief poem previously published by their own press. Furthermore the manuscript and the Ferrar edition of George Herbert's *Temple*—the latter was the product of Buck and Daniel—are both extant. A comparison of these proves that the Cantabrigian compositors adhered to an author's text with extreme fidelity.[2]

The alternative is that Fletcher was responsible for the mechanical changes, a theory in harmony with what we already know about his habits. Thus Fletcher seems to have renovated his systems of spelling and punctuation at some time between 1610 and 1633. It might be argued that the poet was a victim of the disorder and want of method in these matters which are sometimes supposed to have been the attributes of Elizabethans and Jacobeans. I suspect, however, that individuals of those eras adhered to private standards of punctuation and orthography more rigidly than is generally believed. Certainly the changes Fletcher introduced into his punctuation and spelling were not accidental, because in each he was proceeding in a definite direction. His new principle of punctuation is discernible in the two editions of the poem we are considering: it is a tendency toward greater closing, particularly at the end of the line, and the semicolon is, for the larger part, the tool on which he most depended. In the same way he undertook the rectification of his 1610 spelling and carried it out with a heavy hand, rewriting more than 10 percent of the total words. I have made a random selection of the orthographical improvements in the second printing: ladds, lads; poasting, posting; chaunt, chant; and chast, chaste.

By means of the repetitious passages, it is possible to fix more closely the date of Fletcher's new notions about punctuation and spelling. Upon comparing any one of the many parts of *The Apollyonists* with its duplicate, for instance, the basanite or touchstone illustration used in both *The Apollyonists* and *The Purple Island*,[3] we shall meet a contrast quite as significant as that between the two editions of "Upon my brother, Mr. G.F." etc. The Gunpowder

[2] Palmer has collated the manuscript and the Ferrar text of Herbert's poems, and finds that the variations between the two are extremely rare. In his edition of Herbert's works, he praises Buck and Daniel for their careful printing.

[3] *Apollyonists*, I, st. 14; *The Purple Island*, VIII, st. 8.

Plot poems were printed in 1627 by Thomas and John Buck, while the others were issued by Thomas Buck and Daniel in the collected edition of 1633. The modernizing must have taken place within that six-year interval and at the time when Fletcher prepared his *Purple Island, Piscatorie Eclogs,* and *Poeticall Miscellanies* for publication. Here, too, is additional proof that the university printers took no hand in the alterations, because the archaisms of 1627 and the modernizings of 1633 were both issued by Thomas Buck.

Added to the mechanical improvements, there were four changes of wording in the 1633 issue of the address to Giles Fletcher. If the various repetitious passages are set one against the other, the verbal changes prove to be more numerous than those of punctuation and orthography. Some of the former were the necessary result of adaptation, for the borrowing had to be fitted into its new environment. On the other hand, most of the alterations in wording seem to be improvements and could only have been made for that purpose. A study of the whole body of repetitions convinces one that Fletcher polished his work with considerable patience and labor. There is a close connection between reproduction and polishing, as they were practiced by Fletcher. In certain cases it is difficult to determine whether the author has fallen into the first or has risen to the second. Such is true of the five *Apollyonists-Locustae* poems when they are considered as integrals. There are four complete and variant versions of the latter—the Harleian MS. 3196, the Sloane MS. 444, the Egerton MS. 2875, and the printed edition of 1627. These were different drafts of the same poem and not only are examples of Fletcher's refinings, but are also indicative of the extremity of industry he underwent in his furbishings and refurbishings. The English *Apollyonists* is, and is not, a translation of *Locustae,* but compares with it in much the same way as the Orpheus and Eurydice accounts compare with one another. It is more detailed than any of the four Latin versions and is more properly a paraphrastic expansion of them. The *Apollyonists-Locustae* group are instances of Fletcher's revision and possibly of his self-plagiarism, but they reflect still a third trait which we shall consider soon—his wavering between Latin and English as a literary medium.

As there are three autograph manuscripts and a printed text of *Locustae,* so there are two manuscripts and a printed text of *Sice-*

lides that involved Professor Boas in difficulties of collation such
as only a scholar of his judiciousness could have overcome. The
distinction between the poem and the drama, however, is that
neither the Additional MS. 4453 nor the Rawlinson MS. 214—the
two versions of the comedy—is in Fletcher's hand. Professor Boas,
with all the other authorities, thinks that the quarto was pirati-
cally printed and was entirely unauthorized; but we have noticed [4] that there is reason for believing that Fletcher delegated
an agent to take his play to a publisher. If he did so, it was that he
wished to keep it anonymous; and for the same reason he left the
proofs uncorrected, with the result that the 1631 text is corrupt.
The same is true of the twin manuscripts which were evidently the
work of inaccurate copyists. On the other hand, there are variations between all three versions which cannot be inaccuracies, but
rather are someone's intentional changes. It is a temptation to
ascribe these differences in *Sicelides* to Fletcher's passion for revision. If the trio represent stages of the author's improvements, the
quarto must have been the latest, for, according to our theory, he
sent that copy to Sheares, the printer.[5]

It is apparent from Fletcher's practice that he wavered between
Latin and English as a literary medium, and many of his Latin
poems seem to date from his early years at King's College.[6] In
1603, when he was still a boy, he composed "Now Did the Sunne
Like an Undaunted Hart" and also "Quae, sicut rutilis Cynthia
curribus," each in honor of Elizabeth and her Scottish successor.
"Upon the picture of Achmat the Turkish tyrant" and its translation, "In effigiem Achmati Turcarum tyranni," are a similar
combination. He produced at least one Latin parallel for nearly

---

[4] See above, pp. 96-97.

[5] Self-repetition may assist in determining the relationship between the individual
manuscripts and the printed texts in this supposed evolution of the play. I have
collated the twenty-four instances of this in *Sicelides,* as they are found in each
version, with their parallels in the other Fletcherian poems. (Of course these latter
passages may have been altered after the final preparation of the manuscript
which Sheares used and, if such was the case, this comparison is of no value.) The
following is a tabulation of the total variations between the particular *Sicelides* text
and Fletcher's poems: Additional MS., 12; the quarto, 21; and the Rawlinson MS., 27.
Do the three represent three stages of revision?

[6] Important exceptions are "Elisa Vincenta—Anagramma," "Amicissimo et Candidissimo Edvardo Benlowes," "Dom. Observandissimo H.W.," "Fusca Ecloga,"
"Collegiis Regalibus," "In celeberrimam Theophilam," and *Locustae.*

every type of English poem he wrote. One senses caution in this duplication of genres, the elegy for the *elegiam,* the epigram for the *epigramma,* and the eclogue for the *eclogam.*[7] The poet was much like a man going forth upon a cloudy morning, armed with sun glasses and umbrella.

In the neighborhood of 1608, when he began his *Purple Island,* Fletcher seems to have resolved his doubts and decided that the vernacular was to be his medium. His entire experience in the matter is analogous to Milton's, and although Fletcher did not write an "At a Vacation Exercise," with its purposeful decision, his *Purple Island* seems to convey a similar message. This, Fletcher's most ambitious poem, was not only composed in English, but apparently was written for the very purpose of turning the knowledge of anatomy into English. This fact is evident in the studious avoidance of all Latinities throughout the twelve cantos, as, for instance, in the following marginals:

Within, the Pleura (or skinne which clotheth the ribs on the inside) compasses this middle region.

The Purple Island, IV, st. 14, marg. k.

Next is that Septum lucidum, or bright wall, severing these hollow caverns.

The Purple Island, V, st. 16, marg. k.

No university man of the Jacobean era needed to be told that a *septum lucidum* was a bright wall. The author was making the facts of anatomy available to the uneducated reader.

Fletcher has a place in any history of the pastoral tradition for two or three solid reasons. Most of his major poems—*Sicelides, The Purple Island,* the *Piscatorie Eclogs,* and the *eclogae* of *Sylva Poetica*—belong to the genre. He was a prominent member

---

[7] Of course the duplication of genres may not have been a case of caution. Academic training would lead Fletcher into Latin versification during his undergraduate years. Furthermore, poems like *Locustae* and "Dom. Observandissimo H.W." appear to have been designed for the sake of impressing their readers with the author's scholarly attainments, while a poem like "Amicissimo et Candidissimo Edvardo Benlowes" was obviously prepared for an unusually formal occasion. Although there is much to obscure the issue, two facts are clear enough: we know that an academic poet of 1610 faced the option of writing in Latin or English (witness Milton's problem a generation later), and we know that Fletcher's longest poem, *The Purple Island,* and most of his subsequent writing was in English.

of the little pastoral society at the university, and he introduced several interesting variations into the customary conventions. Above all, he concentrated upon the rarest outgrowth of the form, the piscatory, and became its leading exponent in the history of English literature. His treatment of the pastoral is distinguished for its originality.

The pastoral disguise and that personal element, one of the piquant features of Fletcher's poems, go hand in hand, and perhaps without the first we should never have had the second. In his poems, and preëminently in the *Piscatorie Eclogs,* Phineas Fletcher deals with himself, his father, his brother, his wife, and other relatives. He does not hesitate to narrate incidents of the utmost intimacy concerning these persons—their achievements, their failures, their love affairs, and even their wrongdoings and sins. Thus there is a semi-Pepysian flavor about the Latin and English eclogues. Both the diarist and the poet confided family privacies to paper, but each veiled them, the one by means of a cipher, the other by disguising names and events under a pastoral screen, less involved than the code but more effective. By a solution of the shorthand system, it was possible to lay bare the contents of the diary at one stroke; but Fletcher's cryptogram has been decoded bit by bit, through the discoveries and conjectures of various persons. Certain of the names and allusions will, I fear, remain forever dark.

According to the traditions, the pastoral poet entered his trade by taking to himself a boyish or rustic name, proceeded to re-christen his relatives and acquaintances, and finally enrolled himself in a little society of poets, all of whom had similarly altered their names. This transformation in nomenclature was one of the circumstances of the pastoral which made it usable as a cipher. Greg speaks of a kind of pastoral freemasonry that sprang up at the close of the sixteenth century, whose chief dignitaries were Colin Clout, Astrophel, Amyntas, and Rowland. Fletcher was a leader in a similar organization, a younger chapter of the society which flourished at Cambridge, fostered there by the university poets. The fraternity has not been recognized in subsequent historical writings, perhaps because the real names of so many of its members were unknown. Some of them—Giles Fletcher, Phineas' brother; John Tomkins; Francis Quarles; and Samuel Collins—have been unmasked with more or less success in the earlier half of the present work. Each had his peculiar nickname: Thomalin only slightly conceals its original, Tomkins; and I was able to connect Melite with Tomkins' wife, Margaret Griffiths, by the initial, M. But unfortunately the names given out by Phineas Fletcher contain clues to the identities of the owners only rarely. This has made the lot of the biographer a thorny one, which was exactly what the poet intended it to be. He had no right, however, to change his own title more than once; that was against the rules. And yet he godfathered himself into no less than four different names. Starting the pastoral life in 1603 with Coridon, he shifted to Myrtilus, then to Thirsil, and finally to Algon. It was Thirsil, however, who composed *The Purple Island,* and thus Thirsil he must ever be to the brethren of the cult. Although the string of aliases cannot be easily explained, I have concluded that he had a theory. He required a poet to assume a new pastoral designation with each fresh love affair; and since his own heart was not overconstant, his name was no more so. With his marriage to Nicaea, the alterations ceased abruptly; perhaps his wife would have no more of such nonsense.

The second deception in the pastoral of which Fletcher made the most, had to do with professions, dwelling places, account books, indeed with all the facts of life in the seventeenth century. Like his brethren, he alluded to these as if they were phases of a shepherd's or fisherman's experiences, but in one respect his practice was unique. In his references to the Thomalins and Thenots and their fellowship, he makes it obvious that he does not propose to include among them every Tom, Dick, and Harry. So far as Fletcher was concerned, it was a fraternity open only to two sorts, the vicars and rectors of the parish and the fellows and doctors of the university. Furthermore, he divided the chosen into two groups, the fishers and the herdsmen. The shepherd swain, his safe and lowly cottage and his sweet contentedness, are praised in *The Purple Island.*[8] He is definitely the parish cleric, for he has a faithful spouse and a little son who creeps into his bosom. Distinctions between the two régimes of life are drawn at the beginning of *Sicelides,*[9] distinctions which are explained in the seventh piscatory

---

[8] *The Purple Island,* XII, st. 2 ff.
[9] *Sicelides,* I, 1.

eclogue.[10] Here it is stated that the fisher boys are the university men, while the shepherds are those erstwhile fishermen who have since cast loose from the shore to enter parish livings.[11]

Interesting facts about Fletcher and his nearest kin have lain hidden under a pastoral disguise devised by the poet himself, while his prose works—*Joy in Tribulation, The Way to Blessednes,* and *A Father's Testament*—have remained little known, because of their rarity, until they are now almost forgotten. It would increase Fletcher's fame if they were reprinted and read, particularly *A Father's Testament.* The other two are typical seventeenth-century devotional treatises: *Joy in Tribulation,* as its title implies, describes the solace that religion can offer to the mourner; while *The Way to Blessednes* is a sort of Baedeker to guide the believer along the highway of religious life. As in other tracts of the age, the style rides from extreme to extreme, for there are dull levels heavily "bumbasted" with biblical quotations and there are occasional inspired pages. Some angel, eloquent like Raphael, must have hovered over the prose writers of the seventeenth century, and now and then Fletcher was under the angelic aegis. When he takes his readers to task for their drunkenness, wantoning, and Sabbath-breaking, his sentences crackle and flame; the lightning of *The Apollyonists* flares anew. At other times he falls into the question-and-answer method, and what should have been a prosaic treatment stirs with life and becomes almost as dramatic as an Elizabethan play. The best in these works is the product of strong, simple emotions, rather than of original thought. The author himself calls attention to this, for he begins by condemning those tracts designed to promote new ideas, dismissing them as idle pamphlets. As for him, he preferred to restate and reëmphasize the good old ideas, but his sincerity made him unexpectedly fluent.

[10] *Piscatorie Eclogs,* VII, st. 5.

[11] The chorus of the second act of *Sicelides,* where the joys of the piscatory life are painted, seems to cast doubt upon this conclusion:

> "There shall I quiet fearelesse raigne,
> My boyes my subjects taught submission,
> A boat my court, my sonnes my traine."

It appears that the fisherman has his children also and that he is accordingly something other than a university fellow. I believe, however, that the fisher's "sonnes" and "boyes" are his undergraduate students.

A Father's Testament is a beautiful book. Its charm began with its origin, since Fletcher wrote it to be read only by his children and, so far as we know, made no move toward publication. In the main it is no more original than the other two, such treatises of fatherly advice being common during the Jacobean era. Its prose, however, occasionally burns with lyricism, as in the following sentence:

> What an Heaven is that soul where all these glorious stars of Prophets, and Apostles are fasten'd in the understanding, and the Throne of God set up in the heart, where the Lord Jesus reigns, attended by all Saintly thoughts, and Heavenly graces?
>
> *A Father's Testament*, p. 155.

Set at intervals in the text of *A Father's Testament* are poems, reprinted by Boas, which, few and brief as they are, include some of Fletcher's best work. Lyrics such as "Vast Ocean of Light," "Great Fount of Light," and "Fond Soul! Is This," with their "shoreless thoughts" and "vast tenter'd hope," to use Vaughan's own words, remind one strangely of the Silurist. In them nature is presented with a sweep and a spirituality which contrast with the rather mincing descriptions of the *Piscatorie Eclogs* and *The Purple Island*. Not the least interesting feature of these late poems is their prosodic variety.

"Fidgety" seems to be the term accepted by critics for describing Fletcher's prosody. A consideration of the Fletcherian stanzas as a whole and in their chronological development will prove that there were order and climax in the poet's metrical experiments. His prosody began in servility, rose with a steady increase in artistry and independence, and reached a triumphant culmination. At first the reader will see none of this progression, but will be confounded by the multiformity. He will find blank verse, couplets of four and five feet, stanzas of three, twelve, thirteen, fourteen, sixteen, and even twenty-four and thirty-six lines. He will encounter half a dozen varieties of the ten-line strophe and a like number of eight-liners. All in all, there are no fewer than thirty-six different metrical types among the Fletcherian poems.

Fletcher's stanzas are like a small heaven of stars that seem to be scattered aimlessly about or else to be wandering nowhere. Any-

one, however, patient enough to study them briefly, will find the
principles underlying the apparent confusion. The great bulk of
the Fletcherian works were composed in staves of six to ten lines,
while those of other lengths are seldom used in more than one
instance. It is not accidental that the Spenserian stanza and rhyme
royal are barely overlapped at either of these extremes, for they
were the two bases from which Fletcher ventured in his early
experiments and, for the most part, he was unwilling to wander
far from them. The Spenserian and rhyme royal are like two
poles, and almost every Fletcherian strophe revolves about either
the one or the other.

Some critics have referred to "Phineas Fletcher's stanza" as if
he had one favorite, but they are in error, for the poet was devoted
to five different types. These all belong to those two orbits, and
nine-tenths of the Fletcherian poetry was framed in some one of
the five molds. The first of them is a six-line stanza rhyming
a b a b c c, with a final pentameter. It was not used in any important poem, but no fewer than sixteen minor pieces employ it.
Secondly there is a seven-liner, rhyming *a b a b b c c;* it was the
stanza of "Elisa" and seven less important poems. This and the remaining three conclude with an Alexandrine, which is the characteristic, though not inevitable, mark of the Fletcherian stave.
Another stanza of the same length, the *a b a b c c c,* is the so-called
Fletcher stanza, and was used throughout *The Purple Island* and
in three additional instances. A fourth stanza of eight lines, an
a b a b b c c c, is found in *Brittain's Ida* and in four shorter works.
Lastly *The Apollyonists* and seven minor poems employ a nine-
liner, rhyming *a b a b a b c c c.*

No one of these five strophes is especially original, for they were
either taken over bodily or modeled closely on the rhyme royal
and the Spenserian stanza. They contain, however, one notable
element of independence. Although Phineas Fletcher was eager to
echo Edmund Spenser as accurately as he possibly could in all
other phases of the poetic art, he never used the exact stanza of
The Faerie Queene. The first, or the six-line stave, is the one which
served Colin Clout in "Teares of the Muses," "Astrophel," a part
of *The Shepheardes Calender,* and elsewhere. The third, found in
"Elisa," is straight rhyme royal except for the lengthening of its

final verse. The eight-liner of *Brittain's Ida* was probably borrowed from Giles Fletcher, who had invented it for "A Canto on the Death of Eliza" and resurrected it for *Christs Victorie and Triumph;* there is little likelihood that the elder brother could have devised it before 1603. The poet was also more or less dependent upon outside sources for some of his less common stanzas. A great many of these were loosely modeled upon those of Spenser, and more particularly on the nine-line stanza that bears Spenser's name. In two works Fletcher enlisted the ottava rima, once with perfect regularity and again with a final Alexandrine.

With Phineas Fletcher the prosodic art was not static, but wholly fluid, because his stanzas grew more and more complex with the passing of the years. He began by imitating Spenser; yet as his craft developed, it steadily moved away from the Elizabethan's to produce staves that had little or no similarity with the master's. The only poems by Fletcher which we know, with a reasonable degree of certainty, to have been written long after the productive era of 1608-1611, are those of *A Father's Testament.* The prose work contains twenty-one verse interludes, and nine of these employed entirely new stanzas. Only five of the group repeat any of the characteristic five. It seems that the more mature Fletcher, as Spenser's influence on English letters waned, had begun to imitate the prosody of George Herbert and the other Caroline poets.

The "Epithalamium" is the climax of Fletcher's entire prosodic development. Probably written in 1614, it is earlier than *A Father's Testament* but later than *The Purple Island, The Apollyonists,* and most of the others. Its form was evidently suggested by the eighteen-line stanza of Spenser's "Epithalamion," but Fletcher adventured far beyond the comparative simplicity of his predecessor. Miss Seaton's description of this marriage song, which, she said, consisted of "regular stanzas of seven, eight, and nine lines interspersed with passages irregular in length and structure," is somewhat misleading. Actually, it contains nineteen strophes which are set off by breaks in the manuscript, and the regularity mentioned by Miss Seaton is decidedly limited. There are two nine, two twelve, and two seven-line stanzas, which correspond with one another; but all the rest differ. The first stanza of the poem is never repeated, but the second and fourth are paired, as are the third and fifth. A nineteen-line passage of rhymed couplets follows, and from then on diversity reigns supreme. There is even one stretch of seventeen lines devoted to a single rhyme. Furthermore a like variety is encountered among the verses, for there are lines of three, four, five, and six feet. Feminine rhymes, a characteristic of Fletcherian prosody, are omnipresent in the poem, and lend it a sugared ornateness which is not unappropriate to a hymeneal song. The total effect of Fletcher's experiments in his "Epithalamium" is one of loveliness, and it resembles a basket of variegated blossoms.

To offset his skill in prosody, Fletcher had certain failings which leave their marks again and again upon his poems. He delighted in the conceit, and some of his are as unhappy as that one perpetrated by his brother:

> His [Christ's] cheekes as snowie apples, sop't in wine.
> "Christs Victorie on Earth," st. 11.

In "Elisa," at a moment heavy with tragedy, Fletcher addresses the widow with the following behest:

> These raining eyes into thy bottle gather.
> "Elisa," I, st. 13.

The poet had a fondness for the paradox, which is a phase of the conceit:

> Most strong he is, because he will be weak.
> The Purple Island, X, st. 14.

Intentional archaisms, artificialities at best, present themselves not only in the form of vocabulary but also of grammatical structure: e.g., "with softly pace," [12] "simple as we been," [13] "learne me that sacred art," [14] and "there had he fell." [15]

These were the faults of the age, and for them Fletcher is not to be censured unduly. Of another nature is the defect in his genius which operated more widely and more heavily upon his writings. Each of the poet's major works suffers from some large structural infirmity, and thereby falls short of the true masterpiece. The persons who make up the drama, Sicelides, act without adequate cause,

---

[12] The Purple Island, VI, st. 77.
[13] Ibid., VI, st. 65.
[14] The Apollyonists, V, st. 18.
[15] The Purple Island, XII, st. 17.

and no skill of stage interpretation could ever make them live. *The Apollyonists* gets off to a masterful start, rises slowly to a climax, not too well constructed, and fades away to an abrupt and somewhat inept end. The latter half of *The Purple Island* is surrendered to an allegory which, despite its occasional charm, is often wooden and always interminable.

Despite its weaknesses, there are many reasons why Fletcher's poetry has been and will be read. There are recurring trills of music in its measures and flashes of color in its similes. When the poet hammers out lines in righteous anger, his phrases become forceful, never spiteful, but strong and true as steel. There is a manly vigor about all these poems which has been overlooked and which should recommend *The Apollyonists*, particularly, to more readers. It seems to me that just one work is unspoiled by any structural weakness: cantos I-V of *The Purple Island*. Here the material is original and here the author's technic is perfectly adapted to its presentation.

XI

A BACHELOR OF ARTS AND DIVINITY, TURNED
MASTER OF SCIENCE

CURIOUSLY enough the most original feature of Phineas Fletcher's life and writings is that which has been the least investigated —his scientific interests. These converge upon the anatomical cantos of *The Purple Island*, though their influence was by no means restricted to that poem. The historians of literature and medicine have treated the versified anatomy with a scorn that gave way only to neglect.

The chroniclers of anatomical history, who, unlike the literary men, possessed the proper equipment for such an analysis, have not directed it upon *The Purple Island*. We seek vainly through surveys like Sir Michael Foster's *Lectures on the History of Physiology in England during the Sixteenth, Seventeenth, and Eighteenth Centuries,* which do not even mention the poem. Nor do we fare much better among the nearly endless pages of periodicals such as *The Annals of Medical Science* and *The British Medical Journal,* works devoted wholly or partly to the history of discovery in this field. The medical profession has given us only two articles on *The Purple Island:* an anonymous jotting entitled "A Poet's Anatomy," [1] and a more extended treatise, *The Purple Island, A Seventeenth Century Poetical Conception of the Human Body,* by Augustus T. Pohlman.[2] These physicians, with a commendable taste for literature, chanced upon a work which, for obvious reasons, arrested their attention. Each went into print upon the presumption that *The Purple Island* was a sort of bibliophile's rarity to be rescued from oblivion. Although it is true that Fletcher's works, since his death, were at no time widely popular, they have never been unobtainable.

The non-scientific literary scholar has hunted down their arti-

[1] *British Medical Journal,* May 9, 1925.
[2] *Johns Hopkins Hospital Bulletin,* Vol. XVIII, No. 197, 1907.

cles, hoping for an expert measurement of the Jacobean author's place in the annals of anatomic pioneering. Perhaps he was resigned to being told that the information was sadly antiquated, had been gathered from Greek and Roman authorities, and was out of touch with the Renaissance discoverers. Or he may have hoped vaguely that Fletcher would be proved not altogether obsolete as a scientist. Neither the anonymous writer nor Pohlman attempts to analyze Fletcher's facts. The first passes them over with amused contempt, while the other makes several erroneous guesses about the origins. Pohlman's general conclusion, flung off airily, is that Fletcher has conned some standard text such as Galen, but he avoids specifying a particular work.

The reason why no one has suspected the real significance of *The Purple Island* is obvious enough. Nothing could be less scientific than the half-allegorical, half-philosophical, and entirely fanciful method chosen by Fletcher for presenting the cold facts of the laboratory. On the purple isle the veins and arteries become rivers and brooks, the heart a city, the head a tower, the liver a well, the gall a conduit, the kidneys twin mountains, and so on throughout. The entire body is an index that

> Briefly should impart
> The summe of all; the whole, yet of the whole a part.
> *The Purple Island,* I, st. 43.

We have found that Fletcher derived his Man, who at one and the same time was the Whole and a part of the Whole, from Renaissance Platonism. Although Fletcher seems to have regarded him as entirely Platonic, the creature is also connected with another concept, medieval in origin and less innocent than the Platonic to which it was remotely related.[3] In his *Advancement of Learning,*

---

[3] See above, pp. 147-49. The chief difference between the medieval and the Neoplatonic concepts seems to be that the former was practical, whereas the latter was mystical. Fletcher, on more than one occasion (see above, p. 148), uses the ideas of Spenser's *Fowre Hymnes* to give his man a Platonic character. On the other hand, his scheme for *The Purple Island* was derived from Du Bartas, Sylvester, and Spenser's *Faerie Queene.* The theme, as treated by those writers, is a practical application of the microcosm-macrocosm theory, without noticeable Neoplatonic implications. Both concepts seem to have sprung from a common origin in early Greek philosophy, but they had long followed divergent paths of development when Fletcher reunited them in his *Purple Island.*

Francis Bacon wrote that the heathen writers "supposed the world to be the image of God, and man to be an extract or compendious image of the world." [4] Bacon alluded to the concept of the micro-cosm-macrocosm, born among the earliest Greek philosophers— the idea that the microcosm, man's body, repeats in miniature all the structural details of the greater world, the macrocosm. It follows that the contemplation of God and his universe would serve as an adequate substitute for the study of the body. This brain child, nurtured in the schools of Gentile philosophy, lived on harmlessly through the green ages of Plato, of Aristotle, of the Peripatetics, of Claudius Galen, but all the while it was waiting for the redemption it was to find in Christianity. The medieval scholiasts took it to their bosoms, cherished it, and made of it something pernicious. The theory of the microcosm-macrocosm, more than any other factor, paralyzed anatomical study from the death of Galen to the birth of Mundinus.[5] It gave rise to a false conception of the human body, and at the same time turned men away from the investigation of the flesh, blood, and bones—the only real text of the physiologist. Surgery became, for the most part, the art of knaves, and medicine the profession of fools like the "Phisicien" of *The Canterbury Tales*.

If Fletcher really had supposed "the world to be the image of God, and man to be an extract or compendious image of the world," then he deserved the neglect dealt his science. We shall learn, however, that the poet was far from subscribing to the microcosm-macrocosm speculation. His allegorical scheme of presentation is superficial, so that instead of penetrating the scientific facts, it hovers over and around them like a cloak. The unhappy author, seeking an artistic structure, built himself a mausoleum where he concealed the genuine worth of his work. Once a reader bursts the heavy doors, the values of *The Purple Island* lie spread before him. The first is its large autobiographical significance. Fletcher's anatomical enthusiasm is not only the truest expression of his individual genius, but it is the one phase of his work which reveals him as sympathetic toward the forward-looking intellectual movements of his age, which was also the age of Francis Bacon, Robert Burton,

[4] *The Advancement of Learning*, p. 91.
[5] Singer's *Evolution of Anatomy*, pp. 14, 64.

William Harvey, Sir Thomas Browne, and Robert Boyle. That the poet's coevals found no great novelty in his poem is made plain in the complimentary verse they wrote. The two Benlowes, Roberts, and Featly remarked upon nothing unusual, other than its excellence; and although Quarles describes the author as "ingenious," he later states that it is the very kind of work which "jumpt" with his own genius. Their complacence is less mysterious when we find that other anatomical and medical poems were composed within one hundred years of Fletcher's day.

The first anatomical poet seems to have been Girolamo Fracastoro, Italian astronomer, physician, and man of letters, who was born in 1483 and who wrote *Syphilidis, sive morbi Gallicis*. It is medical in subject matter and gave origin to the term, "syphilis." [6] Dr. David Kinloch, a Fletcher contemporary, composed Latin verse entitled *De hominis procreatione,* and accordingly became the first Scotch writer on obstetrics.[7] A third work, *Roberti Grovii carmen de sanguinis circuitu, a Gulielmo Harvaeo Anglo primum invento. Adjecto sunt, miscellaneo quaedam,* published in London in 1685, is strikingly similar to *The Purple Island*. The resemblance lies all in the spirit of the *Carmen,* and not at all in its form or subject matter. The same eagerness for anatomy inspired Grove's work, although it is likely enough that he had never heard of Phineas Fletcher. The *Carmen* describes the vivisection of a dog so minutely that the writer might be jotting down his observations from a chair in the anatomical theater. Although slighter than its predecessor, its scientific information is more advanced. The greater enlightenment is natural enough, since the *Carmen* was written seventy-four years later. Our poem is on a larger scale, is better known, and more capably written than any of these. It is the climax of a little genre of Renaissance literature.

Of more importance to our purpose is the fact that the anatomical cantos were likewise a normal expression of Fletcher's scientific temperament. Perhaps this interest has gone unnoticed because of the superstitions which are met frequently in the poet's pages, and which might deceive the reader. As a psychologist, Fletcher

[6] See an unsigned article entitled "Fracastorius," *British Medical Journal,* September 18, 1926.
[7] See R. C. Buist's "Dr. David Kinloch," *British Medical Journal,* May 1, 1926.

allowed himself to believe that a lunatic was possessed with legions of devils; [8] and as a natural scientist, he subscribed to the age-old concept of the four elements.[9] He accepted such impossible animal lore as the fable attached to the pelican,[10] a bird said to feed her young upon her own blood. He was even assured of the existence of witches and of their prophetic powers.[11] Credence in witchcraft and persecution of old hags are two different matters, and certainly Fletcher must not be classed with a minister like Cotton Mather. One is not to be blamed, however, for questioning whether this gullible young Cantabrigian had a proper scientific attitude. In the modern sense of the term he had not, but our knowledge of Sir Thomas Browne and even of William Harvey reminds us that superstition and enlightenment dwelt in conjugal intimacy during the seventeenth century. The *Pseudodoxia epidemica* was a sort of mixed frenzy which could simultaneously slay and nurture vulgar errors. Similarly *The Purple Island* is able to repeat the grossest delusions, and yet we shall find it to be a manifesto of the new inductive science.

We have more than the anatomical cantos to demonstrate that Fletcher had this scientific bent, because astronomy, a pseudo chemistry, and the natural sciences provide a notable amount of illustrative material throughout his writings. Despite the fact that the devotional prose tracts do not lend themselves to such inclusions, their author insists upon them. It was a strange harvest within the walls of a Cambridge that, for the most part, had become giddy with philosophical and logical disputation.

Next to anatomy the poet's chief interest was astronomy, and his pages are alight with the glow of stars and planets. True enough, he was a Ptolemaist, but one scarcely expects Copernican views in poetry older than *Paradise Lost* by fifty years. In addition to several references to the planets,[12] we come upon a lengthy and well-informed discussion of the magnitudes of heavenly bodies.[13] The reader is put in mind of Milton, when *The Apollyonists* describes the moon as the "Florentine's new world." [14] Since Galileo began

---

[8] *The Way to Blessednes*, p. 137.   [9] *The Purple Island*, I, st. 41-42.
[10] *Ibid.*, VII, st. 3.   [11] *Ibid.*, VII, st. 31.
[12] *Ibid.*, III, st. 9; *The Apollyonists*, V, st. 20-21; *The Way to Blessednes*, p. 212.
[13] *The Way to Blessednes*, dedicatory address.
[14] *The Apollyonists*, II, st. 33.

his epochal lunar study only a year or so before the completion of *The Apollyonists,* it is evident that Fletcher was conversant with some of the latest developments in the science. Although he was no specialist in this, as he was in anatomy, his astronomical information and ardor distinguish him from the average writer of his day.[15]

More delightful is the enthusiasm for curious facts from the field of knowledge that lies midway between science and nature lore. Modern natural sciences were without dignity at the time, and the poet would have been astonished to hear his anecdotes about plants and animals described as horticultural, ichthyological, and zoölogical. Nevertheless, in these references we can sense the same curiosity concerning the processes of life that motivated *The Purple Island.* They are scattered so widely throughout his writings that the reader would hardly notice them, but gathered together, they appear important. In *The Way to Blessednes* we come upon a practical discussion of the art of tree-grafting,[16] and elsewhere there are short passages dealing with wild animals.[17] The poet's delight in the sport of angling and his familiarity with the habits of fishes are unmistakable. His verses provide an exposition on the art of fishing for pike with withe traps,[18] a comment upon the habits of the salmon,[19] and a reference to the training of an otter to assist the fisherman like a hunter's retriever.[20] Here is the revelation of a pleasant

[15] A passage in *Sicelides,* written in 1615, is of little or no value as proof of the poet's inclination toward astronomy:

> "First ah first the holy Muse
> Rapt my soules most happy eyes,
> Who . . .
> . . . learne those sacred misteries,
>
> .   .   .
>
> The flowing of the sea and Moone
> And ebbe of both, and how the tides
> Sinke in themselves and backward run.
> How palled Cynthia closely slides,
> Stealing her brother from our sight."
> *Sicelides,* II, chorus, lines 13-23.

The lines appear to mean that the poet studied this science with some zeal and at an early age. Actually, they are a literal translation from Vergil's *Georgics* (II, lines 475-86). It is possible, of course, that Fletcher seized upon the Vergilian passage because he recognized it as more or less true of his own experience.

[16] *The Way to Blessednes,* p. 131.
[17] "Elisa," I, st. 1; *The Purple Island,* XI, st. 25, 31-32.
[18] *The Purple Island,* I, st. 55.   [19] *Piscatorie Eclogs,* V, st. 3.
[20] *Sicelides,* III, 3.

and human phase of the clergyman's personality, which has lain half-buried beneath the theology and allegory of his works. During his visits in London, he may have stretched his legs up Tottenham Hill while walking toward Ware with Piscator. Certainly we now understand more clearly why he had so many warm friends.

The poet even exhibits an inclination toward chemistry, still-born because the science was as yet nonexistent. Alchemy had been more or less discredited, and Robert Boyle was unborn. Neverthe-less we find the same curiosity prying into the elements and their interrelations,[21] where it could express itself only in questioning and wonder. If *The Purple Island* had never been written, it could still be asserted that its author had a scientific turn of mind. It was the most natural thing for his type of intellect to produce an ana-tomical poem. Another circumstance corroborates this conclusion. Fletcher's ardor for physiological studies, instead of being a ca-price of the several years surrounding 1609, had its inception in his early youth and continued into his late middle age. Not only was he interested in science in general, but he was long captivated by anatomy in particular.

"Anni temporum mutationes, variorum causa morborum," an insignificant item of *Sylva Poetica,* alone provides a clue to the year of Fletcher's first interest in matters anatomical. Like in form to Milton's "Naturam non pati senium," it is obviously a responsion or opponency, and thus the author composed it for the commence-ment exercises of some year between 1604 and 1607, certainly be-fore he had turned twenty-three. The thirty-one lines deal with the effects of the seasons upon human health, an inquiry that is dis-tinctly physiological. There can be little doubt that the author was influenced by Hippocrates' *Aphorisms,* an extensive section of which [22] catalogues the various maladies caused by seasonal changes. What is more, Fletcher's imitation, though less thorough than its model in enumerating ailments, follows it with some fidelity. For instance, Fletcher, instead of welcoming the spring for her yellow cowslips and pale primroses, warns against her "mille papulae" and her equally numerous "exanthemata." The Hippocratic vernal

---

[21] *The Apollyonists,* I, st. 14; II, st. 11; IV, st. 5; V, st. 22-25; *The Purple Island,* I, st. 41-42; II, st. 35; IV, st. 29; VIII, st. 5; IX, st. 16; *Sicelides,* V, 5, lines 137-39.
[22] *Aphorisms,* pp. 66-68.

season also dances in, attended by a large company of diseases, but among them are "impetigines" and "pustulae ulcerosae," which are the same as Fletcher's "papulae" and "exanthemata." The *Aphorisms* stood among the first books on the reading list of the seventeenth-century medical student, and thus Fletcher, while still a pensioner, may have entertained the idea of becoming a physician. At any rate, *The Purple Island* was the fruit of a considerable period of reading and thought.

It is likewise significant that Fletcher's interest in physiology stayed with him far into his Hilgay years. In his *Joy in Tribulation* he wrote of "ill humours which through distemper either of ayre and dyet have crept in upon us," and recommended for them various "Physicall purgations." [23] These included a "sowre sallat" which, he says, is good for the melancholy man, Robert Burton's "miserabilis homuncio." He dedicated *Joy in Tribulation* to Sir Walter Robarts and to the welfare of the spirit, yet he found it difficult to forget the old house of mortality. Throughout, one notes the author's fondness for analogies between the spiritual and the bodily functions. The most significant of these is his reference to the head and heart, that yield "animall spirits; which being sent by them and diffused into every particular member, quicken, and move it." [24] Thus he still adhered to his early belief in the false doctrine of the three spirits, despite the fact that it had been largely discredited. He had not kept in touch with physiological discovery during his later life, nor had he renovated his anatomical system along with his spelling and punctuation. But he was a prisoner to the mud and water of the fenland, where he had no chance of knowing about the discoveries of Borelli, Wirsung, and their fellows. On the other hand, he did maintain his interest in the subject for at least twenty years after the completion of his masterpiece. There can be no doubt that the mechanics of the human body was one of the profound intellectual curiosities of Fletcher's entire life.

To all appearances, Fletcher was an unscientific poet-clergyman (we have found that his temperament was distinctly scientific), who could only have acquainted himself with anatomy by means of the conventional, outmoded authorities. He studied in a university

[23] *Joy in Tribulation*, pp. 1-2.
[24] *Ibid.*, p. 202.

criticized by Milton for its medievalism,[25] and his England of 1600 was reputed to be one thousand years behind Italy in anatomical enlightenment.[26] His anatomical knowledge must have been outworn, but we shall learn that an amazing amount was as modern as the Paduan dissection theater. Attaching discovery dates to the various details—the vermiform appendix or the aqueduct of Sylvius, for example—of the human structure, as it was presented in *The Purple Island,* is the crux of the entire problem. The first task is the ascertaining of the true intent of each detail, and to this end it will be necessary to analyze the five cantos systematically. Instead of a precise anatomical text, we are confronted with science in allegorical poetry, which offers a perilous footing, and where the highly colored phraseology will often suggest more than the reader has any right to infer. With care, however, I believe we can avoid the pitfalls, because *The Purple Island* anatomy is clarified by concise prose marginals. Once Fletcher's meaning is established, we shall be in a position to consider when the fact in question was discovered. Finally it will be necessary to seek out the immediate sources of the poet's information.

During the seventeenth century, the situation in the related fields of anatomy and physiology was in certain respects analogous to that in the study of astronomy. Most of the sidereal knowledge of the era belonged to the old-fashioned or Ptolemaic school of thought, and the great majority of Fletcher's contemporaries were Ptolemaists; not that they had read Ptolemy—they were simply the victims of the errors to which he had given currency. A Jacobean might have gathered his astral conceptions from any one of ten thousand sources, because until 1530 practically every writer for a millennium had been Ptolemaic. The same traditional school was to be found in anatomy, where it was called the Galenist. It clung to

[25] Milton's "Of Education."

[26] Such is the opinion of the authorities on the early history of anatomy in England. For this and subsequent remarks on the state of anatomical, physiological, and medical studies in Elizabethan and Jacobean England, I am principally indebted to Foster's *Lectures,* Singer's *Evolution of Anatomy,* Herringham's "Life and Times of Dr. William Harvey" (a series of articles), Griffiths' "Shakspere and the Practise of Medicine" (an article), Wyatt's *William Harvey,* Da Costa's *Harvey and His Discovery,* Gunther's *Early Science in Oxford* (Vol. III), Allbutt's *Science and Medieval Thought,* and Larkey's "The Vesalian Compendium of Geminus and Nicholas Udall's Translation" (article).

the principles laid down by the Greek physician in the second century of the Christian era. Unfortunate it is that such stigma has gathered about the term "Galenist," since Claudius Galen was a splendid scientist who experimented in the Baconian manner. As in astronomy, so in anatomy we cannot assume that a Jacobean who was stuffed with the traditional doctrines had read them in their ancient author. Practically every anatomical writer from the third to the fourteenth century repeated, parrotwise, the ideas of the Greek master. The analogy with astronomy is not complete, for in anatomy there was no Copernicus. Galileo, Kepler, and other captains of the Renaissance who sailed the uncharted seas of the sky, were known as Copernicans. They believed in the concepts of a man who, with solitary strength, had torn apart the epicycles and had shattered the spheres. On the other hand, the transition from Galenism to modern physiology was accomplished by slow and painful accretion, by the fragmentary discoveries of many individuals. Only after several centuries of such advance was it clear that man's understanding of "the purple island" had undergone as great a revolution as his comprehension of the heavens.

All of the foregoing will determine how the anatomical details of *The Purple Island* are to be estimated. The poem was composed when anatomical progress had reached a stage where there was no gray—a man's thinking was black or white. He was either a blind worshiper at the altars of tradition, or he countenanced experiment and the new. If it can be proved that Phineas Fletcher accepted Renaissance and anti-Galenist theories, we will have found in him the open mind which has been the secret of all the progress in anatomy from the day of Mundinus to our own. The reader cannot expect innovations on every page of the poem, because at the time there had not been that many discoveries. He must be prepared to meet much of the traditional, but then Galen is often present in the writings of the greatest Renaissance anatomists—Fabricius, Vesalius, and William Harvey.

Fletcher begins his poem with the common structural features of the body: namely, skin, flesh, fat, muscles, and bones. He describes the flesh as blood indifferently dried, and the skin as a mixture of the seed and blood. He defines the cuticle that covers it as the means of touching. The poet now digresses into an elaborate exposition of the mythical four humors, and the effect of each—the melancholy, the phlegmatic, the choleric, and the sanguine—upon the color of the skin.[27] The allusion to the humors is the first diagnostic, and by such, as they appear every so often throughout *The Purple Island,* it will become possible to date the ultimate origins of the poet's material. Our criteria are of two sorts, the fundamental principles of Galenism, like this matter of the humors, and the doctrines of the new age, the era that began close to 1500. The poet has more or less hidden these clues beneath his mountains, kitchens, rivers, pipes, and the other geographical and mechanical stuff of his allegory. The belief in humors prejudices us, since it temporarily establishes the author as a Galenist.

Continuing, we learn that the fat springs from the airy portion of the blood, serves as a defense against bruises, and maintains the heat of the inward parts.[28] In emphasizing temperature, Fletcher has provided us with a second diagnostic, because the earliest Greeks taught that the working principle of the living body was heat. Galen's explanation of cardiac action was founded upon the high temperature which he attributed to the inner chambers of the heart.[29]

The lacteals are rather curiously combined with the skin and fat in the poet's treatment. He says that the peritoneum has many holes through which the "veins, arteries, and other needfull vessels might have passage." [30] By "other needfull vessels" he probably means the lacteals. This was the one trace of modernity credited to Fletcher by Pohlman, who stated that these ducts were discovered by Gaspar Aselli in 1622. Actually *The Purple Island* was completed in 1611, and Herophilus described the lacteals in 300 B.C.

It has been a poor beginning, because so far Galenism has given way only to pre-Galenism, to material no more advanced than that of Aristotle and the first Greek anatomists. Of course this discussion of the tissues is a slight section of *The Purple Island,* and further-

[27] *The Purple Island,* II, 17, marg. o.
[28] *Ibid.,* II, 19, marg. r.
[29] Both Foster's *Lectures* and Singer's *Evolution of Anatomy* provide an analysis of the beliefs held by the Galenist, or traditional school, in medieval and Renaissance anatomy.
[30] *The Purple Island,* II, st. 22, marg. u.

more the Renaissance had made no progress in the field. Not until chemistry and the microscope were united in a common effort did dermatology become a science.

Similarly the problem of muscular motion was not solved until Borelli's work in 1622, and it was again the microscope which made possible the accomplishment. Earlier scientists, even the leaders of the new school like Fabricius, accepted the superstition that the nerves carried animal spirits which provoked the muscle fibers, which, in turn, produced a contraction of the sinew. If muscular motion remained a mystery, at least the individual muscles had been catalogued with great accuracy. Galen described three hundred of them, and this account has been called the best part of his work. Fletcher falls far short of the Greek physician. He does not attempt to explain the operation of the organ, but that is characteristic of *The Purple Island,* which, for the most part, avoids physiology in favor of anatomy. He states that the muscle is dry or cold, and is made by the virtue generative through the heat of the thicker portion of the seed. He mentions eight muscles of the abdomen and sixty-five of the thorax, although he does not name or treat any of these individually.

What little is said about the bones in *The Purple Island* is similarly old-school. The author traces them to much the same origin as the muscles: they are dry or cold, and are made by the virtue generative, etc. With the exception of several parts of the cranium, Fletcher does not describe, does not even name, a bone of the human skeleton. In contrast to this meagerness, Galen gave an elementary but accurate accounting of almost all the bones, and the sixteenth-century anatomists, like Vesalius, went into the greatest of detail in cataloguing them.

Now that we are ready to pass on to Fletcher's presentation of the digestive, circulatory, and nervous systems, the worst has been said about the anatomical material of *The Purple Island.* The author has given us scraps of Galenism in his discussion of the structural tissues and organs, but some allowance must be made for the form of his work. Do we demand that he name and classify each of the three hundred muscles set down by Galen and the two hundred odd bones pictured by the artist, Vesalius? Fletcher's meagerness is clearly the result of poetic judgment. because in

this district of the isle thoroughness and artistry were interexclu-
sive. The digestive, circulatory, and nervous systems, on the other
hand, held dramatic possibilities. With them there was no listing
of score upon score of uniform items; rather they offered sequence, suspense, and climax. Fletcher rose to the challenge, and
the first half of *The Purple Island* became a work of art as well as
of science. In our present analysis, it is fairer to judge his familiarity with anatomy on the basis of his treatment of the three great
organizations where he could entertain completeness and sym-
metry at the same time.

The first of the major systems in Fletcher's arrangement is the
digestive, but along with it he discusses the ventral organs not
directly connected with the processes of assimilation. Had his
material been one unbroken chain of the best Renaissance knowledge—and it would be absurd to expect as much—the reader
would still be amused by its blunders. The Renaissance had no
chemistry, and even an elementary understanding of the digestive
organs is dependent upon the test tubes and formulae of the sister
science. One sixteenth-century alchemist, Paracelsus, suspected its
importance in bodily functions; but Vesalius, with all his clear-
sightedness, deemed Paracelsus a charlatan. Fletcher calls the pancreas the "all flesh" and says it acts as a pillow to support the
stomach and the veins that are spread from the gate or portal vein.
Here is a physiology that is comic enough. Still none of his coevals
knew any more about the gland, the function of which was not
determined until 1643, when Wirsung discovered its duct. In
1610 the ventral cavity was like a contemporary map with many
a tract labeled "Terra incognita."

Fletcher tells us that the stomach is a kitchen and the ventral
organs are its sinks and sewers, with Concoction the ruler of all
that nether region. The reader is at first inclined to think Galen
the real lord. The poet talks about the concoction of the meat,
the perfecting of the chyle, and the three excremental liquors
that are drawn off: one that is too light and fiery, a second that is
too earthy, and a third that is too wheyish. Such were Galen's
dicta on assimilation, handed on to the Arab physicians, thence
down through the Middle Ages, to be generally accepted during
the seventeenth century. One of Fletcher's conceptions seems to

have been borrowed directly from Galen's *On the Natural Faculties,* which insisted upon "the digestive faculty in the stomach." [31] The poet explains the same functioning as the result of "an innate propertie and speciall vertue." [32]

The two cities of Hepar and Splenion, the liver and spleen, are also largely under the suzerainty of Greece. The liver, we are told, is appointed to contain, concoct, and distribute the blood; all the fluid that runs in the veins springs from it; and, in addition, it yields three poisonous liquors: a choleric, an earthy, and a wheyish, which are drawn to the gall, the spleen, and the kidneys respectively—again that pervasive error of the humors. The spleen is notable as the seat of melancholy, and it attracts an earthy humor from Hepar, the liver. One of the first hints that Galen is not the unbridled tyrant of "the purple isle," comes in the form of an omission. The old school held a curious belief concerning the veins which link the stomach and the liver. They thought of them as tidal estuaries, capable of a two-way flow, sometimes carrying chyle from the stomach and intestines to the liver, and then reversing themselves to convey a venous nutriment from Hepar back to Koilia and its pipes.[33] Although the poet did not repeat this fantasy, there remains much in the furnishings of his kitchen that was out of date.

His presentation of the bladder and genitals suffers from another fault, a mincing modesty. With him they were indecent topics, to be avoided after several words:

> From thence with blinder passage, (flying name)
> These noysome streams a secret pipe conveys.
> *The Purple Island,* II, st. 26.

Nowhere else is Fletcher so much the clergyman-moralist and so little the scientist. *Paradise Lost* provides a model of dignity to the poet who would deal with such subjects, and when measured by this Miltonic standard, Fletcher is found wanting.

On the other hand, he has no shame about the umbilical vessels, which he explains with great thoroughness.[34] He describes

[31] Galen's *On the Natural Faculties,* I, 4.
[32] *The Purple Island,* II, st. 34, marg. k.
[33] Galen's *On the Natural Faculties,* III, 13.
[34] *The Purple Island,* II, 23, marg.

the nurse, the two arteries, the ourachos, and the amnion, all of which is apt to be unduly impressive. From the Greeks on, a particular interest was taken in the processes of the body during parturition and pregnancy, functions which soon were understood accurately. Galen described each of the organs mentioned by Fletcher; and the sixteenth-century anatomist, Fabricius, in his *On the Formed Foetus,* treats the subject more thoroughly than either Fletcher or Galen. Though it is impossible to credit *The Purple Island* with any Renaissance umbilical discoveries, we must admit its information to be admirably detailed.

One citizen of Koilia is to all appearances a fellow of no moment, and the author passes him off as a little groom. He proves to be more important than any of the dignitaries who rule the great provinces of the isle, because he is an alien in the land, an undeniable child of the Renaissance who has wandered into what seems to be a world of Galenism. In Fletcher's marginal note, he is identified as "Vas breve, or the short vessel, which sending in a melancholy humour, sharpens the appetite." [35] These short branches of the splenic artery and vein were a discovery of the new age.[36] Not that the little serving-man was the only one of his kind on the island, nor that he was a true alien. We shall find him one of a fully naturalized group of citizens, but because he is the first mentioned, he is outstanding. He appears early in the second canto; and when the poet's critics came upon "Vas breve," they might have recognized his racial traits—then *The Purple Island* would not have been called the flotsam and jetsam of medieval science.

There are other modernisms in the section of the poem devoted to the ventral organs. There can be little doubt that the poet intends the vermiform appendix in his description of the intestines, though he is not altogether explicit: "The first of the baser is called blinde: at whose end is an appendant, where if any of the thinner chyle do chance to escape, it is stopt, and by the veins of the midriffe suckt out." [37] Jacobus Berengarius, who died in 1530, was the

[35] *Ibid.,* st. 32, marg. h.

[36] See Herringham's "Life and Times of Dr. William Harvey." Herringham (p. 122) quotes Seth Ward's *Vindicia academiarum* (1654), where the author lists certain "modern" discoveries including the "vas breve."

[37] *The Purple Island,* II, st. 42, marg. q.

discoverer of the organ.[38] Fletcher's delineations of what he calls the "epiploon" and the "mesenterium" also have about them traces of inductive science:

> The first from over-swimming takes his name,
> Like cobweb-lawn woven with hundred stripes, *etc.*
> *The Purple Island,* II, st. 45.

The marginal note carries the description further: "Epiploon (or Overswimmer, descends below the navill; and ascends above the highest entrails, of skinny substance all interlaced with fat." [39] "The Mesenterium (or midst amongst the entrails, whence it takes the name) ties and knits the entrails together: it hath a double tunicle." [40] As far as can be determined, no equally accurate accounts of the gastrocolic omentum and the mesentery are to be found prior to those of Vesalius.[41]

If there were but one or two fragments of Renaissance discovery in *The Purple Island,* it might be argued that their presence was more or less accidental. They are appearing, however, with considerable frequency, and thus constitute a fundamental element in the poem. At the same time they imply a sympathy for experimental science in its author.

These convictions are strengthened when we quit the lowlands for that double Nephros mountain. The poet's exposition of the kidneys is not only Renaissance, but also suggests that he was familiar with a fact supposed to be unknown until considerably after his death:

> The third bad water, bubbling from this fountain,
> Is wheyish cold, which with good liquors meint,
> Is drawn into the double Nephros mountain;
> Which suck the best for growth, and nourishment:
> The worst, as through a little pap, distilling
> To divers pipes, the pale cold humour swilling,
> Runs down to th' Urine-lake, his banks thrice daily filling.
> *The Purple Island,* III, st. 20.

[38] Singer's *Evolution of Anatomy,* p. 97.
[39] *The Purple Island,* II, st. 45, marg. x.
[40] *Ibid.,* marg. y.
[41] Fletcher's description seems to be as capable as that of Vesalius, which Ball finds both modern and admirable (Ball's *Andreas Vesalius,* p. 108).

I add the marginal note on the foregoing passage: "The Ureters receive the water separated from the bloud, as distilled from little fleshie substances in the kidneys, like to teats." The author's word for the functioning of the kidneys, namely distillation, implies a better knowledge of the nephritic glands than was owned by Galen, Mundinus, or Vesalius, each of whom believed that the urine was literally filtered off." [42] Vesalius thought of the glands as two sieves, and represented them as such diagrammatically. I do not see how Fletcher's "distillation" can be a loose or figurative synonym for filtration, particularly when it far more aptly describes the elaboration and elimination that actually goes on in these organs.[43] Possibly in 1610 more was known about the working of the kidneys than medical historians have indicated.

We pass from the ventral regions of the island to the imperial city of Kerdia and its neighbor, Pneumon—that is, to the heart, lungs, circulatory and respiratory systems. At the same time, our investigation becomes still more of an adventure. In 1610 knowledge concerning this section of human anatomy was in the process of complete upheaval, a revolution in thinking that was to alter all physiology. Fletcher's cantos were written in the years when William Harvey was doing the research and compiling the notes which made possible the heroic publication—*Exercitatio de motu cordis et sanguinis in animalibus.*

There has never been a hint of a connection, personal or otherwise, between Fletcher and Harvey. None the less, I began the survey of Kerdia with eagerness, because I hoped to find some broken reflections from Harvey's light, some gleams of the principle of circulation, but I met with temporary disappointment. Two factors seemed to rob the situation of all its promise. The first was that Harvey left Cambridge for Padua in 1598, whereas Phineas Fletcher was admitted to King's on August 25, 1600. A bare two years separated the authors of *The Purple Island* and the *Exercitatio* at Cambridge, but so far as I could see, it might as well have

---

[42] Foster's *Lectures*, p. 101.

[43] In the marginal note on the kidneys, Fletcher alludes to "little fleshie substances like to teats." He is undoubtedly referring to the Malpighian pyramids. I have not been able to determine whether or not the ancients and medievalists had seen and described these pyramids. At least it shows Fletcher to be admirably familiar with his subject.

been a hundred. Then I was discouraged by *The Purple Island* itself, wherein Fletcher steadily hammered upon the Galenist doctrines of blood flow. Further study of the poem, however, disclosed a scientist who rebelled against Galen's tyranny over Kerdia, as well as the other precincts of the isle. Here, too, a mass of traditional material was crowding down important lumps of Renaissance leaven. Familiarity with Harvey's life, his kinsmen, and his companions, revealed that a personal connection between the poet and the scientist was not alone possible but almost probable. Thus we quit the shores of the island for an unexplored part of Fletcherian biography, which may give us the key to Kerdia, the imperial city.

All along it has been a temptation to seek the source of the poet's unusual anatomical interest in some relative or friend. The list of his intimates, as well as it can be formulated, offers the name of no anatomist, no scientist, and not even of a physician. On the other hand, there is an outer circle of acquaintances, a group of persons bound to his biography by ties that are both indefinite and indubitable. Almost any one of the individuals in the group might have been more intimate with Fletcher than surviving evidence indicates. Furthermore there is no denying that a man's whole life can be inspired and directed by the view of a noble soul, even at a distance. Neither of the transcendent scientific spirits of the Jacobean era has been hitherto connected with the poet, and yet both are found in the shadowy outer regions of his acquaintanceship.[44] The first, Sir Francis Bacon, was attached closely to Fletcher's father and was the patron who guided and employed the younger Giles throughout his later life. The second, William Harvey, was the greatest Renaissance physiologist, and either or both of these immortals may have aroused the interest in human anatomy and the passion for experimental science that created *The Purple Island*.

It has already been stated that Harvey left Caius College in 1598 for Padua. He returned to England in 1602 and, so far as we know, resided in the London which Fletcher frequented between

[44] I might have included a third person, but I hesitated to mention him, important Jacobean as he was, in the same breath with Bacon and Harvey. There is reason for believing that Sir Henry Wotton had an interest in science. In 1610 John Wodderburn, a Scotch student of Galileo, wrote to Sir Henry with reference to the compound microscope and its use. Fletcher's connection with Wotton has already been discussed.

1602 and 1610 during his holidays. Furthermore Harvey was not only a young alumnus with the usual desire to return to the scenes and friendships of his university days, but he was also a dissector carrying on the traditions taught him at Caius. As such, he would have adequate reasons for going up to Cambridge during the years when the poet was in residence. An acquaintance between the two was physically possible. Add to this the fact that Harvey attended Sir Francis Bacon in the capacity of physician and visited Percival Willoughby at Derby as a friend (Percival Willoughby of Wollaton Hall, famous obstetrician, was related to the Willoughbys of Risley, Fletcher's patrons), and the inquiry takes on interest.[45]

The vital link between Harvey and Fletcher is not to be found in either Bacon or the Wollaton Willoughbys, but in a more obscure associate of the poet, Lewis Roberts. His little encomium was among the complimentary verses that introduced *The Purple Island,* where it was entitled, "To The Unknown Mr. P.F. Upon Survay of his Isle of Man." The opening words, "To The Unknown," were composed in huge letters, as if to warn off those who would seek a connection between the writer and "Mr. P.F." The anatomical poem, however, was published without the author's name, and Quarles' commendatory verses suggest that he and the other admirers had been instructed to preserve its anonymity. Subsequent students seem to have been thrown off the track by these professions of unacquaintance. Oddly enough, Roberts' peculiar emphasis of the word, "unknown," may be irony, and therefore an indication that he was well acquainted with the author. He must have been bound to Fletcher in some fashion, because otherwise his rhymed couplets would never have found their way to these island shores.

Harvey had five brothers, each of whom was a prosperous London merchant. It was a concentration of specialized ability similar to the strain of poetic genius which ran strong in John Fletcher, Dr. Giles Fletcher, the younger Giles, and Phineas. Thomas Harvey was born in 1585, Daniel in 1587, Eliab in 1590, and the twins, Michael and Matthew in 1593. The eldest two, Thomas and Daniel, succeeded notably, became very rich, and were famous

---

[45] These and subsequent facts about William Harvey and his family have been derived largely from Herringham's "Life and Times of Dr. William Harvey" and from Willis' *Works of William Harvey* (the latter has a valuable memoir).

within the countinghouses, upon the exchanges, and along the wharves of the city. Thomas must have begun his apprenticeship close to 1600, a date that will assume importance, and Daniel not long afterward. These two were later characterized as "farmers of the preëmption of Tynne," although their business seems to have been more varied than that would suggest. In June, 1624, Daniel was already a freeman of the East India Company; and in 1628, Eliab, Michael, and Matthew were admitted to the same privileges. Lewis Roberts was the apprentice of Thomas Harvey.

The bond between Roberts and the brothers was very close—that much is certain. He was born in 1596, came to London from Beaumaris in Anglesey, and in 1617 sought service with the East India Company. Six years later, when he applied for admission to the Levant Company, he was described as an apprentice of Thomas Harvey, lately deceased. After his brother's death, Daniel had refused to pay a fine to the company, and in consequence the young man's application was denied. Probably he began his apprenticeship closer to 1610 than 1623. In December, 1625, Daniel Harvey met his obligation, Roberts was made a freeman of the company, and began a rapid rise. Five years later he was appointed assistant, one of the court of directors, and in 1632/3 he became husband, *i. e.*, secretary and manager. He was the author of several works on trade: *The Merchant's Map of Commerce*, 1638; *Warfare Epitomized*, 1640; and *The Treasure of Traffic*, 1641. His daughter, Delicia, married John Nelson and gave birth to Robert Nelson, the divine. The veteran merchant was buried at St. Martin's Outwich on March 12, 1640/1. He dedicated his first book, *The Merchant's Map of Commerce*, to the Harveys in the following words:

to the thrice worthy and worshipful William Harvey, Dr. of Physic, John Harvey Esq., Daniel Harvey, Mercht., Michael Harvey, Mercht., Matthew Harvey, Mercht., Brethren, and John Harvey, Mercht., onely sonne to Mr. Thomas Harvey, Mercht., deceased.

It is evident that if Phineas Fletcher knew Roberts with any degree of intimacy, he had access to some or all of the Harvey brothers.

Our information about the importer is not so full as we might like, but the place and date of his birth, the identity of his wife, and other pertinent facts are on record. In none of these is there an indication as to why he was the author of a commendatory poem on *The Purple Island*. True enough, he had a friend in Izaak Walton, through whom he could have come to know the poet, but there is more reason for thinking that one of the Harveys was the go-between. In other words, it is possible that Fletcher was acquainted with the anatomist's family before he met their apprentice, that what we have assumed to be a cause was an effect. The brothers came out of Folkstone, twenty miles from Cranbrook, and their mother, Joan Halke, was born in Hastingleigh, removed by only fifteen miles from the poet's birthplace. It is not inconceivable that the two families, the Fletchers and the Harveys, were friendly before they went up to London, or that arriving in the metropolis at about the same time, were drawn together by Kentish ties. Of equal significance is the elder Giles Fletcher's place on the contemporary map of commerce, to use Roberts' figure. No man was more intimately associated with all phases of England's foreign and domestic trade than Fletcher, the remembrancer of the city and the ambassador for the Merchant Adventurers. Had he lived until 1620 when the Harveys became barons of trade, there could now be little question of his acquaintance with them. Although he died when the eldest Harvey mercer was only twenty-five, it is still possible that Thomas or Daniel was apprenticed to some one of his friends, and that Phineas Fletcher was thus brought into contact with the discoverer's family and later with their employee, Roberts.

All this has been a case of pyramiding conjecture upon conjecture, but there is a chance, and an intriguing one, that the authors of *The Purple Island* and *Exercitatio de motu cordis et sanguinis in animalibus* were on speaking terms. If the two works were utterly remote from each other, the foregoing would be idle, but the little island is just offshore. From its high buildings and hilltops, the mainland of the *Exercitatio* is plainly visible.

At the same time, the lower levels of Kerdia are littered with relics of the old régime, the Galenist empire that had passed. Thus it becomes necessary to set down the classical doctrines and then to trace the various steps of discovery to the time of Harvey's pronouncement. As in other phases of anatomy, the truth about circulation was learned only after a tedious hundred years' war upon the forces of error. At times it seems very natural that Fletcher devoted the latter half of his poem to a battle between the vices and the ultimately triumphant virtues. Our survey will not be easy, because the circulatory system has been one of the most disputed fields in the history of anatomy. Other scientists saw the verities dimly before Harvey flooded them with light, and there have been many spiteful and nationalistic attempts to rob him of his glory.

To Galen and his followers, the lungs were a sort of glorified chimney, serving the purposes of refrigeration and ventilation. Their first function was to carry off the fumous superfluities from the heart; the second, to draw down cool air, which would both temper the all-important heat of the organ and take part in the generation of the vital spirit in the left ventricle. In their ignorance, the ancients could only describe the substance of the lungs as parenchyma, which was an impressive word, like the phlogiston of the chemists, meaning nothing. It was not until the mid-seventeenth century that Malpighi, again aided by the microscope, discovered the minute capillaries and air vesicles.

The Galenist explanation of the heart and blood system was like the image in King Nebuchadnezzar's dream, with head of gold, breast and arms of silver, but feet of clay. The complicated structure was founded upon errors which prevented an understanding of circulation, and which will serve as signposts in our passage along the avenues of Kerdia. The prime mover of the whole contraption was the doctrine of the three spirits, natural, vital, and animal—a sort of holy trinity. The natural spirit, concocted in the liver out of the chyle conveyed there from the intestines, formed the venous blood; and hence the liver was supposed to be the great spring of all the dark-colored blood. From its source, the spirit was carried to the right ventricle. Here it gave off impurities, which passed through the so-called artery-like vein to that ventilating chimney, the lungs. Part of the blood sent to the right ventricle returned upon itself through the valves (known as early as 340 B.C. but supposed to work fitfully), and the remainder trickled through the minute foramina of the septum into the left ventricle. The entirely erroneous theory of the seepage through the mythical pores of the septum, and the equally erroneous but more dangerous delusion of the ebb and flow from the right ventricle, were twin fundamentals of Galen's explanation. So long as they were maintained, a true understanding was impossible, because the old fluctuating, seeping fabrication and Harvey's complete circulation are antagonistic.

The second or vital spirit was manufactured in the left ventricle. The blood, arriving through the septum, was elaborated by the air brought from the lungs along the so-called veinlike artery. The vital spirit was sent out into the arterial system by coronary expansion and contraction, an action caused by the heat which rarefied the contents of the heart. The third or animal spirit was communicated to the blood as it passed through the brain, whence it was emitted along the nerves.

Instead of being the first to attack the old order, William Harvey was the last and greatest of a line of Renaissance scientists who had been peering into the heart, arteries, and veins. They found matters to be different from what Galen had led them to expect: Servetus denied the existence of the foramina of the septum, explaining that the blood passed from the right to the left ventricle by way of the lungs. His *Restitutio Christianismi,* published in 1553, did not influence the anatomists of his day, with one exception. That was Mattheus Columbus who repeated Servetus' views in his *De re anatomica* of 1559, and who is generally accused of plagiarizing the *Restitutio.* Andreas Cesalpinus, in a work published in 1601, expressed much the same opinions. Indeed he seems to have hit upon the idea of the complete circulation from the veins, to the right ventricle, through the lungs, to the left ventricle, through the arteries, and back to the veins. He had no proofs for his hypotheses, which were evidently the product of idle opinion rather than experiment. Hieronymus Fabricius, Harvey's teacher, was fascinated by the little swinging doors of the veins, investigated them, and published his results in his *De venarum ostiolis* of 1574. It was a thorough study of the venous valves, but he failed to recognize the one important implication of his work: that his conclusions and the ebb and flow of the blood were incompatible. His tiny doors had, without his knowing it, closed forever upon the fluctuation theory.

From the supposedly barbarous northern island came Fabricius' pupil, who familiarized himself with these new views, coördinated them, drew his own stunning conclusion, and proved it. Foster has aptly said that Harvey was not so much the discoverer of circulation as its demonstrator. He showed that the vena cava and the pulmonary vein fill the auricles during diastole and that the ventricles empty into the pulmonary artery and the aorta during systole. He was the first to prove that *all* the blood of the right ventricle passed through the lungs, and that there was a complete and constant circulation throughout the entire body. Almost every subsequent step toward an understanding of the human structure was based upon that law. Therefore, although Harvey's discovery dealt with a comparatively small section of the total area of the body, his name is first on the rolls of anatomical achievement. Even though he gave the old falsity its deathblow, it was widely accepted for many years after the publication of the *Exercitatio*.

Such is the pattern into which *The Purple Island* must be fitted. One's first impression is that the author drones out each of the clauses of the timeworn credo. He tells us that the flesh of the lungs is light and spongy, and although he does not actually use the term, that is much the same as calling it parenchyma. He mentions the air they send into the left ventricle. He asserts that the heart gives "out load to the vitall spirits," [46] thereby acknowledging that unholy trinity. Finally he writes in no uncertain terms about the septum, "if it be well viewed, we shall see it full of many pores, or passages." [47]

After seemingly surrendering Kerdia to Galen, he proceeds to reclaim it for Harvey and the Renaissance. Traditionally coronary pulsation had been explained as the result of rarefaction and heat.[48] Fletcher writes, "The flesh of the heart is proper and peculiar to it self, not like other muscles." [49] He seems to have been familiar with the new, muscular explanation of the rhythmical contraction. The poet gives more prominence to the valves than they received in the Galenist texts, and he specifically mentions the tricuspid,[50]

[46] *The Purple Island*, IV, 24, marg. y.
[47] *Ibid.*, 20, marg. r.
[48] Foster's *Lectures*, pp. 12, 57-59.
[49] *The Purple Island*, IV, 17, marg. n.
[50] *Ibid.*, 22.

the mitral,[51] and the semilunar.[52] We have found that even Fabricius, the pioneer of the little doors, believed that every one of the structures allowed an ebb and flow; [53] but Fletcher takes the opposite view: "Here also is the like three-folding doore, made like half-circles; giving passage from the heart, but not backward." [54] All signs point to the conclusion that the poet's understanding of the blood system was much closer to Harvey's than we have heretofore suspected, but the climax is to be found in the following lines:

> Circling about, and wat'ring all the plain,
> Emptie themselves into th' all drinking main;
> And creeping forward slide, but never turn again.
> *The Purple Island,* II, st. 9.

Surely the author of those words had some intimation of the doctrine of complete circulation. The "never turn again" is an unequivocal assertion. The discoverer's great principle has been enunciated by one who may have known him, by one who—as we shall soon find—learned anatomy at the Caius College which had trained Harvey a few years before; yet the science of *The Purple Island* has been tossed off as froth and bubbles, floating upon a stagnant pool of Galenism.

The third of the great systems described in the poem is the nervous, and Pohlman assures us that Fletcher's knowledge of the brain and sensory organs was "undoubtedly drawn from the Greeks." Here, as in other parts of the isle, the reader is confronted with a heterogeneous collection derived from Galenist tradition and Renaissance dissection, but Pohlman's generalization proves most harsh. It is true that among the market-places, courts, caves, and tunnels of the city on Cephal mount, the three spirits have a more complete and malevolent ascendency than anywhere else. According to Fletcher, the sole function of the cerebrum is to manufacture the animal spirit. He avoids the nerves, probably because his knowledge concerning them was meager. After defining them as a spermatical part arising from the brain and conveying the animal spirit, he briefly describes the spinal cord, and then quits the subject.

[51] *Ibid.,* 23.   [52] *Ibid.,* 24.   [53] Foster's *Lectures,* p. 37.
[54] *The Purple Island,* IV, 23, marg. Fletcher gives no indication that he was familiar with the subject of Fabricius' work, the venous valves.

On the other hand, the tide of Renaissance influence has risen even to the top of Cephal mount, where it left several prominent marks. The first is negative in character, a virtue of omission, for Fletcher refuses to admit either the *rete mirabile* or the special functions traditionally assigned to the cerebral ventricles. This mythical network, Galen supposed to be literally an intricate criss-crossing of nerves inside the brain, and also the vital working part of the organ. His followers had never found it, but their master said it was there, and so they all described the structure. That was the way of the medieval anatomical writer, who took not only his religion but also his science on faith. Even Vesalius drew a picture of the wonderful network in 1538; yet not long afterward Berengarius opened the brain, looked for the thing, failed to find it, and had the courage to say so.[55] Fletcher's silence is significant because the *rete* was a picturesque detail admirably suited for allegorical treatment. He might have depicted it as a divine fish net, or as the casement lattice of Intellect's window, or as a maze where little men (the thoughts) wandered like Rosamand.

Even better adapted to the fanciful arrangement of the poem was the long-lived delusion about the functions of the three ventricles. To the first was assigned the seat of sensation, to the second imagination, and to the third memory.[56] What an opportunity for building castles in Spain, with architecture fitted to their tenants—gray, lichen-covered stones for Eumnestes, and many-colored crystal for Phantastes—but they were never erected. Fletcher's failure to repeat these superstitions is an almost sure indication that he had rejected them.

Besides a praiseworthy thoroughness, the poet's account of the brain is lighted by one positive gleam from the new sunlight. He makes a reference to what seems to be the aqueduct of Sylvius, an item of considerable interest, because modern historians think that the cerebral passage was not known until many years after *The Purple Island* was written.[57] Following an orderly description of the three ventricles, these marginal notes appear:

[55] Singer's *Evolution of Anatomy*, p. 97.
[56] Foster's *Lectures*, pp. 256-57.
[57] In his *Lectures on the History of Physiology*, Foster states, "we owe to him [Franciscus Sylvius], it is true, and not to his older namesake, the aqueduct of Sylvius" (p. 147). Franciscus Sylvius was an anatomist of the mid-seventeenth century.

By the third cavitie are two passages; and at the end of the first is the (Infundibulum or) tunnell, under which is (Glans Pituitaria or) the Rheugm-kernell, as a spunge sucking the rheugms, and distilling them into the palate.

The Purple Island, V, 17, marg. n.

The other passage reaches to the fourth cavitie, which yeelds a safe way for the spirits.

The Purple Island, V, 18, marg. o.

The other passage, the "safe way," appears to be the duct to which the name of Franciscus Sylvius has been given. Surely this was an item which he did not take from the Greeks!

The most consistently modern part of the anatomical *Purple Island* is its closing stanzas, devoted to the sensory organs and primarily to the watchtowers of Visus and the caves of Auditus. So full is the author's dealing with these latter precincts, that it contrasts strangely with the slighting sentences paid to Tactus and Gustus. Fletcher had no opportunity to be more courteous, because touch and taste had to await Malpighi's microscope and genius.

In 1610, more was known about the working of the eye, and the poet was abreast of the latest discoveries. He lists correctly the six ocular muscles,[58] his work comparing favorably with that of Vesalius, who erroneously described seven, the extra one being found only in animals.[59] The mistake is a reminder of the obstacles met by these early anatomists in their efforts to secure bodies for dissection. One of them, for example, needed certain bones to complete the skeleton he was setting up for his studies. Repeatedly he went to the public execution place in the deep of night, there to feel through the mouldering corpses for what he sought. *The Purple Island* became possible because men defied such horrors, but it conceals the gruesome scenes and the stenches under a covering of allegory. Fletcher proceeds by mentioning the three humors of the eye: watery, crystalline, and glassy; and the six tunicles: "conjunctive, cornea, uvea, cobweb, reticularis, and glassy." In Galen's expounding of the eye, the chief fallacy, to which his followers and also most of the Renaissance anatomists succumbed, was the assigning of the seat of vision to the crystalline lens. Even Fabricius, who was the

[58] *The Purple Island*, V, 26, marg. z.
[59] Singer's *Evolution of Anatomy*, pp. 126, 132-33.

first to perceive the true form of the crystalline, agreed that it was
the dwelling place of Visus. Johann Kepler corrected the error in
his *Ad Vitellionem, paralipomena* of 1604, where he announced
that the crystalline refracted the rays of light, brought them to a
focal point, and painted the images upon the retina. Fletcher's exposition, designed for the common man, was less technical than the
German astronomer's, but there can be no question that he was
aware of the basic principles of the discovery:

> The fift, Reticularis, netty tunicle, framed of the substance of the
> brain: this diffuseth the visil spirits, and perceives the alteration of the
> crystalline; and here is the mean of sight.
>
> *The Purple Island,* V, 33, marg. k.

The poet explores the caves of Auditus with similar thoroughness, mentioning the tympanum, the ossicles, including the stapes,
the Eustachian tubes, the labyrinth, the cochlea, and the auditory
nerves. One is tempted to praise his familiarity with the cartilagi-
nous tubes named after the Roman physician, Eustachius, who
died in 1574. Actually they were known as early as 500 B.C., but the
stapes was certainly discovered by Ingrassias during the sixteenth
century.[60] It is fitting to find in this last reach of the isle a marker
as substantial as granite, that bears the date, 1548:

> The first an Hammer call'd, whose out-grown sides
> Lie on the drumme; but with his swelling end
> Fixt in the hollow Stithe, there fast abides:
> The Stithes short foot doth on the drumme depend,
> His longer in the Stirrup surely plac't;
> The Stirrups sharp side by the Stithe embrac't,
> But his broad base ti'd to a little window fast.
>
> *The Purple Island,* V, st. 43.

---

[60] Foster's *Lectures,* p. 30.

XII

THE MAGNIFICENT ENTHUSIASM

WE HAVE seen that almost every division of the scientific part of *The Purple Island* contains ancient, Renaissance, and late-Renaissance material. The intermixing of the old and the new is one of the confusing characteristics of the poem, and for it there are several explanations. The author lived in an age when the scales were falling from men's eyes, but they had not quite fallen. Thus the same hodgepodge is found in the writings of the greatest contemporary anatomists. Fletcher was not only a scientist but also a poet, and perhaps his problem was somewhat like that of Milton, who chose the Ptolemaic system for *Paradise Lost,* although he was familiar with the Copernican. We go to the *Exercitatio* or the *De re anatomica* to find, not the traditional, but the novel; passing over the one, we underscore the other. *The Purple Island* may be treated in the same fashion, because it contains a continuous train of Renaissance interpretations that forms the essential substance of the poem. Obviously Fletcher did not make each discovery personally—to demand that were the same as asking him to be a composite Mundinus, Vesalius, Fabricius, Columbus, and Harvey. The facts of his work represent the findings of many investigators. What, then, were the poet's immediate sources?

Having become acquainted with the ultimate origins, we are already a long way on the road to an answer. Galen, Hippocrates, Aristotle, Avicenna, and their commentators can be promptly set aside. These were the authors of volumes frequented by the medical students of the time, although no amount of usage could free their pages from the dust of centuries and error. The new portions of the *Purple Island* anatomy must have been gathered in books of the sixteenth century, if they came from books at all.

The readiest avenue to an author's sources is his own references to other works, but with *The Purple Island* it proves to be a blind alley. In his extensive marginals, Fletcher acknowledges the following authorities, some of them frequently: Hippocrates, Plato, Aristotle, Stratonicus, and Trajan. He also refers to the "Peripateticks," which was the school of the Stagirite, its leaders being Theophrastus of Lesbos, Eudemus and Andronicus of Rhodes, and Strato of Lampsacus. Finally there are allusions to persons whom he calls the "Physicians and Anatomists." [1] It is interesting to know that Fletcher had read in these ancients, but of course the poet's admissions are not of the slightest value in solving our present problem. The prominence given to the gray-bearded fathers of anatomy was for the most part pedantic embellishment, designed to impress the reader. Possibly Fletcher was not so familiar with the Greek writings as he would have us believe. If he had only enlarged upon those allusions to the "Physicians and Anatomists"!

Our last and most promising resort is the sixteenth-century books. We know most of those that Fletcher could have found in the libraries on the banks of the Cam. The reading lists of men like Harvey [2] indicate the authors that were obtainable, and that were deemed worth while: Columbus, Sylvius, Vesalius, Fallopius, Fabricius, Fernelius, Laurentius, Massa, and Bauhin. If the poet's library made any pretense at collecting the anatomies printed in England, and it probably did not, it might have contained Thomas Geminus' plagiary of Vesalius, Udall's later translation of the same, and Bannister's or Vicary's works.

There is no telling whether Fletcher read Vesalius, Fabricius, Columbus, or the other available Renaissance texts, with the single exception of Vicary. Distinct parallelisms of phrasing, organization, or subject matter, between *The Purple Island* and any of these are altogether wanting. On the other hand, it can be said with absolute certainty that the major source for which we are seeking is not to be found among them. No one of the works contains the bulk of *The Purple Island* facts, nor does the poem embrace all or even a significant part of the material in any. It seems

---

[1] In a prose work, Fletcher refers to Vincent of Beauvais, the great author of a medieval compendium of science. Thus Vincent may be viewed as another acknowledged authority for *The Purple Island,* but he was as Galenist and as unenlightened as the others.

[2] Harvey's reading list included the following authors: Aristotle, Galen, Hippocrates, Avicenna, Averroes, Oribasius, Herophilus, Vesalius, Columbus, Fallopius, Fabricius, Bauhin, Fernelius, and Cardano (Malloch's *William Harvey,* pp. 12-13).

impossible that Fletcher could have read them, discriminated between them, and used their substance for his own work without leaving some indication of his processes.

Among these more recent anatomical writings, Thomas Vicary's work alone bears some resemblance to the poem, although it is far from being the fountain head of our quest. *A Profitable Treatise of the Anatomie of Man's Body* was a textbook for medical students that ran into ten editions, a popular work that might have been found in any hall of Cambridge.[3]

There seem to be a few indisputable similarities between the textbook and the poem. Each starts in the same way, because Vicary's opening pages deal with "simple members, the Bones, Cartylages, Nerves, Pannykles, and Lygaments." The two methods of procedure, however, differ immediately, Vicary's passing from the simple members to the head, which is the final division of Fletcher's study. More notable are certain similarities of phrasing:

The Bone is a consimile member, simple and spermatike, and colde and drye of complexion.
> Vicary, *A Profitable Treatise*, p. 18.

Bones are a similar part of the body, most dry, or cold.
> *The Purple Island*, II, 5, marg. a.

The fyrst portion of the Guttes is called Duodenum for he is xii ynches of length.
> Vicary, *A Profitable Treatise*, p. 65.

This is called Duodenum (or twelve finger) from his length.
> *The Purple Island*, II, 40, marg. n.

for to him lyeth ever more the chest of the Gal, beating him sore, and draweth forth of him al the drosse, and clenseth him clene.
> Vicary, *A Profitable Treatise*, p. 65.

and by the way takes in a bitter brook,
That when the chanel's stopt with stifeling mire,
Through th' idle pipe with piercing waters soking,
His tender sides with sharpest stream provoking,
Thrusts out the muddy parts, and rids the miry choking.
> *The Purple Island*, II, st. 40.

---

[3] There may even have been a slight connection, hitherto unrecognized, between Fletcher and the author of *A Profitable Treatise*. Thomas Vicary died close to 1561, but he left behind him a nephew resident in Tenterden, one of the outlying hamlets of Cranbrook.

These likenesses do not go very deep or very far. *A Profitable Treatise* keeps to the main highway of Galenist tradition, and it does not share any of the Renaissance discovery found in *The Purple Island*. Fletcher probably read Vicary's anatomy, but it had only the slightest influence upon his poem.

So long as we seek in books for the fountains of the versified science, our quest will be as fruitless as was Ponce de Leon's. On the other hand, if the poet did not derive his material from the printed page, he may have had it by word of mouth. The only persons in England who could have told him about the aqueduct of Sylvius and the vermiform appendix were the progressive physiologists, and they were not to be found in the libraries. Though William Harvey drew up a reading list for himself, he spent little time thumbing over pages. Where was Harvey and where were his fellow experimentalists? To answer that question, it will be necessary to survey the state of anatomical studies in the England of Fletcher's day.[4]

One is not surprised that the remnants of Galenism are superficially dominant in *The Purple Island* after becoming acquainted with the physicians and medical schools of Renaissance Britain. With them, the Greek author was the oracle who had spoken, and his word was a religion. As late as 1559, Dr. John Geynes was cited before the Royal College of Physicians "for impugning the infallibility of Galen." Almost all of the physicians, and even a large number of the anatomists, held dissection to be a defilement of human hands and an abomination unto Jehovah. During surgical operations and dissections, they stood far enough off to keep their skirts clean and gave orders to some rude boy or barber who wielded the scalpel. The medical arts were a cult open to none but the initiate, and consequently there were almost no books on the subject in English. The inventory of an Edinburgh medico's library, made as late as 1700, revealed only 4 works in the vernacular out of a total of 136 tomes.[5] The men of position, those who dictated the professional codes, who ran the medical courses at the universities, and who held the public eye, were the apostles of Claudius Galen.

[4] See above, p. 176, n. 26.
[5] "A Medical Library Two Hundred Years Ago," by J.W.B., *British Medical Journal*, September 8, 1923.

Beneath all this, and hidden by it, was new life. At the root of its virulence was a single agent—dissection before an audience or, as it was then called, the public anatomy. The whole renaissance in science and the rebirth of physiology were inevitable, when men awoke to a truth expressed by Bacon in the following sentence:

Another error hath proceeded from too great a reverence, and a kind of adoration of the mind and understanding of man; by means whereof men have withdrawn themselves too much from the contemplation of nature and the observations of experience, and have tumbled up and down in their own reason and conceits.

The Advancement of Learning, p. 59.

The pompous professors of the universities and the fellows of the Royal College had tumbled up and down among the conceits of Galen until they were quite out of their wits. It took well over one thousand years for the world to realize that the human body was more like the human body than like Galen's account of it. Those who saw the light ceased tumbling, got their feet on solid ground, and began to anatomize and discover.

The author of *The Advancement of Learning* recognized that dissection, even vivisection, were applications of the inductive method, to which he had devoted *The Great Instauration:*

into the deep, fruitful, and operative study of many sciences, specially natural philosophy and physic, books be not only the instrumentals. . . . some places . . . do likewise command the use of dead bodies for anatomies.

The Advancement of Learning, p. 77.

though the inhumanity of anatomia vivorum was by Celsus justly reproved; yet in regard of the great use of this observation, the inquiry needed not by him so slightly to have been relinquished altogether, or referred to the casual practises of surgery; but might have been well diverted upon beasts alive.

Ibid., p. 106.

The achievements of Vesalius, Servetus, Columbus, Sylvius, Harvey, and all their successors, became possible only after they had resorted to the unpleasant but necessary use of dead bodies and dissection of living beasts. The only men who could have communicated to Fletcher the important facts of his *Purple Island* were not in the libraries, but were in the anatomical theaters.

In England, as elsewhere, the right to dissect had to be established. The practice offended the deep-lying superstitions of the ignorant and the religious principles of their betters. The medieval Church had taught that post-mortem molestation of the body was an abuse, and her commandment survived the Reformation. Although legally permitted in Fletcher's day, dissection was regulated with great strictness. We have reason to be thankful for such stringency, because it makes possible our knowing where and when the poet might have seen such spectacles.

What was evidently the first English law concerning dissection was the license issued by Henry the Eighth in 1540. The Barber Surgeons Company was permitted to anatomize the bodies of four felons each year, and about 1560 it erected a theater for the purpose. The College of Physicians secured the same right, and in London these two held a monopoly on public anatomies. It is true that parliamentary acts were passed, enabling surgeons to dissect with the permission of either of the two monopolists, but they were to perform in privacy.

Considering the prejudice latent in sixteenth-century England, it is somewhat extraordinary that such acts, severely limited as they were, could be got past Parliament and king. Perhaps the part of the scientists was taken by the influential lords, whose curiosity led them to the anatomical theater. Samuel Pepys heard a lecture at Surgeons' Hall and wrote an account of his visit under the date of February 27, 1662/3:

About 11 o'clock, Commissioner Pett and I walked to Chyrurgeon's Hall (we being all invited thither, and promised to dine there); where we were led into the Theatre; and by and by comes the reader, Dr. Tearne, with the Master and Company, in a very handsome manner: and all being settled, he begun his lecture, this being the second upon the kidneys, ureters, etc., which was very fine; and his discourse being ended, we walked into the Hall, and there being great store of company, we had a fine dinner and good learned company, etc.

If what he describes was a dissection as well as a lecture, the diarist had not only an excellent digestion but also some of that insatiable curiosity. Even Charles the Second amused himself by anatomizing with his own hands in the privacy of his closet. Serious medical students were present in the anatomical theaters, but they were outnumbered by the gentlemen and ladies on holiday.

There are engravings depicting the chambers erected for public dissections, solid, sumptuous places with oak paneling. Sharply banked steps run up on all sides from a small area at the bottom, where the table and lecturer's desk are located. The drawings always show a throng of spectators who jostle one another on the stairs, fill the balconies, while Cupids hang and gape from the chandeliers. The last may be a fiction of the artist's imagination, but the fashionable ladies and the fops were real enough. Anatomy theaters were theaters in the fullest sense of the term.

One of Vesalius' beautiful sketches presents the instruments and the table used in the performance. We expect a small number of crude tools, but the variety is amazing. In addition to a saw, mallet, needle and thread, sponges, syphon, and scissors, there are any number of variously shaped scalpels. The table pictured is one used for the vivisection of animals, and accordingly it is provided with a complexity of cords and appropriate holes through which they may be passed in fastening down the unhappy pig or dog. During the Renaissance the ritual of the public dissection underwent an evolution. It began as a two-man affair, the assistant performing upon the body, while the physician read from the work of some famous author. As time went by and new discoveries were made, the professor's eye wandered more and more from his book, until he finally left the book at home and lectured from his notes. Later he began to leave his assistant at home also that he might work with his own hands.

There was no means of preserving the body, and time could not be wasted. It was Harvey's custom to settle beforehand the exact number of minutes he would give to each member and then to adhere rigidly to his schedule. Despite such precautions, there remained olfactory inconveniences. Approximately three days were allotted to the complete anatomizing, with morning and afternoon lectures.

An excellent idea of the discourses may be obtained from the plans laid down by the founders of the Lumleian Lectureship. In establishing their famous foundation at the College of Physicians, Lord Lumley and Dr. Caldwell prescribed a broad and farsighted program: lectures were to be given on two days of the week,

Wednesday and Friday, all the year round, and a definite cycle was plotted out for a six-year period. During the first year, the professor was to deal with the whole art of surgery, with swellings, wounds, ulcers, and bonesetting, and was to dissect the entire body. It is to be presumed that the Wednesday-Friday rule was in abeyance at the time of the latter performance. The second year was marked off for the reading of the more advanced works of surgery and the dissection of the muscles. During the following two years he was to discourse first on wounds, and then on ulcers, and to dissect the head and later a leg and arm. The fifth and sixth years were set aside for an anatomizing to show the bones, the reading of one work—to be selected by the lecturer—and another on surgery and medical knowledge requisite to surgery.

Throughout the period when Fletcher was composing his masterpiece, he made infrequent trips to London, where he could have visited the anatomical theaters at Surgeons' Hall or at the College of Physicians. *The Purple Island,* however, can hardly be the result of half-hearted and occasional adventures; it is rather the fruit of a sustained and unified portion of the writer's life. Apparently Fletcher received his inspiration, gathered his material, and wrote his poem on the bank of the Cam. After completing it, the author could justly boast of the laurels he had set upon the brow of Alma Mater Cantabrigia. If it were possible to prove that public anatomies were regularly given at the university between 1600 and 1610, we should have a clue of the utmost significance.

Our investigation has invariably led us below the surface, for superficially *The Purple Island* was swimming with Galenism and so was the England of 1600, but the heart of each belonged to the new age. The same was true of Cambridge during the poet's residence, but to a still greater degree.[6] In a university, with its youth and freedom from restriction, one would expect a thriving of the new induction. Actually, the distinguished professors and fellows were dumb, deaf, and blind to all the recent achievements in

---

[6] The following works have proved valuable for this study of the state of medical and anatomical investigation at Cambridge during Fletcher's day: Herringham's "Life and Times of Dr. William Harvey"; Cooper's *Annals;* Gunther's *Early Science in Oxford* (Vol. III); Venn's *Annals of Gonville and Caius College, Gonville and Caius College,* and *Biographical History of Caius College.*

physics, astronomy, and the other sciences. The study of physiology and anatomy belonged to the school of medicine, but there the courses were notoriously backward, unpopular, and meager. As late as 1654, John Webster's *Examen academiarum* charged the twin founts of light with teaching nothing but Galen. There are no available Cantabrigian statistics for the period, but from 1571 to 1600 Oxford gave less than fifty medical degrees—men like Harvey had sense enough to go off to Padua for their doctorates. The statutes of Cambridge required the candidate to attend readings on Johannicius, Philaratus' *De pulsibus,* Theophilus' *De urinis,* Isaac, Nicolaus' *Antidotarium,* Galen's *Tegni,* Hippocrates' *Prognostics* and *Aphorisms,* and the *Regimen acutorum.*

The lectures were evidently given by the Regius Professor, the Queen's Reader in Physic, who in 1601 was Sir William Ward. There is no indication, however, that this savant felt the need of tempering his erudition with dissection. It was not until 1623 that a readership in anatomy was endowed at Oxford, with provisions for anatomizing, apparently the first official opportunity of the kind offered by either school. In the poet's day the Queen's Readers were interested not in experimental studies, but in logical and philosophical disputations on subjects like "Mors est malum" or "Anni temporum mutationes, variorum causa morborum." Logomachia of the kind were in high regard as entertainments and drew Queen Elizabeth herself on at least two occasions. Such was the wind and rank mist which the English universities offered the youth who were to be entrusted with the health of the nation.

The foregoing is a glimpse into an intellectual life moldy with the passing of the centuries. Amidst all this decadence, one little anatomy theater, whose size was no measure of its importance, has been overlooked. Buried among the liberties accorded to Gonville and Caius College by a sixteenth-century foundation license is the annual grant of the bodies of two felons. The college statutes set aside the sum of one pound, six, and eightpence to be expended each twelvemonth on the dissections. The cadavers were finally to be interred in St. Michael's, the whole college reverently attending. It is a curious picture—the solemn master, the fellows, and the scholars in their blue gowns giving the last rites to almost every rogue hanged in the county. The brief sequence of regulations and privileges has been regarded as no more than a quaint antiquity, but to us it is by all odds the most significant detail of the world in which Fletcher lived.

In 1557, a bare seventeen years after the Barber Surgeons had acquired from Henry the Eighth the right to perform the first legal dissection in the history of England, a similar allowance was made to an obscure college. Was anything else in the entire life of the university so dynamically progressive? The official university deserves small credit for the advanced views of its college, which had their origin in the mind of one man, John Caius, actually a splendid rebel but considered a fool. The dons suffered him to pursue his crotchets, so-called, because he was independently wealthy and poured his riches into the lap of Alma Mater. He died in 1573 and was buried in the college chapel, but by 1600 experimental investigation had become a tradition in the buildings over his tomb. The little college, designed for pre-medical students, was adjacent to the great foundation of King's. Twice every year a body was dissected, some eighty yards from Fletcher's lodgings.

The positive, short man who came up to Cambridge and reorganized old Gonville seems to have been the real though remote originator of *The Purple Island*. Probably the poet gathered some of his information from the Caius College lectures and was therefore indebted to the scientists who performed the semi-annual dissections between 1600 and 1610. Unfortunately we cannot be certain as to who the demonstrators were, but they may have been Thomas Grimston or John Gostlyn, two fellows of Caius.[7] Grim-

---

[7] A third fellow of Gonville and Caius possibly played a part in Fletcher's biography. John Fletcher, the astrologer, was a notorious member of the university community, and he may have been a distant relative of the poet. He was born at Hebden, Yorks., the son of Thomas, a husbandman. He studied under a Mr. Hargraves at Leeds, and was admitted to Caius as a pensioner on February 5, 1577/8. He was a fellow of the same college from 1587 to 1613. He had a penchant for strange scientific exploits, and also for involving himself in personal scandals. Phineas Fletcher's grandfather, too, came down to Cambridge from Yorkshire, and it is quite possible that his family and the Hebden Fletchers were related. Of course there is no reference to the astrologer in Phineas Fletcher's works, but then the poet was equally silent about his dramatist cousin, John Fletcher. It is not impossible that this kinship first attracted the student of King's to the Caius College dissections, although natural curiosity would be enough to lead him across the intervening eighty yards.

ston was famous throughout the university as a dissector and held his fellowship from 1582 to 1595, quitting it at least five years before Fletcher could have begun his attendance at the anatomies. There is still a chance that the young pensioner of King's absorbed some of Grimston's teaching, because, according to Venn, Grimston went no further than the town of Cambridge where he practiced physic. Furthermore, we know that he maintained contact with the university until his death in March, 1607/8: he took his M.D. there in 1601 and, by testament, he left his books to Caius and Clare Colleges. So distinguished was Grimston as an anatomist, that he may have continued the semi-annual dissections after 1595.[8]

If Grimston did not prolong his appearances in the Caius anatomical theater, John Gostlyn was probably his successor.[9] The younger physician matriculated at Caius as a pensioner in 1592 and held a fellowship from 1591/2 until July 12, 1607, when he was elevated to the mastership of his college. The election was disputed, and Gostlyn, evidently provoked, retired to Exeter and to a private practice. In 1618/19 he was successful in a new vote, which remained unquestioned, and returned to Cambridge in triumph. After being made Regius Professor of Physic in 1623, he died on October 21, 1626.

Knowing of Fletcher's opportunities, we shall recognize an entirely new element in *The Purple Island*. Throughout every canto, on every page, there runs a positive indication that the author's information came from the anatomical theater and the dissection of the human cadaver. Fletcher's program or scheme of presentation is a very handwriting on the wall.[10] The first five cantos of his poem are an accurate though allegorical account of a public anatomy,

---

[8] Venn's *Annals*, pp. 209-13.　　　[9] *Ibid.*, p. 215.

[10] The division of the poem into days has some relation to this matter of dissection. *The Purple Island* is marked off into seven days in the following manner: I, first day, morning; II, first day, afternoon; III, second day, morning; IV, second day, afternoon; V, third day; VI, fourth day; VII, fifth day, morning; VIII, fifth day, afternoon; IX, sixth day, morning; X, sixth day, afternoon; XI, seventh day, morning; XII, seventh day, afternoon. The arrangement, of course, was suggested by such poems as Du Bartas' *Semaines*. On the other hand, the apportionment of the opening cantos is remarkably similar to the time schedule for a contemporary dissection, such as those performed by Grimston. During the afternoon of the first day and the morning of the second, the poet describes the abdominal viscera; the thoracic, during the afternoon of the second day; and the cerebrum and sensory organs, during the morning and afternoon of the third day.

every move of the dissector being set down with complete fidelity. When the felon's body was laid out upon the table in the Caius theater, Grimston invariably began with the abdominal viscera, because experience had taught him that they were the first to decay. He then proceeded to the thoracic cavity, leaving the cerebral organs, least subject to corruption, until the last. *The Purple Island* advances through the three "metropolies" in like manner, starting with the lowest, passing to the middle, and concluding with the highest.

When the cantos are examined more closely, we find that the author was governed by the same principle in his setting forth of each of the triple regiments into which he parted his isle. In general he works from the outside of the body inward, as if he were actually handling the scissors, sponges, and scalpels. After brief remarks about the skin, flesh, and muscles, he discusses the parts of the ventral cavity in the following order: skin, fat, "panniculus carnosus," muscles, vessels of the tunicle, bladder, stomach, intestines, pancreas, liver, blood vessels of the liver, gall, spleen, and kidneys. They have been treated in the sequence of their appearance under the instruments of the dissector. Fletcher discloses the organs of the thorax and cerebral cavity in the same realistic succession: the breasts, thoracic muscles, diaphragm, pleura or skin inside the ribs, heart, tunicle covering the lungs, and lungs; the cranium, first, second, third, and fourth ventricles, and the beginning of the spinal cord. Every shadow of doubt concerning the wherefore of the author's scheme vanishes when we find him again hanging on the movements of the anatomist in his presentation of the individual organs. For instance, Grimston picked apart the heart before the gaping scholars of Caius, passing from the walls to the substance, cavities, septum, blood vessels, and concluding with the valves. That, too, is a history of the visitor's progress through Fletcher's city of Kerdia. One is not only convinced that *The Purple Island* sprang from the anatomy theater, but also that its author had an extraordinary familiarity with each act of the performance.

Throughout the poem there is another significant element, a type of remark that also has gone unnoticed, despite the fact that it is omnipresent in the anatomical stanzas. For instance, the author elaborates his account of the cave of Auditus with a marginal, "The last passage is called the Cochlea, snail, or Periwincle; where the nerves of hearing plainly appeare." [11] He might have read about the spiral canal and even about the organ of Corti, but how did he know that the spiral rods were to be seen "plainly"? Elsewhere he describes the flesh of the liver as

> Built all alike, seeming like rubies sheen,
> Of some peculiar matter . . .
> *The Purple Island,* III, st. 6.

Vesalius and others sketched the organs, but one whose acquaintance with the liver was limited to an artist's illustrations could not draw distinctions about the quality of its redness. Cochlea and Hepar must have been opened before his eyes, and so with the other parts of human anatomy, because the poet depicts them with the same ocular discriminations. Perhaps the most convincing instance of the habit is found in his account of Cephal mount:

> Next these, the buildings yeeld themselves to sight;
> The outward soft, and pale, like ashes look;
> The inward parts more hard, and curdy white.
> *The Purple Island,* V, st. 13.

This aspect of *The Purple Island* is corroboration of our earlier conclusion—that the verses were the harvest of the anatomical theater—but it is much more than that. We have finally cornered the elusive object of our investigation, the essential source of Fletcher's anatomical knowledge. Parts of his information seem to have come from Aristotle, Galen, and Greece; from Ingrassias, Italy, and the sixteenth century; from Kepler and the young seventeenth century; from Vicary; from John Caius and Gonville and Caius dissectors; but the intrinsic core was the product of no book, ancient or modern, nor of hearsay. Nothing intervened between the cadaver and the poet, and his writing was a reporting of what he had seen with his own eyes.

Bacon condemned adoration of the mind and understanding of man, which had paralyzed scientific progress through long ages of history. Fletcher had none of this reverence; no men walked between him and the purple isle to obscure his vision of that land.

[11] *The Purple Island,* V, 46, marg.

Instead of withdrawing from nature like the Galenists, he devoted himself to contemplating her in her nudity. Rather than tumbling up and down in reason and conceits, he was clear-headed, realistic and scientific. Whatever may be the factual connection between Phineas Fletcher, William Harvey, and Francis Bacon, and whatever may be the inequalities in their individual geniuses, they were fundamentally brethren. The poet and his work were wedded to the laboratory, to experiment, and to the entire renaissance in science.

History has been unjust in many ways to Phineas Fletcher. His rabid anti-Romanism has been condemned by those who were ignorant of the heritage handed down by Vicar Richard Fletcher. The drying up of his poetic vein during later life at Hilgay has not been linked with his disappointment at Cambridge, and thereby excused. The borrowings from Spenser have been emphasized, but no one has called attention to Fletcher's conscientious admissions of dependence upon Colin Clout and others. Far too much has been made of the curiosity of his writings and too little of the normality of his life as an earnest pastor and a loving father. The greatest of the wrongs done him, however, has been the failure to recognize the first half of *The Purple Island* for what it is.

These cantos are the climax of the poetry and the life of Phineas Fletcher. They rescue him from the slough of the commonplace and set him upon the high plain where he walks, humbly as was his wont, with Sir Francis Bacon, Galileo Galilei, William Harvey, and the other soldiers of science who warred against holy edicts, superstitions, lethargies, and all that vagrant rout. *The Purple Island* is a vindication of England's share in the progress of anatomical study, of certain mute, inglorious anatomists of Caius College, and of Phineas Fletcher's original genius. The remaining years, many though they were, added little to his fame. He was to grow in moral rather than in creative stature, and it is fitting that we should part from Phineas Fletcher in this, the shining hour of his life.

APPENDIX A

A TABULATION OF THE PASSAGES IN FLETCHER'S WORKS REVEALING SELF-REPETITION

1. "Amicissimo et Candidissimo," l. 24.		Locustae, dedication to Henry
2. The Apollyonists		Locustae
3.	I, st. 3	The Apollyonists, II, st. 4
4.		Piscatorie Eclogs, III, st. 7
5.		st. 17
6.		A Father's Testament, p. 10
7.		The Purple Island, VII, st. 25
8.	st. 9	IV, st. 22
9.		III, st. 5
10.	st. 11	VI, st. 72
11.	st. 11-12	XII, st. 27-29
12.	st. 12	st. 31
13.	st. 13	VII, st. 25
14.	st. 14	VIII, st. 8
15.		Sicelides, V, 5, lines 137-43
16.	st. 15	The Purple Island, XII, st. 32-34
17.	st. 18	VII, st. 10
18.	st. 25	I, st. 40
19.	st. 40	Locustae, lines 101-6
20.	II, st. 4	Piscatorie Eclogs, III, st. 7
21.		The Apollyonists, I, st. 3
22.		Piscatorie Eclogs, III, st. 17
23.	st. 11	The Purple Island, XII, st. 25
24.	st. 40	VII, st. 32
25.		XI, st. 18
26.	III, st. 1	"Elisa," I, st. 27
27.	st. 3	II, st. 39
28.	st. 10	The Purple Island, VIII, st. 40
29.	st. 18	VII, st. 4
30.	st. 21	Piscatorie Eclogs, IV, st. 28
31.	st. 22	st. 14
32.	st. 23	st. 17
33.	st. 25	st. 20
34.	st. 27	The Apollyonists, IV, st. 1
35.	st. 28-29	The Purple Island, VII, st. 40-43
36.	IV, st. 1	The Apollyonists, III, st. 27
37.		V, st. 1
38.	st. 4	The Purple Island, XII, st. 30
39.	st. 5	VII, st. 56
40.	st. 13	VI, st. 23
41.	st. 17	VII, st. 47
42.	V, st. 1	The Apollyonists, IV, st. 1
43.	st. 14	"An Hymen," lines 2-3

98. *Piscatorie Eclogs,* I, st. 6
99.   st. 15-16
100.   st. 18
101.   III, st. 1
102.   st. 7
103.
104.
105.   st. 10-12
106.
107.
108.   st. 17
109.
110.
111.   IV, st. 10
112.   st. 14
113.   st. 17
114.   st. 20
115.   st. 28
116.   V, st. 2
117.   st. 5
118.   VI, st. 4
119.   st. 11
120.   st. 12
121.   st. 11-13
122.   st. 14-16
123.   st. 25
124.   VII, st. 1
125.   st. 16
126.   st. 32
127. *The Purple Island,* I, st. 1
128.   st. 2
129.
130.   st. 13
131.   st. 40
132.   st. 42
133.   III, st. 5
134.   IV, st. 5
135.   st. 22
136.   V, st. 61-68
137.
138.
139.   VI, st. 1
140.   st. 5
141.   st. 23
142.   st. 68
143.   st. 72
144.   VII, st. 4
145.   st. 10
146.   st. 25
147.
148.
149.
150.   st. 32
151.   st. 40-43

Piscatorie Eclogs, III, st. 1
Sicelides, III, 6, lines 21-32
II, chorus
Piscatorie Eclogs, I, st. 6
III, st. 17
The Apollyonists, I, st. 3
II, st. 4
Sicelides, III, 2, lines 1-12
Brittain's Ida, V, st. 2-3
"Venus and Anchises," st. 42-44
The Apollyonists, I, st. 3
II, st. 4
Piscatorie Eclogs, III, st. 7
Sicelides, II, 1, lines 4-5
The Apollyonists, III, st. 22
st. 23
st. 25
st. 21
"Edward Benlowes Sun-warde"
The Purple Island, VII, st. 25
Sicelides, III, 6, lines 69-73
"Fusca Ecloga," lines 62-66
lines 75-80
Sicelides, III, chorus
"Fusca Ecloga," lines 92-113
The Purple Island, XII, st. 11
VI, st. 1
Sicelides, III, 6, lines 193-94
"Lusus Ecloga," lines 35-36
The Apollyonists, V, st. 27
Locustae, lines 828-30
dedication to Henry
"Venus and Anchises," st. 1
The Apollyonists, I, st. 25
V, st. 25
I, st. 9
"Epithalamium," lines 199-203
The Apollyonists, I, st. 9
Sicelides, IV, chorus
"A translation of Boethius"
A Father's Testament, pp. 62-64
Piscatorie Eclogs, VII, st. 1
"To my beloved Thenot," lines 17-24
The Apollyonists, IV, st. 13
"Elisa," II, st. 34
The Apollyonists, I, st. 9
III, st. 18
I, st. 18
st. 3
A Father's Testament, p. 10
Piscatorie Eclogs, V, st. 5
The Apollyonists, I, st. 13
II, st. 40
III, st. 28-29

204. "To my ever honoured Cousin,"	
lines 19-21	"To E. C.," lines 26-28
205. lines 25-27	*A Father's Testament,* p. 178
206.	*Sicelides,* II, chorus
207. "A translation of Boethius"	*The Purple Island,* V, st. 61-68
208.	*Sicelides,* IV, chorus
209.	*A Father's Testament,* pp. 62-64
210. "Upon the picture of Achmat"	"In effigiem Achmati"
211.	*Locustae,* lines 236-50
212. "Venus and Anchises," st. 1	*The Purple Island,* I, st. 13
213. st. 42-44	*Piscatorie Eclogs,* III, st. 10-12
214.	*Sicelides,* III, 2, lines 1-12
215.	*Brittain's Ida,* V, st. 2-3

APPENDIX B

A TABULATION OF THE APPARENT SOURCES OF OCCASIONAL PASSAGES IN FLETCHER'S WORKS

1.	"Against a rich man," *etc.*		Tasso, *Jerusalem Delivered*, p. 133
2.	"Anni temporum mutationes"		Vergil, *Georgics*, III, lines 440-556
3.	*The Apollyonists*,	I, st. 1	Sylvester, *Du Bartas*, p. 189
4.		st. 9-16	Vergil, *Aeneid*, VI, lines 273-81
5.		st. 13	Marlowe, *Hero and Leander*, I, line 59
6.		st. 15	Spenser, *The Faerie Queene*, I, ix, st. 21-22
7.		st. 39	"Virgils Gnat," line 344
8.			Tasso, *Jerusalem Delivered*, p. 63
9.		II, st. 4-5	Vergil, *Aeneid*, VII, lines 528-30
10.		st. 9-38	Tasso, *Jerusalem Delivered*, pp. 63-66
11.		st. 21-22	Spenser, *The Faerie Queene*, VI, xii, st. 24
12.		st. 29	I, viii, st. 47
13.			Sylvester, *Du Bartas*, p. 97
14.		st. 39	Spenser, *The Faerie Queene*, II, iii, st. 19
15.		st. 40	Ovid, *Metamorphoses*, I, lines 264-66
16.		III, st. 9	Spenser, "Prosopopoia," lines 950 ff.
17.		st. 18-19	Ovid, *Metamorphoses*, XV, lines 420-33
18.		st. 18-20	Spenser, "Ruines of Time," lines 64-77
19.		st. 27	*The Faerie Queene*, I, iv, st. 4
20.		IV, st. 4	Ovid, *Metamorphoses*, IV, lines 495-505
21.			Sylvester, *Du Bartas*, p. 219
22.		st. 4-5	Vergil, *Aeneid*, VII, lines 341-59, 462-66
23.		IV, st. 11	Spenser, *The Faerie Queene*, V, x, st. 7-14
24.		V, st. 10	Sylvester, *Du Bartas*, p. 189
25.		st. 13	Tasso, *Jerusalem Delivered*, p. 192
26.		st. 14	Spenser, *The Faerie Queene*, IV, xi, st. 34
27.		st. 25	Ovid, *Metamorphoses*, I, lines 18-20
28.		st. 32	Vergil, *Aeneid*, VIII, line 202
29.			Spenser, *The Faerie Queene*, V, x, st. 9
30.	*Brittain's Ida*,	I, st. 1	VII, vi, st. 36
31.		st. 2	Marlowe, *Hero and Leander*, I, line 59
32.			Tasso, *Jerusalem Delivered*, XIV, st. 61-67
33.		st. 6	Sidney, *Arcadia*, p. 223
34.		II, st. 3	Marlowe, *Hero and Leander*, I, lines 191-93
35.		st. 4-5	Spenser, *The Faerie Queene*, II, xii, st. 70-71
36.		st. 5	Tasso, *Jerusalem Delivered*, XVI, st. 14-21
37.		st. 6	st. 9-10
38.			Daniel, "Complaynt of Rosamond," lines 380-82
39.		st. 1-6	Spenser, *The Faerie Queene*, II, xii, st. 42
40.		II	Giles Fletcher, "Christs Victorie on Earth," st. 39-52

41. *Brittain's Ida,* II
42.   III, st. 2
43.
44.   st. 10
45.   st. 11
46.   st. 13
47.   IV, st. 1
48.   VI, st. 6-7

49.   st. 10

50. "Elisa," I, st. 7
51.   st. 27
52.   st. 16-40
53.   st. 45

54.   II, st. 38-40
55. "Epithalamium," lines 23-26
56. *A Father's Testament,* pp. 62-64
57.
58. "Fusca Ecloga," lines 12-26

59.   lines 12-27
60.   lines 58-59
61.   lines 84-88
62. "An Hymen," lines 13-14
63.   lines 43-49
64. *Locustae,* p. 104

65.   p. 110

66.   p. 120
67.
68. "Lusus Ecloga," lines 35-36
69. "Myrtillus Ecloga," lines 20-23
70.   lines 27-29
71.   lines 37-40
72. "Nisa Ecloga," lines 86-92

73. *Piscatorie Eclogs,* I, st. 5
74.   st. 6
75.   st. 7-9

76.   st. 12
77.   st. 13-15
78.   st. 18

79.   II, st. 1
80.   st. 8

81.   III, st. 1
82.
83.   st. 4

Ariosto, *Orlando Furioso,* VII
Spenser, *The Faerie Queene,* II, vi, st. 32
                              xii, st. 77
Sidney, *Arcadia,* p. 224
Spenser, *The Faerie Queene,* VI, viii, st. 43
                              II, xii, st. 77
                                   st. 68
Marlowe, *Hero and Leander,*
                    II, lines 61-69
Daniel, "Complaynt of Rosamond,"
                    lines 796-98
Spenser, "Daphnaida," lines 150-54
Sidney, *Astrophel and Stella,* st. 47
Spenser, "Daphnaida," lines 262-94
Daniel, "Complaynt of Rosamond,"
                    lines 796-98
Spenser, "Ruines of Time," lines 50-56
Vergil, *Aeneid,* IV, lines 143-48
Spenser, "Virgils Gnat," lines 433-80
Vergil, *Georgics,* IV, lines 453-527
Spenser, *Sheapheardes Calender,*
                    Feb., lines 77-83
                    Aug., lines 16-17
                    Mar., lines 80-82
                         lines 61-64
Spenser, "Epithalamion," lines 145-46
                         lines 185-90
Giles Fletcher, "Christs Triumph over
                    Death," st. 43
                "Christs Victorie on Earth,"
                    st. 49
Tasso, *Jerusalem Delivered,* p. 192
Vergil, *Aeneid,* I, lines 297-301
Sannazaro, *Eclogues,* I, lines 45-48
                    III, lines 50-53
                    I, lines 24-28
                       lines 72-75
Spenser, *Sheapheardes Calender,* June,
                    lines 108-12
Sannazaro, *Eclogues,* III, line 12
                        line 10
Spenser, *Sheapheardes Calender,*
                    Dec., lines 19-50
                    May, lines 39-40
                    Apr., lines 23-24
                The Faerie Queene,
                    VI, ix, st. 19-25
Sannazaro, *Eclogues,* III, lines 1-10
Spenser, *Sheapheardes Calender,*
                    April, lines 13-16
                    July, line 81
Sannazaro, *Eclogues,* III, lines 1-10
Spenser, *Sheapheardes Calender,*
                    Jan., lines 39-40

BIBLIOGRAPHY

Academia Cantabrigiensis lacrymae. Cambridge, 1587.

Allbutt, Sir Thomas Clifford, *Science and Medieval Thought.* London, 1901.

Ariosto, Ludovico, *Orlando Furioso in English Heroical Verse.* Translated by Sir John Harington. London, 1591.

Bacon, Francis, *The Works of.* Cambridge, 1863.

Ball, James Moores, *Andreas Vesalius.* St. Louis, 1910.

Benlowes, Edward, *Sphinx theologica.* Cambridge, 1636.

―――― *Theophila or Love's Sacrifice.* London, 1652.

Birch, Thomas, *Memoirs of the Reign of Queen Elizabeth from 1581 till Her Death.* London, 1754.

Bloxam, John R., *Register of the Presidents, Fellows, Demies . . . of St. Mary Magdalen College.* Oxford, 1863-81.

Boehme, Traugott, "Spenser's literarisches Nachleben bis zu Shelley." *Palaestra,* No. 93, Berlin, 1911.

Boethius, *De consolatione philosophiae.* London, 1823.

Brown, Eleanor Gertrude, *Milton's Blindness.* New York, 1934.

Bush, Douglas, *Mythology and the Renaissance Tradition in English Poetry.* Minneapolis, 1932.

Collier, John P., *Bibliographical and Critical Account of the Rarest Books in the English Language.* London, 1865.

Cooper, Charles H., *Annals of Cambridge.* Cambridge, 1842.

―――― *Athenae Cantabrigiensis.* Cambridge, 1858.

Cox, John Charles, *Notes on the Churches of Derbyshire.* Chesterfield, London, and Derby, 1875-79.

Cranbrook, a Brief Historical Account of. Cranbrook, 1789.

Da Costa, J. M., *Harvey and His Discovery.* Philadelphia, 1879.

D'Ewes, Sir Simonds, *A Compleat Journal of . . . the House of Lords and the House of Commons.* London, 1693.

Drayton, Michael, *Works.* Edited by J. William Hebel. Oxford, 1932.

Ellis, Sir Henry, *Original Letters of Eminent Literary Men.* Printed for the Camden Society. London, 1843.

Epicedium Cantabrigiense in obitum immaturum. Cambridge, 1612.

Faulkner, Thomas, *An Historical and Topographical Description of Chelsea.* Chelsea, 1829.

Fletcher, Giles the Elder, *De literis antiquae Britanniae.* Cambridge, 1633.

―――― *Israel Redux; or the Restauration of Israel, exhibited in two short treatises. The first contains an essay upon some probable ground, that the present Tartars near the Caspian sea, are the posterity of the Ten Tribes of Israel.* London, 1677.

―――― *Licia and other love poems and the rising to the crown of Richard the Third.* Edited by Alexander Grosart. "Miscellanies of the Fuller Worthies' Library." Blackburn, 1870-76.

Of the Russe Common Wealth. London, 1591.

Fletcher, Giles the Younger, *Christs Victorie and Triumph.* Cambridge, 1610.

―――― *Christs Victorie and Triumph.* Cambridge, 1632.

―――― *Christ's Victory and Triumph.* Cambridge, 1640.

―――― *Complete Poems.* Edited by Alexander Grosart. London, 1876.

―――― *The Reward of the Faithfull.* London, 1623.

Fletcher, Phineas, *Brittain's Ida*. Ascribed to Edmund Spenser. London, 1628.
———— *A Father's Testament*. London, 1670.
———— *Joy in Tribulation*. London, 1632.
———— *Locustae vel pietas Iesuitica*. Cambridge, 1627.
———— *Piscatory Eclogues with Poetical Miscellanies*. Edinburgh, 1771.
———— *Poems*. Edited by Alexander Grosart. Printed for private circulation. 1869.
———— *Poetical Works of Giles and Phineas Fletcher*. Edited by Frederick S. Boas. Cambridge, 1908.
———— *The Purple Island, or the Isle of Man: Together with Piscatorie Eclogs and Other Poeticall Miscellanies*. Cambridge, 1633.
———— *Sicelides*. London, 1631.
———— *Sylva Poetica*. Cambridge, 1633.
———— *Venus and Anchises and other Poems*. Edited by Ethel Seaton. Oxford, 1926.
———— *The Way to Blessednes*. London, 1632.
Foster, Sir Michael, *Lectures on the History of Physiology*. Cambridge, 1924.
Fox, John, *Book of Martyrs*. London, 1811.
Fuller, Thomas, *History of the Worthies of England*. London, 1840.
Galen, *Oeuvres*. Paris, 1854.
———— *On the Natural Faculties*. Translated by Arthur J. Brock. London, 1916.
Greg, Walter W., *Pastoral Poetry and Pastoral Drama*. London, 1906.
Griffin, Ralph, *Visitation of the Arms of Kent—1594*. London, 1924.
Griffiths, Lemuel Matthews, "Shakspere and the Practise of Medicine." *Annals of Medical History*, O.S., III, 50 ff.
Grove, Sir George, *Dictionary of Music and Musicians*. London, 1878.
Grove, Robert, *Carmen de sanguinis circuitu*. London, 1685.
Gunther, R. T., *Early Science in Oxford*. Oxford, 1925.
Hakluyt, Richard, *The Principal Navigations, Voyages . . . of the English Nation*. London, 1598.
Harrison, John Smith, *Platonism in English Poetry*. New York, 1903.
Hartopp, Henry, *Index to the Wills of Leicestershire*. Vol. XXIX of the "Index Library." Printed for the British Record Society. London.
———— *Leicestershire Marriage Licenses*. Vol. XXIV of the "Index Library." Printed for the British Record Society. London, 1910.
Harvey, William, *Works*. Translated by Robert Willis. Printed for the Sydenham Society. London, 1847.
Hasted, Edward, *The History and Topographical Survey of the County of Kent*. Canterbury, 1790.
Headley, Henry, *Select Beauties of Ancient English Poetry*. London, 1810.
Herbert, George, *The English Poems*. Boston, 1916.
Herringham, Sir Wilmot, "The Life and Times of Dr. William Harvey." *Annals of Medical History*, N.S. Vol. IV, 1932.
Heywood, James, and Thomas Wright, *The Ancient Laws of the Fifteenth Century for King's and Eton Colleges*. London, 1850.
Heywood, John, *Proverbs*. London, 1874.
Hippocrates, *Aphorisms*. Translated by Elias Marks. New York, 1817.
Hutchinson, Lucy, *Memoirs of Colonel Hutchinson*. London, 1846.
Igglesden, Sir Charles, *A Saunter through Kent with Pen and Pencil*. Ashford, 1900.
Koeppel, E., "Der Englischen Tasso-Ubersetzungen." *Anglia. Zeitschrift fur Englische Philologie*, XI, 33 ff.
Larkey, Sanford V., "The Vesalian Compendium of Geminus and Nicholas Udall's Translation." *The Library*, Vol. XIII, June, 1932.
Leigh, Augustus A., *King's College*. 1899.
Macdonald, George, *England's Antiphon*. London, 1868.

Malloch, Archibald, *William Harvey*. New York, 1929.
Milton, John, *Works*. Edited by Frank A. Patterson. New York, 1931 —.
Molineux, Gisborne, *Memoir of the Molineux Family*. Privately printed. London, 1882.
Morgan, R. B., *Readings in English Social History*. Cambridge, 1923.
Morton, Edward P., "The Spenserian Stanza before 1700." *Modern Philology*, May, 1907.
Mullinger, James B., *The University of Cambridge from the Earliest Times*. Cambridge, 1873-1911.
Mustard, Wilfred P., *The Piscatory Eclogues of Jacopo Sannazaro*. Baltimore, 1914.
Ovid, *Metamorphoses*. London, 1916.
Pepys, Samuel, *The Diary*. London, 1928.
Plato, *Dialogues*. Translated by Benjamin Jowett. New York, 1899.
Plotinus, *Enneades*. Paris, 1855.
"A Poet's Anatomy," *British Medical Journal*, May 9, 1925.
Pohlman, Augustus T., "The Purple Island, a Seventeenth Century Poetical Conception of the Human Body." *Johns Hopkins Hospital Bulletin*, 1907, Vol. XVIII, No. 197.
Pownall, Nathaniel, *The Young divines Apologie for his Continuance in the Universitie*. Cambridge, 1612.
Quarles, Francis, *Emblemes*. London, 1635.
Roberts, Lewis, *The Merchant's Map of Commerce*. London, 1638.
Sackville, Thomas, *Mirror for Magistrates*. London, 1870.
Sidney, Sir Philip, *The Countess of Pembroke's Arcadia*. Cambridge, 1926.
———— *Miscellaneous Works*. Boston, 1860.
Singer, Charles J., *The Evolution of Anatomy*. New York, 1925.
Sorrowes Joy. Cambridge, 1603.
Spedding, James, *The Letters and Life of Francis Bacon*. London, 1861-74.
Spenser, Edmund, *Complaints*. Edited by W. L. Renwick. London, 1928.
———— *The Complete Poetical Works*. Boston, 1908.
Strype, John, *Annals of the Reformation*. Oxford, 1824.
———— *Ecclesiastical Memorials Relating Chiefly to Religion*. Oxford, 1822.
———— *Life and Acts of John Whitgift*. Oxford, 1822.
Sylvester, Joshua, *Du Bartas His Divine Weekes and Workes*. London, 1641.
Tasso, Torquato, *Jerusalem Delivered*. Translated by Edward Fairfax. New York, 1901.
Thoroton, Robert, *History of Nottinghamshire*. Nottingham, 1790.
Threno-Thriambeuticon. Cambridge, 1603.
Todd, Henry J., *Account of the Deans of Canterbury*. Canterbury, 1793.
Tomkins, Thomas, *Songs of 3, 4, 5, and 6 Parts*. London, 1622.
Upham, Alfred H., *The French Influence in English Literature*. New York, 1908.
Venn, John, *Annals of Gonville and Caius College*. London, 1904.
———— *Biographical History of Caius College*. Cambridge, 1897.
———— *Gonville and Caius College*. London, 1901.
Vergil, *Bucolica*. London, 1737.
———— *Aeneid*. Oxford, 1930.
———— *Georgica*. London, 1774.
Vesalius, Andreas, *De humani corporis fabrica*. Venice, 1568.
Vicary, Thomas, *A Profitable Treatise of the Anatomie of Man's Body*. Published for the Early English Text Society. London, 1888.
Walton, Izaak, *The Compleat Angler*. London, 1655.
Warwick, Sir Philip, *Memoirs*. Edinburgh, 1813.
Webster, John, *Academiarum Examen*. London, 1654.

Weibel, Karl, "Phineas Fletcher's Purple Island in ihrer Abhangigkeit von Spenser's Faerie Queene." *Englische Studien*. Leipzig, 1924, LVIII, 321-67.

Wheeler, John, *A Treatise of Commerce*. Middleburgh, 1601.

Winstanley, William, *Lives of the Most Famous English Poets*. London, 1687.

Witts Recreations. London, 1640.

Wood, Anthony, *Athenae Oxonienses*. London, 1820.

Wyatt, Raymond B. H., *William Harvey*. Boston, 1924.

INDEX